PATHS TO
THE PRESENT

The cover design by William Barss includes the following symbolic landmarks along our path to the present: an engraving of the Boston Tea Party by Daniel N. Chodowiecki from *Calender für 1784* (Berlin), property of the Metropolitan Museum of Art; a nineteenth century tobacco wagon from *Field Book of the American Revolution* by Benjamin Lossing, property of the Metropolitan Museum of Art; vignettes of a mill and of women making butter, two woodcuts by Alexander Anderson, property of the New York Public Library; an American eagle from a newspaper masthead of the same century; and finally the twentieth century's contribution to architecture, the skyscraper.

Arthur M. Schlesinger

PATHS TO
THE PRESENT

What's past is prologue.

SHAKESPEARE, *The Tempest*
Act II, Scene I

SENTRY EDITION
REVISED AND ENLARGED
with a Foreword by
Arthur M. Schlesinger, Jr.

HOUGHTON MIFFLIN COMPANY BOSTON
The Riverside Press Cambridge
1964

The Riverside Press
CAMBRIDGE • MASSACHUSETTS
PRINTED IN THE U.S.A.

FOR
ELIZABETH

And what is writ is writ;
Would it were worthier!

BYRON, *Childe Harold's
Pilgrimage*, Canto IV

Foreword

THIS VOLUME contains the conclusions of an historian who has meditated for half a century on a number of critical issues of our national development. *Paths to the Present* was first published in 1949 (the text and notes have been brought up to date for this edition, and two essays have been added); but its intellectual roots stretch far back in my father's personal as well as scholarly experience. Thus "The Role of the Immigrant" appeared in an earlier form in *New Viewpoints in American History* in 1922, but the prefatory anecdote shows that the seed was planted in the 1890's. The present version extends and enriches what was in 1922 an unorthodox thesis and is now universally accepted as an essential dimension of our history.

New Viewpoints had a sharp impact on the writing of American history both because of the author's own insights and preoccupations and because of his cogent presentation of the emergent scholarship of his generation. Above all, my father was concerned with redefining the scope of American history, with emancipating American scholarship from the Victorian conviction that "history is past politics," and with emphasizing the nonpolitical forces which had so vitally shaped the evolution of American society. Many books were inspired by the new trails opened up here, among them my own *The Age of Jackson*. By the 1940's, with the completion of the *History of American Life* series, which he edited in association with Dixon Ryan Fox, the battle for "social history" was won. *Paths to the Present* is, in part, the ripened summation of the effect on American development of such social factors as immigration, the city, the voluntary associations, food, and currents from the globe outside, along with a discussion of America's contributions to world civilization.

But social history, as my father conceived it, never implied the dictum "history is *not* past politics." Both as an historian and as a citizen, he has believed that the inchoate impulses of society reach moments of truth in decisions of public policy. The well-known essay "Rating the Presidents" reports the judgment of the historical fraternity on the relative success and failure of our chief executives. "Persisting Problems of the Presidency" discusses unresolved dilemmas of the presidency as an institution. "The Tides of National Politics" began in rudimentary form as an essay in *New Viewpoints,* evolved into a lecture in the later 1920's and became a controversial essay in the *Yale Review* in 1939; it has had the distinction of influencing not only the writing of American history but also perhaps the making of a President.

The opportunity for one historian to express admiration for the work of another who happens to be his father is probably rare. I make no apologies for seizing this chance. My father has had a profound effect on his associates and students not only for scholarly but for moral reasons — not only because of his vision of the American past but because of his vision of the American future. He has embodied, or so it seems to me, the fundamentals of the American democratic temper — its sober optimism, its sagacious moderation, its skeptical sense of human limitation and human frailty, its abiding faith in the ultimate wisdom of the democratic experience. *Paths to the Present* might as well have been entitled *Paths to the Future*; for the factors and forces here defined and illuminated will continue to answer Crèvecœur's question — "What then is the American, this new man?" — for generations to come.

ARTHUR M. SCHLESINGER, JR.

September 1963

Contents

Contents

NATIONAL
TRAITS

1

"What then is the American, this new man?"

THE question which forms the title of this essay has never ceased to arouse interest since Crèvecœur posed it in the last years of the Revolution. If we can learn why the American has come to be what he is, how he reacts instinctively to life, wherein he differs from other peoples, we shall have gained a deep insight into the springs of national behavior. Crèvecœur's own answer, the considered opinion of a Frenchman long resident in the New World, may still be read with profit. The American, he said, "is either an European, or the descendant of an European, hence that strange mixture of blood which you will find in no other country. . . . *He* is an American, who leaving behind him all his ancient prejudices and manners, receives new ones from the new mode of life he has embraced, the new government he obeys, and the new rank he holds. . . . From involuntary idleness, servile dependence, penury, and useless labour, he has passed to toils of a very different nature. — This is an American."

I

Crèvecœur, of course, was one of a long procession of Europeans who have tried to describe and appraise the American. Their writings, though of varying merit, possess the common advantage of presenting an outsider's point of view, free from the predilections and prepossessions which blur the American's vision of himself. Viewing the scene from a different background, they are also sensitive to national divergences of which the native-born are usually unaware. Though bias may influence the individual observer's judgment, the total number of visitors has been so great as to render far more significant their points of agreement.

The composite portrait that emerges deserves thoughtful consideration. The attributes most frequently noted have been a belief in the universal obligation to work; the urge to move from place to place; a high standard of average comfort; faith in progress; the eternal pursuit of material gain; an absence of permanent class barriers; the neglect of abstract thinking and of the aesthetic side of life; boastfulness; a deference for women; the prevalence of spoiled children; the general restlessness and hurry of life, always illustrated by the practice of fast eating; and certain miscellaneous traits such as overheated houses, the vice of spitting and the passion for rocking chairs and ice water.

This inventory, so far as it goes, reveals qualities and attitudes recognizably American. Moreover, the travelers express no doubt as to the existence of a distinctive national character. The native-born looking at their fellow countrymen readily identify them as New Englanders or Middle Westerners or Southerners, as products of old American stock or newcomers of immigrant origin; and they remember that at one period of their history the differences between Northerner and Southerner sharpened into a tragic war. But the detached observer from Europe has always been less impressed by these regional deviations than by the evidences of fundamental kinship, even in slavery times.

James Bryce, most perspicacious of the commentators, goes so far as to say, "Scotchmen and Irishmen are more unlike Englishmen, the native of Normandy more unlike the native of Provence, the Pomeranian more unlike the Wurtemberger, the Piedmontese more unlike the Neapolitan, the Basque more unlike the Andalusian, than the American from any part of the country is to the American from any other part." His conclusion is that "it is rather more difficult to take any assemblage of attributes in any of these European countries and call it the national type than it is to do the like in the United States." The preoccupation of American historians with local and sectional diversities has tended to obscure this underlying reality.

But the particular "assemblage of attributes" recorded by the travelers leaves much to be desired. Not only is the list incom-

plete, but it carelessly lumps the significant with the trivial. Since
the typical European tried to cover as much ground as possible
in a short time, his attention was caught by externals, with the
result that annoying traits and ways assumed undue importance,
much as dust in the eye of a wayfarer distorts the appearance of
the landscape. The gospel of work, for example, hardly deserves
to be equated with the addiction to spitting. Though the more
thoughtful sought to correlate what they noticed with the avowed
ideals of the people, they usually lacked sufficient knowledge of
the deeper historical trends to grasp either the true import of the
ideals or how they manifested themselves in action. Finally,
the traveler gave little attention to the crucial problem of why
the special combination of qualities and attitudes had become
endemic within the borders of the United States.

Hence the judgment of these onlookers, though often clear-
sighted and frequently valuable as a corrective, leaves ample
room for the student of United States history to venture an answer to Crèvecœur's question. If the native-born historian be suspect as a party in interest, he may at least strive to observe that
counsel of objectivity which his professional conscience reveres.

II

What then is the American from a historian's point of view?
The answer, briefly expressed, is so simple as to be a platitude.
This "new man" is the product of the interplay of Old World influences and New World conditions. But just what heritage did
the colonists bring with them from Europe, and why and how
was it changed? Predominantly it involved that part of Europe's
social experience in which they themselves had shared. The great
bulk of the settlers, like the immigrants of later times, belonged
to the poorer classes. They and their ancestors, whether in England or on the Continent, had been artisans, small tradesmen,
farmers, day laborers — the broad foundation which supported
the fine superstructure of European civilization. Shut out from
a life of wealth, leisure and aesthetic enjoyment, they had tended
to regard the ways of their social superiors with misgiving, if not
resentment, and by the same token they magnified their own
qualities of sobriety, diligence and thrift. Even when many of

them, as notably in England, improved their economic position in the seventeenth and eighteenth centuries as a result of the great growth of commerce and industry, they continued to exalt the ancient proprieties.

This attitude found its classic spiritual expression in Calvinism. As Professor Tawney has said, Calvinism was "perhaps the first systematic body of religious teaching which can be said to recognize and applaud the economic virtues." It neatly fitted the glove of divine sanction to the hand of prudential conduct, thereby giving a sense of personal rectitude to the business of getting ahead in the world. But whether in Britain or elsewhere, whether in the religious groups directly concerned or those more remotely affected, Calvinism merely intensified a pre-existing bent. It is similarly true that the stringent code of morals often attributed to Calvinism, and more particularly to the Puritans, represented a lower-middle-class mentality long antedating the Geneva teachings.

This, then, was the type of humanity upon which the untamed New World wielded its influence. It has often been observed that plants and animals undergo modification when removed to America. These mutations arise from differences in climate and geography. But other factors as well affected transplanted people. One was the temperament of the settler, the fact that he was more adventurous, more ambitious or more rebellious against conditions at home than his fellows. It is not necessary to believe with William Stoughton in 1670 that "God sifted a whole Nation that he might send Choice Grain over into this Wilderness," but undoubtedly the act of quitting a familiar existence for a strange and perilous one demanded uncommon attributes of hardihood, self-reliance and imagination. Once the ocean was crossed, sheer distance from the old country and the challenge of new experiences further weakened the bonds of custom, evoked latent capacities and awakened the settler to possibilities of improvement hitherto unsuspected.

The undeveloped continent prescribed the conditions of living the new life, the mold within which the American character took shape. Farming was the primary occupation. At first resorted to to keep from starvation, it quickly became the mainstay of existence. The Revolution was fought by a people of whom nineteen out of twenty tilled the soil. With good land obtainable for more than a century after Independence, agriculture continued, though with gradually diminishing effect, to provide the pervasive atmosphere of American life and thought. "The vast majority of the people of this country live by the land, and carry its quality in their manners and opinions," wrote Ralph Waldo Emerson in 1844. Even when the hosts from Continental Europe began to swell the population after the middle of the nineteenth century, the rural temper of the nation remained pretty much unaltered, for many of the immigrants also turned to farming. This long apprenticeship to the soil made an indelible impress on the developing American character, with results which the modern age of the city has not wholly effaced.

Agriculture in the New World, however, differed from agriculture in the Old. This was the initial lesson which the colonists were compelled to learn. Those who had been farmers in their homelands found many of the traditional methods unsuitable. Those who had worked at urban occupations suffered an even greater handicap. Densely forested land must be cleared; the wildness taken out of the soil; a knowledge gained of indigenous plants and of the best means of growing them. The settlers of Jamestown were barely able to struggle through the early years. "There were never Englishmen left in a forreigne Country in such miserie as wee," wrote one of them. "Unsufferable hunger" caused them to eat horses, dogs, rats and snakes, and instances even of cannibalism are recorded. As is well known, the Plymouth colonists experienced similar trials. Yet in both cases the woods abounded with native fruits, berries, roots and nuts, game was plentiful, and nearby waters teemed with fish.

Had these courageous men been more readily adaptable, they could have enjoyed a gastronomic abundance beyond the dreams of the wealthiest classes at home. But they had never faced such an experience before, and reversion to a stage of civilization which the white man had long since outgrown was not easy. At the very first, all the early settlements actually imported food supplies; the Swedish colony on the Delaware did so for twenty years. A knowledge of self-sufficient farming came slowly and painfully, with untold numbers of men, women and children perishing in the process. In the long run, however, the settlers learned how to master their environment. Utilizing native crops and Indian methods of tillage, they abandoned the intensive

cultivation required by the limited land resources of the Old
World. It was simpler to move on to new fields when the fertility
of the old was exhausted. The typical farm was a small one,
worked by the owner and his family. Even when the system of
staple production developed in the South, the small independent
farmers considerably outnumbered the great slaveholding
planters.

Though the colonial agriculturalist owed much to the savage,
he had no wish to live like one. Accustomed in the old country
to simple comforts and mechanical devices in the home and
about the farm, he duplicated them in the wilderness. Every
husbandman became a manufacturer and every farmhouse a
small factory, producing flour, soap and candles, tanning skins,
preparing the winter's meat supply, making nails, harness, hats,
shoes and rugs, contriving tools, churns, casks, beds, chairs and
tables. Such activities he supplemented with trapping, hunting
and fishing. As cold weather closed in, he used his spare time
getting out rough timber products, such as shingles and planks,
or spent the long evenings before the open fireplace carving
gunstocks or making brooms while his womenfolk knitted, spun
or wove.

Under pressure of circumstances the farmer thus became a
Jack-of-all-trades. As Chancellor Livingston wrote, "being ha-
bituated from early life to rely upon himself he acquires a skill
in every branch of his profession, which is unknown in countries
where labour is more divided." Take the case of a typical New
Englander, John Marshall of Braintree, early in the eighteenth
century. Besides tending his farm, he bought and sold hogs, was
a painter and a brickmaker, as well as a carpenter turning out as
many as three hundred laths in a day, and, in addition, a precinct
constable. The primitive state of society fostered a similar
omnicompetence in other walks of life, as the career of Benjamin
Franklin so well exemplifies. Lord Cornbury, the governor of
New York, characterized Francis Makemie as "a Preacher, a
Doctor of Physick, a Merchant, an Attorney, or Counsellor at
Law, and," he ruefully added, "which is worse of all, a Disturber
of Governments."

The pioneer farmer of later times was the colonial farmer re-
born. Up and down the Mississippi Valley he faced the same
difficulties and opportunities as his forefathers, and he dealt with

them in much the same way. As time went on, to be sure, he managed to buy more and more of his tools and household conveniences. He also took advantage of new inventions like the metal plow and the reaper, while increasingly he raised crops for sale in a general market. Meanwhile along the Atlantic Seaboard similar changes occurred. But whether in the older or newer communities these innovations affected the surface rather than the substance of the traditional mode of life. Nor did the advent of cities at first do much to alter the situation. Mere islands in a sea of forests and farms, they long retained marked rural characteristics and depended for a large part of their growth on continued accessions from the countryside.

III

What elements of the national character are attributable to this long-time agrarian environment? First and foremost is the habit of work. For the colonial farmer ceaseless striving constituted the price of survival; every member of the community must be up and doing. When anyone failed to do his part, the authorities, whether Puritan, Anglican or otherwise, laid a heavy hand upon the culprit. The Virginia Assembly in 1619 ordered the slothful to be bound over to compulsory labor. A few years later the Massachusetts Bay Company instructed Governor John Endecott that "noe idle drone bee permitted to live amongst us," and the General Court followed this up in 1633 with a decree that "noe prson, howse houlder or othr, shall spend his time idlely or unproffitably, under paine of such punishmt as the Court shall thinke meete to inflicte." Such regulations had long existed in England, where it was hoped, vainly, they might combat the unemployment and vagrancy of a surplus laboring class; in America the object was to overcome a labor shortage — that exigent problem of every new country. Of course, most of the settlers, having been inured to toil in the homeland, needed no official prodding. They were the hardest-working people on earth, their only respite being afforded by strict observance of the Sabbath as demanded by both church and state.

The tradition of toil so begun found new sustenance as settlers opened up the boundless stretches of the interior. "In the free States," wrote Harriet Martineau in 1837, "labour is more really and heartily honoured than, perhaps, in any other part of the civilised world." Alonzo Potter voiced the general opinion of the American people when he asserted a few years later, "Without a definite pursuit, a man is an excrescence on society. . . . In isolating himself from the cares and employments of other men, he forfeits much of their sympathy, and can neither give nor receive great benefit." Even when the usual motives for work did not exist, the social compulsion remained. As William Ellery Channing put it, "The rich man has no more right to repose than the poor," for nobody should so live as to "throw all toil on another class of society."

One source of Northern antagonism to the system of human bondage was the fear that it was jeopardizing this basic tenet of the American creed. "Wherever labor is mainly performed by slaves," Daniel Webster told the United States Senate, "it is regarded as degrading to freemen"; and the Kentucky abolitionist David Rice pointed out that in the South "To labour, is to *slave;* to work, is *to work like a Negroe.*" After the Civil War, General W. T. Sherman found public occasion to thank God that now at long last Southern whites would have "to earn an honest living."

Probably no legacy from our farmer forebears has entered more deeply into the national psychology. If an American has no purposeful work on hand, the fever in his blood impels him nevertheless to some visible form of activity. When seated he keeps moving in a rocking chair. A European visitor in the 1890's saw more fact than fancy in a magazine caricature which pictured a foreigner as saying to his American hostess, "It's a defect in your country, that you have no leisured classes." "But we have them," she replied, "only we call them tramps." The traveler's own comment was: "America is the only country in the world, where one is ashamed of having nothing to do."

This worship of work has made it difficult for Americans to learn how to play. As Poor Richard saw it, "Leisure is the Time for doing something useful"; and James Russell Lowell confessed,

> Pleasure doos make us Yankees kind o'winch,
> Ez though 't wuz sunthin' paid for by the inch;
> But yit we du contrive to worry thru,
> Ef Dooty tells us thet the thing's to du.

The first mitigations of the daily grind took the form of hunting, fishing, barn-raisings and logrollings — activities that had
no social stigma because they contributed to the basic needs of
living. As the years went on, the great Southern planters, imitating the landed gentry in England, developed rural diversions of
an elaborate sort; but their example, like that of the fashionable
circles in the Northern cities, merely made the common man all
the more self-conscious when he turned to recreation. Nor did
the mid-nineteenth-century German and Irish immigrants, who
indulged in spontaneous enjoyments when the day was over,
have any other effect upon the native stock than to reinforce
suspicions of the newcomers formed on other grounds. "The
American," wrote the New Yorker Henry T. Tuckerman in 1857,
"enters into festivity as if it were a serious business." And a
serious business it has in considerable degree continued to be
ever since.

Into it goes all the fierce energy that once felled the forests
and broke the prairies. Americans play games not for fun but to
win. They attend social gatherings grimly determined to have a
"good time." Maxim Gorky said of Coney Island, "What an un-
happy people it must be that turns for happiness here." The
"rich gift of extemporizing pleasures," of taking leisure leisurely,
seems alien to the national temper. It is significant that the English Who's Who includes the recreations of the notables listed,
while the American does not.

The importance attached to useful work had the further effect
of helping to make "this new man" indifferent to aesthetic considerations. To the farmer a tree was not a thing of beauty and
a joy forever, but an obstacle to be replaced as quickly as possible with a patch of corn. In the words of an eighteenth-century American, "The Plow-man that raiseth Grain is more serviceable to Mankind, than the Painter who draws only to please
the Eye. The Carpenter who builds a good House to defend us
from the Wind and Weather, is more serviceable than the curious
Carver, who employs his Art to please the Fancy." The cult of
beauty, in other words, had nothing to contribute to the stern
business of living; it wasn't "practical." The bias thus given to
the national mentality lasted well into America's urban age.
One result has been the architectural monotony and ugliness

which have invariably offended travelers used to the picturesque
charm of Old World cities.

IV

On the other hand, the complicated nature of the farmer's
job, especially during the first two and a half centuries, afforded
an unexcelled training in mechanical ingenuity. These ex-Euro-
peans and their descendants became a race of whittlers and
tinkers, daily engaged in devising, improving and repairing tools
and other utensils until, as Emerson said, they had "the power
and habit of invention in their brain." "Would any one but an
American," asked one of Emerson's contemporaries, "have ever
invented a milking machine? or a machine to beat eggs? or
machines to black boots, scour knives, pare apples, and do a
hundred things that all other peoples have done with their ten
fingers from time immemorial?"

As population increased and manufacturing developed on a
commercial scale, men merely turned to new purposes the skills
and aptitudes that had become second nature to them. Thus
Eli Whitney, who as a Massachusetts farm youth had made nails
and hatpins for sale to his neighbors, later contrived the cotton
gin and successfully applied the principle of interchangeable
parts to the production of muskets; and Theodore T. Woodruff,
a New York farm boy, won subsequent fame as the inventor of
a sleeping car, a coffee-hulling machine and a steam plow. In
this manner another trait became imbedded in the American
character.

The farmer's success in coping with his multitudinous tasks
aroused a pride of accomplishment that made him scorn the
specialist or expert. As a Jack-of-all-trades he was content to be
master of none, choosing to do many things well enough rather
than anything supremely well. Accordingly, versatility became
another outstanding American attribute. In public affairs the
common man agreed with President Jackson that any intelligent
citizen could discharge the duties of any governmental office.
He had an abiding suspicion of the theorist or the "scholar in
politics," preferring to trust his own quick perceptions and to
deal from day to day with matters as they arose. In his bread-

winning pursuits the American flitted freely from job to job in marked contrast to the European custom of following occupations which often descended from father to son.

The most casual scrutiny of the *Dictionary of American Biography* discloses countless instances reminiscent of John Marshall and Francis Makemie in colonial times. Thomas Buchanan Read, born on a Pennsylvania farm, was in turn a tailor's apprentice, grocer's assistant, cigar maker, tombstone carver, sign painter and actor before he became a portrait painter, novelist and poet. Another personage is listed as "ornithologist and wholesale druggist"; another as "preacher, railway president, author"; and still another as "physician, merchant, political leader, magazine editor, poet, and critic." The wonder is that, despite such a squandering of energies, they could yet gain sufficient distinction in any phase of their activities to be recalled by posterity.

Even in his principal occupation of growing food, the farmer encountered harsh criticism from foreign observers because of the way he wore out the land, neglected livestock and destroyed forest resources. But Old World agriculture rested on a ratio of man to land which in the New World was the reverse. It was as logical for the American farmer to "mine" the soil and move on to a virgin tract as it was for the European peasant to husband his few acres in the interest of generations unborn. Not till the opening years of the twentieth century, when the pressure of population dramatized the evils of past misuse, did the conservation of natural resources become a set national policy.

Meanwhile the tradition of wasteful living, bred by an environment of plenty, had fastened itself upon the American character, disposing men to condone extravagance in public as well as in private life. Even governmental corruption could be winked at on the ground that a wealthy country like the United States could afford it. In their daily living, Americans were improvident of riches that another people would have carefully preserved. One newcomer from England in the early nineteenth century wrote that the apples and peaches rotting in Ohio orchards were more "than would sink the British fleet." Another said of her neighbors that she wished "the poor people of England had the leavings of their tables, that goes to their dogs and hogs." A great national emergency like that of the Axis war revealed the extent to which the practice still prevails. People learned that by responding to the government's appeal to salvage kitchen fats, old iron and other materials usually discarded they could make a substantial contribution to the war effort.

Toward women the American male early acquired an attitude which sharply distinguished him from his brother in the Old World. As in every new country, women had a high scarcity value, both in the colonies and later in the pioneer West. They were in demand not only as sweethearts and wives, but also because of their economic importance, for they performed the endless work about the house and helped with the heavy farm labor. "The cry is everywhere for girls; girls, and more girls!" wrote a traveler in 1866. He noted that men outnumbered women in thirty-eight of the forty-five states and territories. In California the proportion was three to one; in Colorado, twenty to one. "Guess my husband's got to look after me, and make himself agreeable to me, if he can," a pretty Western girl remarked, "if he don't, there's plenty will." In the circumstances men paid women a deference and accorded them a status unknown in older societies. European observers attributed the high standard of sex morals largely to this fact, and it is significant that the most rapid strides toward equal suffrage took place in those commonwealths whose rural characteristics were strongest.

v

Since the agriculturalist regarded his farm as only a temporary abode — an investment rather than a home — he soon contracted the habit of being "permanently transitory." Distances that would have daunted the stoutest-hearted European deterred "this new man" not at all. Many an Atlantic Coast family migrated from place to place across the continent until the second or third generation reached the rim of the Pacific, then the next one began the journey back. "In no State of the Union," wrote James Bryce in 1888, "is the bulk of the population so fixed in its residence as everywhere in Europe; in many it is almost nomadic."

But for this constant mingling of people and ideas the spirit of sectionalism would have opened far deeper fissures in American society than it did, for the breadth of the land, the regional diversification of economic interests and the concentration of European immigrants in certain areas were all factors conducive to disaffection and disunity. Apart from the crisis of 1861, however, it has always been possible to adjust sectional differences peaceably. The war between North and South might itself have been avoided if the system of slave labor had not increasingly stopped the inflow of persons from other parts of the country as well as from Europe. Denied such infusions of new blood, the Southerners lived more and more to themselves, came to exalt their peculiarities over the traits they had in common with their fellow countrymen and, in the end, determined to establish an independent state.

As the nation grew older and its institutions took on a more settled aspect, the locomotive tendencies of the Americans showed no signs of abatement. On the principle of the man biting the dog, the *New York Times,* June 14, 1942, reported that a resident of Sebastapol, California, had lived in the same house for fifty years, though it admitted that his ten brothers and sisters had left the town. In the 1950's one out of five persons the country over changed his residence, a third of them removing to other states.

With the advent of the low-priced motorcar and the passion for long-distance touring, the rippling movement of humanity came to resemble the waves of the ocean. It seems as though the pursuit of happiness has become the happiness of pursuit. Foreigners had earlier expressed amazement at the spectacle of dwellings being hauled along the streets from one site to another, but in the last twenty years the American people have discovered in the automobile trailer a means of constantly living on wheels. In 1959 alone, sales of these vehicular homes amounted to almost $700,000,000.

Geographic or horizontal mobility, however, has been a less fundamental aspect of American life than social or vertical mobility, though the two are not unrelated. The European conception of a graded society, with each class everlastingly performing its allotted function, vanished quickly amidst primitive surroundings that invited the humblest to move upward as well as outward. Instead of everybody being nobody, they found that anybody might become somebody. In the language of James Russell Lowell, "Here, on the edge of the forest, where civilized man was brought face to face again with nature and taught mainly to rely on himself, mere manhood became a fact of prime importance." This emancipation from hoary custom was "no bantling of theory, no fruit of forethought," but "a gift of the sky and of the forest."

Accordingly, there arose the ingrained belief in equality of opportunity, the right of all men to a free and fair start — a view which in one of its most significant ramifications led to the establishment of free tax-supported schools. This was far from being a dogma of enforced equality. To benefit from equality of opportunity a man must be equal to his opportunities, with the government serving principally as an umpire to supervise the game with a minimum of rules. The upshot was a conception of democracy rigorously qualified by individualism.

This individualistic bias sometimes assumed forms that defied government. The colonists in their relations with the mother country evaded unwelcome regulations and, prompted by their theologians and lawyers, insisted that acts of Parliament contrary to their "unalienable rights" were void. Within the colonies those who dwelt remote from centers of law and order adopted a like attitude toward the provincial authorities. The Scotch-Irish who illegally occupied Pennsylvania soil in the early eighteenth century contended "it was against the laws of God and nature, that so much land should be idle while so many Christians wanted it to labor on and to raise their bread." As a substitute for constituted authority the settlers sometimes created their own unofficial tribunals, which adjudicated property titles and punished offenders against the public peace. In other instances they resorted to the swifter retribution of individual gunplay, or of mob action and lynch law, for from taking the law into one's hands when it could not function it was but a step to taking the law into one's hands when it did not function as one wanted it to.

The tendency to violence so generated has continued to condition the national mentality to the present time. Thoreau, the great philosopher of individualism, knew of no reason why a citizen should "ever for a moment, or in the least degree, resign his conscience to the legislator," declaring that "we should be men first, and subjects afterward." A similar conviction undoubtedly inspired William H. Seward's flaming declaration to the proslavery Senators in 1850 that "there is a higher law than the Constitution," just as it actuated the thousands of churchgoing Northerners who secretly banded together to violate the Fugitive Slave Act. But generally it has been self-interest or convenience, rather than conscience, that has provided the incentive to lawbreaking, as in the case of the businessman chafing against legislative restrictions or of the motorist disobeying traffic regulations. Sometimes the attitude has paraded under such high-sounding names as states' rights and nullification. This lawless streak in the American character has often been directed to wrong purposes, but it has also served as a check on the abuse of governmental powers and as a safeguard of minority rights.

In still another aspect, the individualism of the pioneer farmer does much to explain the intense cultivation of the acquisitive spirit. In the absence of hereditary distinctions of birth and rank the piling up of wealth constituted the most obvious badge of social superiority, and once the process was begun, the inbred urge to keep on working made it difficult to stop. "The poor struggle to be rich, the rich to be richer," remarked an onlooker in the mid-nineteenth century. Thanks to equality of opportunity with plenty for all, the class struggle in America has consisted in the struggle to climb out of one class into a higher one. The zest of competition frequently led to sharp trading, fraud and chicanery, but in the popular mind guilt attached less to the practices than to being caught at them. Financial success was accepted as the highest success, and not till the twentieth century did a religious leader venture to advance the un-American doctrine that ill-gotten wealth was "tainted money," even when devoted to benevolent uses.

VI

It would be a mistake, however, to think of the American simply as a mechanism set in motion by dropping a coin in the slot.

When President Coolidge made his famous remark, "The business of America is business," he quite properly added, "The chief ideal of the American people is idealism. I cannot repeat too often that America is a nation of idealists." This ambivalence puzzled foreign commentators, who found it difficult, for example, to reconcile worship of the Almighty Dollar with the equally universal tendency to spend freely and give money away. In contrast to Europe, America has had practically no misers, and one consequence of the winning of Independence was the abolition of primogeniture and entail. Harriet Martineau was among those who concluded that "the eager pursuit of wealth does not necessarily indicate a love of wealth for its own sake."

The fact is that, for a people who recalled how hungry and oppressed their ancestors had been through long centuries in the Old World, the chance to make money was like the sunlight at the end of a tunnel. It was the means of living a life of human dignity. It was a symbol of idealism rather than materialism. Hence "this new man" had an instinctive sympathy for the underdog, and even persons of moderate substance freely shared it with the less fortunate, helping to endow charities, schools, hospitals and art galleries and to nourish humanitarian undertakings which might otherwise have died a-borning.

The energy that entered into many of these causes was heightened by another national attitude: optimism. It was this quality that sustained the European men and women who with heavy hearts left ancestral homes to try their fortunes in a wild and far-off continent. The same trait animated the pioneer farmers confronted by the hardships, loneliness and terrors of the primeval forest, and served also to spur their successors who, though facing less dire conditions, were constantly pitted against both the uncertainties of the weather and the unpredictable demands of the market. When Thomas Jefferson remarked, "I steer my bark with Hope in the head, leaving Fear astern," he spoke for his compatriots. To doubt the future was to confess oneself a failure since the life history of almost any American documented the opposite view. A belief in progress blossomed spontaneously in such a soil.

If this belief made some men tolerant of present abuses in the confident expectation that time would provide the cure, it fired others with an apostolic zeal to hasten the happy day. As a keen observer in the middle of the last century said of his countrymen, "Americans are sanguine enough to believe that no evil is without a remedy, if they could only find it, and they see no good reason why they should not try to find remedies for all the evils of life." Not even fatalism in religion could long withstand the bracing atmosphere of the New World. This quality of optimism sometimes soared to dizzy heights, impelling men to strive for earthly perfection in communistic societies or to prepare to greet the imminent return of Christ.

It attained its most blatant expression, however, in the national addiction to bragging. At bottom, this habit sprang from pride in a country of vast distances and huge elevations plus an illimitable faith in its possibilities of being great as well as big. The American glorified the future in much the same spirit as the European glorified the past, both tending to exalt what they had the most of. And by a simple transition the American went on to speak of expected events as though they had already happened, being prompted perhaps by an urge to compensate for an inner sense of inferiority. This frame of mind led statesmen to cultivate spread-eagle oratory — a style which the *North American Review* in 1858 defined as "a compound of exaggeration, effrontery, bombast, and extravagance, mixed metaphors, platitudes, defiant threats thrown at the world, and irreverent appeals flung at the Supreme Being."

For the same reason the ordinary citizen resorted to hyperbole. In the thinly settled sections this manner of speech went by the name of tall talk, causing the backwoods to be known as a "paradise of puffers." A Frenchman, however, referred to a national, not a regional, trait when he said Americans seemed loath to admit that Christopher Columbus himself had not been an American, and it was an Easterner writing in an Eastern magazine who soberly averred, "It is easier, say the midwives, to come into this world of America . . . than in any other world extant." In business life this indulgent attitude toward truth lent itself to deliberate attempts to defraud, and made the land speculator with his "lithographed mendacity" the natural forerunner of the dishonest stock promoter of later times. Boastfulness is an attribute of youth which greater national maturity has helped to temper. Still the War Department in its manual of behavior for Yankee soldiers in England during the Axis war thought it prudent to admonish them: "Don't show off or brag or bluster."

This facility for overstatement has lent a distinctive quality to American humor. In the United States humor has never been part of a general gaiety of spirit. It has had to break through a crust of life thick with serious purpose. Hence it has had to be boisterous and bold, delighting in exaggeration, incongruities and farcical effects and reaching a grand climax in the practical joke. Out of a comic mood so induced arose such folk heroes as Mike Fink, Paul Bunyan, Pecos Bill and the myth-embroidered Davy Crockett, whose fabulous exploits flourished in oral tradition long before they were reduced to print. In deference to the national sobriety of temperament the most successful professional humorists have been those who told their yarns while preserving a decorous gravity of expression.

VII

If this analysis of national characteristics is well founded, then certain modifications of the pattern were inevitable when the primacy of rural life gave way to the rise of urbanism. That change began to take place in the latter years of the nineteenth century. In 1860 only a sixth of the people lived in towns of eight thousand or more, but by 1900 a third dwelt in such communities and today well over half do. Along with urban concentration has gone a remarkable development of means of communication and transport — the telephone, rural free delivery, interurban electric transit, good roads, the automobile, the movie, the radio, television — that carried city ideas and ways to "the very finger-tips of the whole land." Though most of the historic traits continued to thrive in this new milieu, some were moderated and a few disappeared. The time is too short to gauge the full consequences, but several of the reversals of attitude are noteworthy.

One is the importance which Americans have come to attach to cultural achievement. The ancient prejudice against "useless" activities could not long withstand the compelling opportunities of the city. In the city were to be found the best schools and colleges, the best newspapers and magazines, and practically all the bookstores, libraries, publishing houses, concert halls, conservatories of music, art museums and theaters. There, too, America made closest contact with the vital thought of Europe. Stimulated by such an atmosphere the writer or artist could also command an appreciative audience and financial support. Who can ever know how dreadful a toll the two and a half centuries of agricultural life exacted in terms of creative advances of the mind and spirit, how many a mute inglorious Milton succumbed to the unremitting struggle with Nature? For persons like these the city meant a glad release, giving them a chance to mature their powers, consort with kindred spirits and enter the lists for fame and fortune. Even in earlier times cultural stirrings had centered in the towns and cities. Now as the urban influence became uppermost, Americans commenced to make contributions to scholarship, science, literature and the fine arts that challenged comparison with the best Europe could offer.

As a necessary consequence, much of the former aversion to specialization of talent vanished. In a civilization rapidly growing more complex, men began to place a higher value on thoroughly mastering a skill or conquering a particular intellectual domain. The business of making a living tended to fall into compartments, with the men best equipped by training or experience reaping the greatest rewards. This trend characterized not only industry and trade but also the arts and sciences. Even in public life expert knowledge steadily played a larger part, notably in the administrative services of city, state and nation. The derisive references to the New Deal's "Brain Trust" came from political opponents who, however, did not intend to forgo the same advantage when they returned to power.

A further result of the altered aspect of American society has been the great impetus given to voluntary associative activity. In a country environment the gregarious instinct was constantly balked by the dearth of neighbors. The hunger for companionship could discover only occasional outlet, as at the county fair or in the agitated throng gathered from far and near for a camp meeting. Now, to the rural birthright of liberty and equality the city added the boon of fraternity. In a crowded community, like could find like. The reformer, the businessman, the wage earner,

the intellectual worker, the sports lover, the ancestor worshiper
— all these and many others gravitated into special groups to
further interests held in common, and these local societies seldom failed to expand into nation-wide federations. Soon the
population became divided between the organized and those
who organized them, until, if the late Will Rogers is to be believed, "Americans will join anything in town but their own
family. Why, two Americans can't meet on the street without
one banging a gavel and calling the other to order." Thus the
passion for associative activity came to be a sovereign principle
of life.

Quite as noteworthy has been another effect of city growth:
the discrediting of individualism as the automatic cure of social
and economic ills. As the nineteenth century advanced, the
increasing domination of the national economy by urban mag-
nates of business and finance caused the farmers to demand that
the government intercede to protect their right to a decent livelihood. In the cities the cramped living quarters, the growing
wretchedness of the poor and the rise of difficult social problems
also created doubts as to the sufficiency of the laissez-faire brand
of democracy. Only the rich and powerful seemed now to profit
from a reign of unbridled individualism. Though the solid core
of ancient habit yielded stubbornly, the average man came gradually to believe that under the changed conditions it was the
duty of the government of all to safeguard the opportunities of
all. After the American fashion it was a doctrineless conviction,
the product of an adjustment to new times for the sake of preserving the traditional spirit of self-reliance and free competition.

Though the gospel of work continued as unquestioned as ever,
willing workers could no longer be certain of regular employment, particularly in the towns and cities. Every sudden jar to
the nation's business structure rendered large numbers idle.
Through no fault of his own, the laborer was being denied an
essential part of his heritage. As early as 1893 the American
Federation of Labor resolved that "the right to work is the right
to life," and declared that "when the private employer cannot
or will not give work the municipality, state or nation must."
But it was not till the Great Depression destroyed the livelihood
of people in all walks of life that this novel view became an

article of American faith. The New Deal assumed the obligation not merely of succoring the hungry, but of creating jobs for the idle and of guarding against such hazards in the future by means of unemployment insurance, retirement pay for aged wage earners and special provisions for farmers. Thus what had started originally because of the community's need that all should work became transformed, first into a doctrine of the right to work, and then into the duty of society to provide the means of work.

VIII

The national character, as we at present know it, is thus a mixture of long-persisting traits tempered by some newly acquired ones. Based upon the solid qualities of those Europeans who planted the colonies, it assumed distinctive form under pressure of adaptation to the radically different situation. "Our ancestors sought a new continent," said James Russell Lowell. "What they found was a new condition of mind." The protracted tutelage to the soil acted as the chief formative influence, dispelling ancient inhibitions, freeing dormant energies, revamping mental attitudes. The rise of the city confirmed or strengthened many of the earlier characteristics while reshaping others. Probably no one of the traits is peculiar to the American people; some occasion apology rather than pride; but the aggregate represents a way of life unlike that of any other nation.

Just as the American character has undergone modification in the past, so it will doubtless undergo modification in the future. Nevertheless, certain of its elements seem so deeply rooted as to withstand the erosion of time and circumstance. Of this order are the qualities that made possible the development of the continent, the building of a democratic society and the continuing concern for the welfare of the underprivileged. These are attributes better suited to peace than to war, yet every great crisis has found the people ready to die for their conception of life so that their children might live it. The American character, whatever its shortcomings, abounds in courage, creative energy and resourcefulness, and is bottomed upon the profound conviction that nothing in the world is beyond its power to accomplish.

2

Biography of a nation of joiners

AT FIRST thought it seems paradoxical that a people noted for individualism should also be the world's greatest example of joiners. How this came about is the object of this inquiry, but the illusion of paradox can be dispelled at once. In the United States individualism has meant not the individual's independence of other individuals, but his as well as their independence of governmental restraint. Traditionally, Americans have distrusted collective organization as embodied in government while insisting upon their own untrammeled right to form voluntary associations. This conception of a state of minimal powers actually made it necessary for private citizens to organize for undertakings too large for a single person. By reverse effect the success of such enterprises hindered the enlargement of governmental authority.

This tendency was reinforced by the absence of fixed social classes. As Alexis de Tocqueville pointed out in the 1830's, men in aristocratic countries have not the same reason "to combine in order to act," since "every wealthy and powerful citizen constitutes the head of a permanent and compulsory association, composed of all those who are dependent upon him, or whom he makes subservient to the execution of his designs." The "independent and feeble" citizens of a democratic society, on the other hand, must "learn voluntarily to help one another."

The real contradiction between individualism (in the American sense) and associative action lies elsewhere — in the disposition of some groups to seek statutory support for imposing their views upon the community at large. Though few started with this intention, a waxing zeal and growing impatience with slower methods led an increasing number to do so. To the extent they succeeded, they enhanced the government's authority and correspondingly reduced the scope of free group enterprise.

The trend toward collective activity began slowly in American history, but it gathered impetus as the years revealed new opportunities and men perceived the advantages to be gained. Broadly speaking, the rise of associations paralleled the development of democratic self-confidence and the greater complexity of social and economic life. Each fresh application of the principle opened the way for further ones and at the same time afforded the experience needed for more extensive undertakings. In the end no department of human existence remained unaffected.

Because the subject is too vast for more than a bird's-eye view in brief space, this account centers upon voluntary bodies of sizable membership, reasonably long duration and fairly large territorial extent, and it proceeds by means of sampling rather than complete coverage. Even as so limited, the theme is unwieldy, for it includes incorporated as well as unincorporated groups, secret societies as well as nonsecret ones, organizations for religious, economic and political purposes as well as those seeking humanitarian, cultural and recreational ends. By a canon of humor the term "joiner" is generally confined to a member of fraternal orders, but in a truer sense it embraces all who for whatever reason choose to "combine in order to act." Viewed against this background, fraternal organizations will be seen as merely a somewhat belated manifestation of a spirit which had already come to dominate great areas of society.

I

During the first century or more of the colonies the people displayed little aptitude for large co-operative undertakings. They had had scant experience in doing things collectively in Europe, and, moreover, towns were few, the population was small and scattered, and communication difficult. Nevertheless, in one important phase of life, that of religion, the principle of association struck quick and effective root. In a majority of the colonies the settlers found they had not escaped the restrictions of an established church by crossing the Atlantic, for in New England the dominant Puritans devised their own counterpart of the Old World system and in the South the Anglicans transplanted the one existing at home. This union of church and state went hard with nonconformists, for these early Americans took their religion more to heart than has any later generation.

Fortunately, the field was open equally to all creeds in the intermediate region — Pennsylvania, Delaware, New Jersey, Rhode Island and most of New York — and there the various groups, including the Catholics, operated on a basis of free association and self-support. Even in the colonies with official churches, the dissidents set up their own places of worship alongside those that were public-supported, even though this subjected them to a species of double taxation. The plan of voluntarism (or voluntaryism) as it was worked out in the different provinces amazed most onlookers from Europe, who could not understand why anyone should pay for the maintenance of religion when not obliged to. The people in organizing their own devotional societies instituted a system which would eventually prevail throughout America.

In other than spiritual concerns, however, men generally acted alone. It was not until toward the middle of the eighteenth century, when towns had grown larger and more numerous, that they ventured somewhat timidly to extend the principle of voluntary action to other interests. Associations for local civic purposes, though not unknown earlier, now assumed greater prominence, as the career of Philadelphia's leading citizen bears witness. Benjamin Franklin, who in so many other ways foreshadowed the modern American, qualifies further as an organizer and joiner. Besides fathering the Junto, a club of artisans and tradesmen, he started a subscription library, an academy for educating youth and a volunteer company of fire fighters, and he also took part in founding a hospital and a fire-insurance company. In addition to these community enterprises, he instituted the American Philosophical Society, America's oldest learned body, served for a time as provincial grand master of the Masons and helped to promote a Western land company.

For various reasons these last three undertakings proved far less successful than the local ones. They were all of interprovincial scope, and distances between the principal towns were still great and communications slow. Most persons, moreover, regarded oath-bound lodges with distrust, if not alarm, and the British government was dubious as to the wisdom of encouraging frontier colonization schemes. The American Philosophical Society languished for some years after its formation in 1743; and the Masonic order, introduced into the leading towns from England in the preceding decade, excited public opposition as aristocratic in spirit and subversive of good morals. On one occasion the New York members were "complimented with Snow Balls and Dirt" while parading the streets. In Philadelphia popular anger over an apprentice's death in a bogus initiation halted Masonic activities from 1738 to 1749. Franklin's land company encountered not only ministerial objections and delays but also intercolonial jealousies.

Nevertheless, this Vandalia project, as it was called, represented a more genuine interest of the times than did the other two undertakings, for it provided an outlet for the surplus capital that was piling up in the towns. Franklin's company was only one of many that were formed up and down the colonies. With most of the coastal lands already in private hands, men with money to invest looked to the vacant tracts beyond the mountains, and a rising speculative fever caused them to league together to obtain government grants. Starting around the middle of the eighteenth century, various groups of provincials, some with English associates, organized such ventures as the Ohio Company, the Mississippi Company, the Illinois Company, the Wabash Land Company and the Transylvania Company. Though none accomplished much, the widespread support they elicited augured the future extension of the associative device to a great diversity of capitalistic projects.

Considerably more effective were the attempts at united political action. For this the home government was unwittingly responsible, for until the British authorities in the 1760's adopted a policy of tighter imperial control, political parties had been unknown on an interprovincial scale and had seldom lasted long in the separate colonies. Now, alarmed by fears of parliamentary taxation and threats to their trade, the people not only formed local groups of opposition, but also acted in concert with similar groups in other places. These interprovincial alliances comprised the first national parties in American history. The Stamp Act emergency of 1764–1765 wove a multifarious network of such agencies along the seaboard: merchants' committees, dedicated to stirring up the legislatures; secret mechanics' organizations of "Sons of Liberty," which sometimes employed mob methods; and other bands of citizens who combined to boycott British imports. The Stamp Act Congress brought many of the leaders face to face for the first time.

As crisis piled upon crisis, these organs were supplemented by still others, notably the committees of correspondence, which in New England were appointed by town meetings but elsewhere usually by unofficial means. When Parliament embarked upon drastic coercive proceedings after the Boston Tea Party, the patriots formed provincial congresses and conventions and proceeded to assemble the First Continental Congress. This body, though not avowedly or constitutionally a government, functioned like one, extending and reinvigorating the local committee system and devising measures of economic opposition which all persons had to obey on pain of boycott. Through the associative process the insurgent elements thus reared a structure which, as a Tory feelingly remarked, "takes the Government out of the hands of the Governour, Council, and General Assembly; and the execution of the laws out of the hands of the Civil Magistrates and Juries." Organized now from center to circumference, the popular party presently took up arms against the British and eventually declared America's independence. Under conditions of extreme provocation the people thus demonstrated their capacity for common political action.

II

In this halting way the colonial era saw the emergence of what was to become a dominant American trait. Prompted originally by a passion for freedom of worship, and for a long time going no farther, the associative impulse began to invade other fields as the break with England approached. Though it achieved decisive results only in the sphere of public affairs, the foundations were laid for future progress in other respects as well. National independence quickened these tendencies. The philosophy of natural rights underlying the Revolution exalted the individual's capacity to act for himself; the military struggle taught men from different sections valuable lessons in joint effort; the mounting sense of national consciousness suggested new vistas of achievement; and Britain could no longer interpose a restraining hand. A little later, after a decade of political instability, the adoption of the Constitution stimulated still further applications of the collective principle.

In the domain of spiritual concerns the complete divorce of church and state was now effected, first in the South and later in New England. Jefferson's famous Virginia statute of religious liberty affirmed that "the rights hereby asserted are of the natural rights of mankind." Such faiths as had maintained Old World connections proceeded to sever them in order to reorganize upon a separate American basis. Moreover, many of the states enacted general laws specifically granting church groups equal opportunities of incorporation — a foretaste of the system that the next generation would apply to business groups.

A further innovation was the formation of nation-wide benevolent societies, religious in inspiration but nonsectarian in personnel and direction. Profiting by British example, these associations labored to awaken an interest in Christianity beyond church circles and even beyond the United States. The principal ones were the American Board of Commissioners for Foreign Missions (1810), the American Bible Society (1816), the American Sunday School Union (1824), the American Tract Society (1825) and the American Home Missionary Society (1826). While each of these agencies discharged a particular function, all stood for a Biblical rather than a doctrinal approach to religion, and they preserved an independence of denominational interference by their financial self-sufficiency. This concern of the devout for the spiritually neglected was a halfway house to the humanitarian reform societies of the Jacksonian period.

Meanwhile, in the economic sphere, the associative spirit flowered in a profusion of community enterprises, notably for building toll roads and establishing banks. The first agricultural improvement societies also arose, some of them state-wide in extent. Though distances continued to favor local projects, yet, as in the case of religious benevolence, larger ones were also undertaken. With British oversight removed, aggressive men, sometimes employing unscrupulous methods, joined forces to secure from Congress or the state legislatures extensive land grants in the Mississippi Valley. Such men as Manasseh Cutler of Massachusetts, Rufus Putnam of Connecticut, Robert Morris of Pennsylvania and Patrick Henry of Virginia participated in some of the earlier schemes. On its own motion the federal government, utilizing powers derived from the newly ratified Constitution, incorporated a Bank of the United States under private control, with branches in the leading coastal cities; and in 1816, five years after the charter expired, Congress set up a Second United States Bank for a twenty-year period with a much larger capitalization. As yet, however, capitalistic undertakings of interstate or national scope were the exception rather than the rule.

The adoption of the Constitution unintentionally provided also a firmer basis for political associations. The framers had thought of parties as temporary combinations of legislators, coalescing and dissolving as new measures were considered, but the device of checks and balances rendered such a system difficult, if not unworkable. The requirement of electing the President, Senate and House in three different manners entailed the danger that these organs of government would each go their separate ways unless some voluntary agency unknown to the Constitution held them together. To supply this unifying element the Federalist and Republican parties quickly took shape, the one looking to Hamilton and the other to Jefferson for inspiration. Thus were instituted those permanent groupings of voters which, as the suffrage was broadened, later generations would mold into even more powerful instruments of political action.

The various extensions of collective enterprise during this first half-century of national independence did not go unchallenged by persons and groups who feared the effects upon either their own or the general welfare. Certain of the churches resented the encroaching activities of the benevolent societies "subject to no ecclesiastical responsibility, and adopting no formula of faith by which their religious tenets may be ascertained." These adjunct bodies were also charged with drying up sources of funds which might otherwise have replenished denominational coffers. The growing rift in the Presbyterian fold over the question of voluntary associations led directly to the great schism of 1837 between the Old School and New School contingents.

Capitalistic associations aroused hostility because of the special legal advantages they often enjoyed at the expense of possible competitors. Few colonial economic enterprises had been incorporated, not even the land companies. But now, enticed by new and more exciting prospects of profit, commercial groups turned increasingly to the legislatures for charters conferring such privileges as rights of way, limited liability for debts and the financial support of numerous shareholders. To many persons the government's action in bestowing exclusive favors seemed to ally it with "large monied interests" and to violate the "natural and legal rights of mankind." They saw no more reason for a union of business and state than of church and state. A Philadelphia pamphleteer in 1792, maintaining that wealth already wielded undue influence, continued, "Laws, it is said, cannot equalize men, — no — but ought they, for that reason, to aggravate the inequality which they cannot cure? . . . It is not the distinction of titles which constitutes an aristocracy; it is the principle of partial association." Although some critics opposed any incorporation at all, most wished to replace the practice of granting special charters with a system of general incorporation open to all who could meet the specified conditions.

In the national arena the dispute concerning corporate privileges centered in the struggle over chartering the original United States Bank. Behind Jefferson's doubts as to Congress's constitutional power in the matter lay deep-seated democratic objections to the creation of a financial monopoly. The Supreme Court in the Dartmouth College case (1819), while not passing upon the issue of equality of privilege, gave great impetus to the associative trend by promulgating the doctrine of the freedom of charters from subsequent alteration by sole action of the lawmaking authority. In time, however, legislatures learned to sidestep the decision by making it a practice to grant charters only on the express condition of their right later to amend or repeal them.

Political associations also incurred opposition, with President Washington particularly outspoken against them. The Democratic Societies, which sprang up in many places during his second term to agitate for popular rights and carry on pro-French propaganda, kindled his fears for the maintenance of orderly government. He classed them with the "self-created societies" that instigated the Whisky Insurrection. Returning to the theme in his Farewell Address, he roundly condemned "all combinations and associations, under whatever plausible character, with the real design to direct, control, counteract, or awe the regular deliberation and action of the constituted authorities." Lest he be understood as not including political parties, he added, "In governments of a monarchical cast patriotism may look with indulgence, if not with favor, upon the spirit of party. But in those of the popular character, in governments purely elective, it is a spirit not to be encouraged."

Local social and literary clubs, on the other hand, excited little criticism, and even the Masonic fraternity seemed to have lived down its earlier disrepute, though portents of future trouble appeared in the increasing strictures by church groups on its unorthodox religious ideals. By contrast, a new secret order, the Society of the Cincinnati, raised a cyclone of rage which the country did not soon forget. Formed in 1783 by Revolutionary officers on the basis of hereditary membership, the organization struck many as a potential military threat to the people's freedom as well as a scheme to perpetuate a species of un-American nobility. The press volleyed against it, Rhode Island considered disfranchising its members, and the Massachusetts legislature proclaimed it "dangerous to the peace, liberty, and safety of the Union." Such fears were doubtless hysterical, but the Cincinnati suffered a blight from which it has never entirely recovered. Nor were the veterans of any of the intervening wars able to establish effective societies.

III

Notwithstanding these occasional dikes of resistance the associative current had steadily gathered momentum during the first half-century of national independence. In the next generation it seemed to many to reach flood proportions. "In truth," wrote William Ellery Channing, one of the most remarkable circumstances or features of our age is the energy with which the principle of combination, or of action by joint forces, by associated numbers, is manifesting itself. . . . Those who have one great object find one another out through a vast extent of country, join their forces, settle their mode of operation, and act together with the uniformity of a disciplined army.

These organizations, he said, constituted the "most powerful springs" of social action. Alexis de Tocqueville, the Frenchman who visited the United States in 1831–1832, quickly sensed their importance. "The power of association," he noted in his diary, "has reached its uttermost development," and as the luminous discussion in *Democracy in America* shows, he marveled at "the extreme skill with which the inhabitants . . . succeed in proposing a common object to the exertions of a great many men, and in getting them voluntarily to pursue it." To posterity, of course, the accomplishments appear less impressive than to people at the time, who compared the situation with earlier America or contemporary Europe.

Channing ascribed the passion for joining to certain new developments in American life: "the immense facility given to intercourse by modern improvements, by increased commerce and travelling, by the post-office, by the steam-boat, and especially by the press, — by newspapers, periodicals, tracts, and other publications." And he added, "The grand manoeuvre to which Napoleon owed his victories — we mean the concentration of great numbers on a single point — is now placed within the reach of all parties and sects." Not long after he wrote, the canal, the railroad and the telegraph greatly augmented these channels of communication.

But the will to make use of these instrumentalities needs also to be accounted for, and here the explanation lies in other basic changes in the nation's life. The rising importance of the plain people, symbolized in politics by Jackson's election as President, made ancient injustices no longer tolerable and inspired the humane, and sometimes the victims themselves, to unite for correcting them. In the Old World, too, a new tenderness was being shown for the underprivileged, and European example, especially that of England, continually encouraged American reform efforts. Besides, as cities increased both in number and size, co-operative action became easier. People of kindred interests could be quickly assembled, agitation organized, mass meetings held, committees put to work. And in addition to being centers of sur-plus enthusiasm, cities were centers of surplus money, furnishing the financial sinews for joint undertakings whether to gird or amend the existing order.

Nowhere did the results prove more striking than in the field of humanitarian reform. The earlier concern for bruised and neglected souls now widened to take in bruised and neglected minds and bodies. Christian altruism combined with democratic idealism to produce what seemed to scoffers an interferiority complex. Typical of the new creations were the American Tem-perance Society (1826), the American Peace Society (1828), the General Union for Promoting the Christian Observance of the Sabbath (1828), the American Lyceum Association (1831), the American Anti-Slavery Society (1833) and the American and Foreign Sabbath Union (1842). If to these national associations be added countless smaller ones devoted to such aims as improv-ing penal methods, advocating universal education and redeem-ing "Females who have Deviated from the Paths of Virtue," one can understand Orestes A. Brownson's sour comment: "Matters have come to such a pass, that a peaceable man can hardly ven-ture to eat or drink, or to go to bed or to get up, to correct his children or to kiss his wife, without obtaining the permission and direction of some . . . society."

Since humanitarian associations espoused views in advance of the times, they had to try to persuade or frighten the majority into adopting the proposals. For this purpose they borrowed and im-proved upon the methods already developed by the nonsectarian benevolent societies. The first step, noted a contemporary, was to choose an "imposing" designation for the organization; next, "a list of respectable names must be obtained, as members and pa-trons"; then, "a secretary and an adequate corps of assistants must be appointed and provided for from the first fruits of collec-tions; a band of popular lecturers must be commissioned, and sent forth as agents on the wide public; the press with its many-winged messengers, is put in operation"; finally, "subsidiary so-

cieties are multiplied over the length and breadth of the land."
These local units were then linked together in state branches,
which in turn sent representatives to a national body. By 1835
the 1,200,000 members of the American Temperance Society
were distributed in eight thousand local affiliates with an over-all
organization in every state but one. Two years later the American
Anti-Slavery Society (whose constituency was in fact strictly
Northern) had grown to more than a thousand local and seven
state associations. In addition, both of these bodies, and the
American Peace Society as well, sponsored youth auxiliaries and
separate branches for women.

To implement their work the crusading groups required funds
as well as zeal. The American Anti-Slavery Society reported an
annual revenue of from $26,000 to $50,000 between 1836 and
1840, not counting the receipts of affiliates. As in the case of
other reform organizations, this income derived partly from
membership dues and collections at public meetings, partly from
gifts and the proceeds of local fairs and sewing circles and
partly from the sale of publications. Publication activities, however, were designed less to raise money than to reinforce oral
propaganda, and hence much of the material was distributed
free. Every aggregation sponsored weekly or monthly organs,
circulated widely the reports of its annual conventions and issued
great quantities of leaflets and pamphlets, including fiction, song-
books, almanacs and "pictorial representations." In the single
year 1840–1841 the American Temperance Union sent out 433,-
000 items. Another practice was to pelt the government with
memorials. The abolitionists' persistence in petitioning the
House of Representatives led the proslavery majority in that
body to adopt a "gag rule" whose repeal ex-President John
Quincy Adams finally accomplished in 1844 after a historic eight-
year battle.

With varying effect the reformers enlisted the support of
church, school and stage. At one juncture more than a thousand
ministers agreed to preach annual peace sermons, and efforts
were made to insert peace arguments in textbooks, while such
books as *Uncle Tom's Cabin* and *Ten Nights in a Bar-room* converted untold numbers to the antislavery and temperance causes.
Use was also made of emblems and ceremonials. Olive Leaf Cir-

cles attracted female foes of war, Cold Water Armies recruited juvenile fighters against the "Demon Rum," and for nearly everybody bazaars, parades, banners and badges mixed fun with serious purpose. So successfully did these pioneer reformers develop the techniques of organization and propaganda that later generations have been able to contribute little beyond taking advantage of new technological devices such as the movies, radio, and television. The South for the most part remained immune to the agitation, fearing lest the institution of slavery perish in an assault on other social abuses.

Some reformers, impatient of gaining their ends through the slow processes of persuasion, ventured to try out their ideas in experimental communities away from the haunts of men. Others, equally ardent but more practical, endeavored to dragoon the unconvinced into conformity through legislation. This helps to explain the interest in petitions and also the emphasis on lobbying. One wing of the abolitionists, discarding halfway measures, launched the Liberty party.

The increasing recourse to political action was a natural consequence of the swift spread of white manhood suffrage in the generation before the Civil War. Parties themselves were transformed by the admission to the polls of persons hitherto considered political outsiders. Party chieftains learned to regiment the vastly enlarged electorate and to flatter and knead the mass mind. As means to this end, these years marked the extension of the spoils system to the federal government, the growth of party machines and the introduction of national nominating conventions as well as of political platforms. Campaign appeals now were slanted at people's emotions rather than their brains. The voter was attracted by such partisan symbols as the log cabin (in which William Henry Harrison was alleged to reside), by torchlight processions and by slogans like "Fifty-four-forty or fight!" It is evident that political associations profited greatly from the example of the humanitarian associations.

The doctrine that every man should have the same chance hastened the adoption of the principle of impartiality in granting incorporation rights to capitalistic associations. On the national stage President Jackson, after carrying his battle to the electorate in the campaign of 1832, stopped Congress from renewing the exclusive privileges of the Second United States Bank,

while in the states his followers and sympathizers strove similarly
to curb the power of legislatures in conferring monopolistic advantages. Many businessmen lent support in order to assure their
equality with competitors in turning to account the expanding opportunities in transportation, manufacturing and banking.
In due course, state after state — a third of them by amending
their constitutions — provided for the future creation of corporations by general law instead of by special acts. Though a large
number of businesses continued to operate as unchartered associations, the legal machinery was made available for that vast
proliferation of corporate enterprise which was eventually to
dominate the American scene.

With far less approval from the commercial classes, indeed
against their stubborn resistance, the rapid growth of industry
begot a new type of voluntary organization, the trade union,
which had long been struggling for birth. Wage earners, confronted with conditions that denied decent standards of living,
resorted to united action in self-defense. Combining here and
there in local crafts, they soon established nation-wide unions in
some trades, and from 1834 to 1837 they kept alive a national
labor federation. At the peak of success, in 1836, the total membership in the five principal cities approximated 300,000 in
160 local unions. Though the movement suffered severe setbacks
and gained only a wavering tolerance from the courts, it nevertheless developed the special techniques that set it apart from all
other kinds of collective undertakings: the walkout, the boycott,
the sympathetic strike, picketing, the closed shop and the trade
agreement. As yet, however, labor's future in the family of associations seemed far from assured.

The zeal for joining also affected professional and intellectual
workers. The motive here was less economic — though the regulation of fees was sometimes an object — than to improve standards of performance, foster research and disseminate the findings
through meetings and publications. These associations differed
from the older American Philosophical Society in not limiting
the number of members and in pursuing more highly specialized
interests. Some were the outgrowth of local or state societies and
"academies." After the American Statistical Association set the
example in 1839, such kindred bodies appeared as the American
Ethnological Society (1842), the American Medical Association

(1847), the American Society of Engineers and Architects (1852), the National Teachers' Association (1857, later the National Education Association) and the American Entomological Society (1859). In 1848 the American Association for the Advancement of Science was formed to unite investigators in all scientific fields. Only research workers in the humanities and social sciences failed to heed the call to national action, but these departments of learning were as yet feebly staffed.

With one section of the population after another succumbing to the associative contagion, the old aversion to secret societies also collapsed. But that came only after a spectacular protest against the principal oath-bound brotherhood. The anti-Masonic uprising was rooted in the antipathy of country to town, where most of the lodges were to be found; in objections of the orthodox to the order's "diluted" Christianity; in lower-class resentment against the well-to-do membership; and in popular alarm at Masonic boasts of a controlling influence in public affairs.

The spark that set off the explosion was the abduction and alleged murder in 1826 of William Morgan of Batavia, New York, a member of the fraternity, who had written a book exposing its secrets. Though the deed was plainly the work of misguided individuals, popular hysteria refused to make the distinction. Churches expelled Masonic clergymen and parishioners. Throughout the rural East lodges disbanded, the number in New York state declining from over five hundred to forty-eight in 1832. The anti-Masons ran their own candidates in state and local elections, several legislatures forbade extrajudicial oaths, while Rhode Island required all lodges to publish their proceedings in annual reports. Astute politicians like Thurlow Weed in upstate New York and Thaddeus Stevens in Pennsylvania saw an opportunity to use the movement as a national rallying point for the forces opposed to Andrew Jackson. In doing so, however, they twisted it so far from the original purpose that in 1832 William Wirt, the party's first and only presidential nominee, did not denounce the order. The anti-Masons won only Vermont's seven electoral votes.

Although the antagonism lived on for several years in a few states, the election marked a decisive turning point in the American attitude toward secret associations. Even if the movement had not been betrayed by political opportunists, it could not

BIOGRAPHY OF A NATION OF JOINERS 39

have gotten far, since what had really offended democratic sensitiveness was not the secrecy but the exclusiveness. More than one public meeting condemned Masonry because, among other things, it destroyed "the principles of equality by bestowing favors on its own members and excluding others equally meritorious." Just as this generation wished to multiply business corporations through a system of general chartering, so it wished to have enough fraternal organizations to go around. The plain citizen sometimes wearied of his plainness and, wanting rites as well as rights, hankered for the ceremonials, grandiloquent titles and exotic costumes of a mystic brotherhood. Moreover, the impersonality of city life put a premium on the comradeship thus afforded. Lodge membership might also help one's business or political ambitions. Add to these motives the financial advantages usually accruing from sickness and death benefits, and the upsurge of fraternal associations following the decline of the anti-Masonic crusade is not hard to understand. Henceforth secrecy and degrees and regalia became an asset instead of a liability.

Within two years of Wirt's defeat, the Order of Druids was introduced from England and the United States had created the first adult secret society of its own: the Red Men — to whose ranks only palefaces were admitted. In 1843 the Odd Fellows, who had been in America for nearly twenty-five years, seceded from the English parent body and swiftly boosted their membership from 30,000 at the time of withdrawal to 200,000 in 1860. "The American," grumbled Henry Thoreau, "has dwindled into an Odd Fellow, — one who may be known by the development of his organ of gregariousness, and a manifest lack of intellect and cheerful self-reliance." Meanwhile the Masons managed a slow recovery which before the Civil War wiped out their earlier losses, while in the colleges and universities national Greek-letter fraternities, most of them recently established, played an increasingly important role.

The great foreign influx of this period added to the variety, contributing the Ancient Order of Hibernians, an importation of Irish Catholics in 1836, and the B'nai B'rith (1843) and similar groups which the German Jews formed after arriving. The foes of immigration returned the compliment by churning up nativist and anti-Catholic sentiment through such secret societies as the

Order of United Americans (1844), the United American Mechanics (1845), the Order of the Star-Spangled Banner (1849) and the Brotherhood of the Union (1850). Even the total-abstinence forces resorted to oath-bound orders, setting afoot the Sons of Temperance (1842), the Templars of Honor (1845) and the Good Templars (1851). Within eight years the Sons numbered 6000 lodges and 245,000 members, a larger total than that of either the Odd Fellows or the Masons. Secret associations, though late in gaining respectability, were henceforth in America to stay.

IV

The progress in associationalism before the Civil War portended far greater advances in the years to come. All the earlier incentives now operated with magnified force. Cities were bigger, more numerous and more generally distributed through the land. They were also bound together by faster communications: the improved telegraph, the expanding railways, the telephone and, somewhat later, the motorcar, the radio and television. Newspapers not only grew in number and circulation but, themselves obeying the associative impulse, developed chains, syndicated features and joint news-gathering methods, thereby reinforcing men's tendencies to think and act together. Moreover, a heightened sense of nationality followed the Civil War. That struggle decided that the Americans were to be one people, not two. The effect upon the triumphant North was greatly to abet far-flung co-operative projects, while the Southerners, no longer hampered by their "peculiar institution," joined in as best they could. So thoroughly did the "habit of forming associations" — James Bryce's phrase — interpenetrate American life that the major political, economic and social developments of the time all bespeak the activity of voluntary organizations.

Capitalistic associations, battening on fast-growing markets, governmental complaisance, and greater access to cheap and abundant raw materials, assumed dinosaur proportions. Within eight years after Appomattox a House investigating committee reported, "This country is fast becoming filled with gigantic corporations wielding and controlling immense aggregations of money and thereby commanding great influence and power."

In the years ahead they strove for monopolistic dominion. By means of pools, rate agreements, interlocking directorates, trusts, mergers, holding companies and other devices, legal or illegal, they reduced large sections of the population to a species of economic vassalage. The United States Steel Corporation, formed in 1901, united under one ownership 228 companies scattered in 127 cities and 18 states, and possessed a capitalization nearly thirty times as great as that of the Second United States Bank. Three years later 318 consolidations (not including transportation lines and other public utilities) represented the fusing of nearly 5300 separate concerns. Henry Demarest Lloyd insisted that the letters U.S.A. had come to mean the United Syndicates of America.

The wage earners responded by extending and strengthening their own associations. They established many new national unions, they experimented for a time with the one-big-union idea as members of the Knights of Labor, and in 1881 they joined in founding the more successful American Federation of Labor, a body which by 1900 represented 82 national unions, 16 state federations, 118 city central unions and 550,000 individual members. These gains came in the teeth of determined opposition from employers' associations, legislatures and courts.

The farmers, who likewise blamed Big Business for their ills, also resorted to organization against the foe, first in the Patrons of Husbandry, then in the more aggressive Northern and Southern Farmers' Alliances. The latter groups launched the People's party to accomplish their political demands and, by capturing twenty-two electoral votes and a million popular votes in 1892, stampeded the Democrats into making free silver their battle cry in the next election. Most important of all, these agrarian bodies accustomed the agricultural population to united action, thereby paving the way for such associations as the National Farmers' Union, the Farmers' Nonpartisan League and the American Farm Bureau Federation in the next century. Aided by modern means of communication, the once isolated husbandman thus also became a joiner.

Meanwhile, in the crowded urban centers, humanitarians intensified their earlier efforts and discovered many new outlets for reform zeal. Typical of these multifarious interests were the American Prison Association, the National Conference of Social

Work, the Women's Christian Temperance Union and the Society for the Prevention of Cruelty to Children, all founded in the 1870's, and the American Red Cross Society, the National Divorce Reform League, the National Arbitration League and the Indian Rights Association, which originated in the eighties. In many of these bodies women were the leading spirits, but they also created special groups for their own advancement. The two nation-wide suffrage associations, formed in 1869, signified one type of activity. Less militant members of the sex congregated in local clubs for self-culture, which became so plentiful by 1889 as to warrant the creation of the General Federation of Women's Clubs.

With even greater energy new associations were instituted for promoting professional and scholarly interests. The ambition of universities to enlarge the sum of human knowledge, combined with industry's incessant demand for improved machines and processes, caused specialization increasingly to dominate the individual workers and the societies they established. Sometimes the organizations arose out of a process of subdivision. Thus the American Society of Civil Engineers, which had grown out of the Society of Engineers and Architects (1852), begot a numerous offspring after the Civil War in the American Institute of Mining and Metallurgical Engineers, the American Society of Mechanical Engineers, the National Association of Power Engineers, the American Institute of Electrical Engineers, the American Order of Steam Engineers, the American Society of Naval Engineers and the American Railway Engineering Association, with more to follow in the twentieth century. In other scientific branches a brand-new start proved necessary, as in the case of the American Chemical Society (1876) and the American Association of Anatomists (1888). Scholars and practitioners in nonscientific fields followed suit. Soon librarians, archaeologists, modern-language specialists, historians, economists, mural painters and musicians, not to mention other groups, were paying dues, electing national officers and flocking to conventions.

Perhaps the most impressive expansion of voluntary associations occurred in the domain of leisure. With more people having more time on their hands, thanks to shorter working hours or larger incomes, numerous organizations rushed in to fill the void. Between 1865 and 1880, 78 beneficiary fraternal orders appeared on the scene, in the next decade 124 more, and between 1890 and 1901 an additional 366. Though some came to an untimely end, well over 5,000,000 names of men and women were inscribed on the rosters of 70,000 local lodges as the century closed, not including the 150,000 college students belonging to 900 chapters of fraternities and sororities.

These leisure-time organizations, however, did not monopolize the field, for, besides the ubiquitous women's clubs, three other types made their bow. The Civil War stimulated both sides to sire commemorative associations of the survivors, with women's branches and, in due course, auxiliaries for the veterans' sons and daughters. The largest of this numerous company, the Grand Army of the Republic, contained 150,000 members in 1887. The centennial celebrations, starting with that for Concord and Lexington in 1875, spawned a second brood of associations. Among the more prominent were the Sons of the American Revolution, the Daughters of the American Revolution, the Colonial Dames, the Society of Colonial Wars and the Mayflower Descendants, all originating in the late eighties or early nineties. If some of the members wished merely to live off the unearned increment of ancestral reputations, others sought to assert the old-time American spirit against the alien influences represented by the then mounting immigration from Southern and Eastern Europe.

Less exclusive in appeal was the third group of organizations, those mirroring the rising popularity of sports. Foreshadowed by the National Association of Base Ball Players (1858), the contagion now spread to nearly all other games and forms of exercise — archery, cycling, canoeing, college football, lawn tennis, croquet, polo, golf. Generally the object was to standardize rules of play for amateurs or to put the contests on a professional and commercial basis. By these various means the American people, after a long period of hesitation and soul-searching, extended the associative principle to their hours of relaxation.

v

To the vast and intricate mosaic of organizations evolved during the nineteenth century the twentieth has as yet added little new or significant. Popular alarm at the overweening power of capitalistic combinations has, however, caused both the state and national governments to place increasing curbs on their freedom of action, while labor's right to organize and to pursue trade-union methods has at last been accorded basic legal sanction.

Secret fraternal orders reached their peak membership of over ten million in the mid-1920's, after which they began to decline, partly perhaps as a result of such competing attractions as the cheap motorcar, the talking movies and the radio. A contributing factor was the rapid growth of International Rotary and similar businessmen's luncheon clubs, founded in the second decade of the century. For the younger generation a special type of association appeared in the Boy Scouts (1910). Sometimes the irrepressible spirit of gregariousness broke out in unexpected forms. Thus the period since the first war with Germany has seen the rise of the National Horseshoe Pitchers' Association, the Guild of Former Pipe Organ Pumpers, the Circus Fans' Association of America, the American Sunbathing Association and the Association of Department Store Santa Clauses.

Related to the associative movement is the revamping of the calendar through the device of designated "weeks." By this dispensation the United States year, according to one recent tabulation, consists of a hundred and thirty-five weeks instead of the traditional fifty-two. Both benevolence and self-interest explain this new dimension of time. Among the occasions which all good citizens are expected to observe are Better Speech Week, Courtesy Week, Fire Prevention Week, Honesty Week, Thrift Week and Walk-and-Be-Healthy Week, while the voice of the advertiser rings through Apple Week, Book Week, Canned Foods Week, Linoleum Week and Pharmacy Week. Thus was devised a mechanism for reaching into the family circle and getting people to think and act in unison when the ties of mutual interest would not support a dues-paying organization and the holding of national conventions. The more influential "weeks" are publicized with badges, seals, stickers and posters. It seems as if social inventiveness has reached its limit.

VI

"At the name of a society," wrote Ralph Waldo Emerson, "all my repulsions play, all my quills rise and sharpen." As he saw it, men clubbed together on the principle: "I have failed, and you have failed, but perhaps together we shall not fail." The historical record shows, however, that his uncompromising stand against the herd instinct neither persuaded his countrymen nor fairly delineated their motives and accomplishments. Out of the loins of religious voluntarism in colonial times had issued a lusty progeny increasing in number and variety as each new stage of the nation's development disclosed fresh needs and opportunities. It usually denoted strength rather than weakness when one person multiplied himself by uniting with others. Disputing Emerson's view, William Ellery Channing declared, "Men, it is justly said, can do jointly what they cannot do singly." It is undeniable that the associative impulse tended to feed upon itself, sometimes leading to an infatuation that provoked the mirth of onlookers, but such excesses should not be permitted to hide the true significance of this powerful force in American life.

Because of it, every community large or small has acquired a cellular structure, intricately interlaced and overlapping. There has evolved what Channing more than a century ago called "a sort of irregular government created within our constitutional government." Day in and day out, these little governments — the chamber of commerce, the trade union, the lodge, the church and the host of other voluntary associations — command the active support of their members, often exerting a greater influence on their lives and eliciting a more constant interest than the regular government.

Nor is the analogy to the political state a mere figure of speech, for these groups actually exhibit many of the attributes of government. Despite their diversity as to function and scope, the fact of membership usually engenders in the individual a pride of belonging and an emotional loyalty that endow the association's purposes and acts with an obligatory character. It is as though the fervor, even the bigotry, once attaching to religious fellowship, has pervaded the National Association of Manufacturers, the AFL-CIO, the Republican party and the Daughters of the American Revolution. Moreover, such organizations generally function on the basis of a written constitution or charter, possess both elected officials and administrative staffs, prescribe standards of conduct, enforce rules and regulations by means of fines, suspensions and expulsions, and impose a species of taxation in the guise of dues and assessments.

Their fiscal operations frequently eclipse those of governmental units. A Senate committee in 1944 pointed out that only six states of the Union have an assessed property valuation larger than the total assets of the Metropolitan Life Insurance Company and that only ten exceed the American Telephone & Telegraph Company, the Chase National Bank or the Prudential Life Insurance Company in this respect. The financial aspect of labor, religious, political and other associations may also be considerable. The International Ladies' Garment Workers' Union in 1947 possessed general funds of over $20,000,000, with aggregate resources of nearly $47,000,000, and as far back as 1919 the fraternal benefit societies had an annual income of $165,000,000.

These unofficial or private governments maintain external as well as internal relations. It might seem that voluntary bodies could be divided between those which mind their own business and those which mind other people's business, but the distinction is unreal since all in some degree impinge upon the interests of outsiders. Recreational, no less than professional and learned, groups seek to uphold codes of ethics and levels of technical competence that indirectly affect the public at large. Capitalistic and labor organizations influence general conditions of employment and, when locked in battle, may disrupt the normal life of a community. Besides, nearly all associations resort at times to pressure tactics in relation to government. Though existing primarily for other purposes, the Methodist Church fronted the movement for national prohibition; the League of American Wheelmen in its day induced many states to provide good roads for bicycling; and the G.A.R. labored successfully for higher pensions.

In recent times such activities have assumed unprecedented importance. By 1942 a total of 628 organizations maintained offices in Washington to supply arguments and witnesses for or against various types of legislation, a number which has since greatly increased. Thirteen spoke for lawyers' groups, 14 for youth or young people's interests, 24 for education, 26 for minority elements, 42 for labor, 42 for one or another kind of political or economic creed, 43 for veterans' or military organizations and 192 for business and finance. And this enumeration omitted political parties, which operate the machinery that alone can gratify the desires of the pressure groups. It need hardly be said that these lobbying activities sometimes injure the public welfare. Only as long as all sides are able to express themselves freely and adequately can the democratic process be regarded as working effectively. In an effort to rob lobbying of its clandestine character Congress in 1946 imposed the requirement of registration upon all such agents with a listing of their purposes, sources of income and expenditures. Within two years over eleven hundred were registered, outnumbering the elected members of Congress nearly three to one.

Emerson's disapproval of group undertakings rested mainly upon the conviction that the many cramp and diminish the one, sapping his self-reliance as the price of acting in concert with others. This view, however, ignores the whole nature of man's evolution from barbarism toward civilization. As Edmund Burke observed, "All government, indeed every human benefit and enjoyment, every virtue, and every prudent act, is founded on compromise and barter." Besides, nothing has been more characteristic of voluntary bodies than the readiness of dissidents to exercise what a president of the American Society of Newspaper Editors has termed "the God-given right of every American to resign, tell why, and raise hell." A process of splitting and splintering, or what sociologists call "schismatic differentiation," has marked the course of practically every sort of association.

The history of religious denominations teems with instances, but hardly more so than that of humanitarian movements, labor organizations, political parties and patriotic societies. Sometimes the cause is an attitude of dogma-eat-dogma, sometimes an internal struggle for power, sometimes a wrangle over such questions as qualifications for membership or the methods of carrying out stated objectives. Fraternal organizations have been torn by similar ructions. For example, the Royal Order of Foresters was the English progenitor of at least ten American brotherhoods containing the words "Foresters" or "Forestry" in their names. If internal strife has wasted a good deal of associational energy, it also indicates the existence of a vigorous spirit of nonconformity.

Probably a graver criticism of voluntary bodies than Emerson's is the extent to which men do things as members that they would be ashamed or afraid to do as individuals. The outstanding example is afforded by capitalistic groups, where a sense of fractional responsibility has often led a stockholder or official to sanction acts contrary to his private ethics. But business and financial corporations are impersonal institutions to a degree that most associations are not, and in recent years, as we have seen, the power of government has been increasingly invoked to keep them within their legitimate bounds.

The same element of diffused responsibility enters into secret conspiratorial organizations. Nearly every great national crisis has hatched one or more of them: the Knights of the Golden Circle and other Copperhead societies in the North during the Civil War; the Ku Klux Klan, the Knights of the White Camelia and similar Southern bands in the period of Reconstruction; the revamped Ku Klux Klan that skyrocketed into prominence in the 1920's; and the jumble of Silver Shirts, United States Fascists, Christian Fronters and German-American Bundists who skulked in the shadows cast by the Great Depression and the ideological conflict over totalitarianism. All of them went in for military discipline and carried on treasonable or terroristic activities. In every instance the members took illicit advantage of the constitutional guarantee of freedom of association, but sooner or later their lawless exploits brought down on their heads the might of government.

The career of these few, short-lived organizations stands in marked contrast to the positive and continuing role in society played by secret fraternal orders of the normal kind. These with rare exceptions have acted as bulwarks of conservatism, their constant endeavor being to emphasize conventional moral and ethical standards, transmit existing social values and avoid political involvements. Furthermore, as a writer in the *Century Magazine* once remarked, their very existence has constituted a "great American safety-valve for those ambitions for precedence, which our national life generates, fosters, and stimulates, without adequate provision for their gratification." The burden of championing minority rights and unpopular causes has fallen on other types of association, notably humanitarian, labor and reform bodies. These have helped educate the public to the need for continuing change and improvement and in their aspect as pressure groups have done much to keep legislatures and political parties in step with the times.

Considering the cardinal importance of voluntary organizations in American history one cannot doubt that they have afforded the people their best schooling in self-government. Through their membership and participation men learned from youth to counsel together, choose leaders, harmonize differences and obey the majority will. Thanks to the "creative magic of mere association," they learned, moreover, to conduct most of the major concerns of life, spiritual, economic, political, social, cultural and recreational. To this fact James Bryce attributed the high level of executive competence he found everywhere in America — talents which he likened to those possessed by "administrative rulers, generals, diplomatists." By comparison, the much-vaunted role of the New England town meeting as a seed-bed of popular government seems almost negligible.

The habits so engendered have also armed the people to take swift and effective steps in moments of emergency. On the advancing frontier the pioneers joined together for house-raisings, for protecting squatters' rights and for vigilante measures against desperadoes. In times of war impromptu organizations spring up as if by spontaneous generation to invigorate the national will and to supplement the government's military efforts in a thousand ways. This instinctive recourse to collective action is one of the taproots of the nation's well-being.

It is with calculated foresight that totalitarian dictators ensure their rise to power by repressing or abolishing political, religious, labor and other voluntary groups. The existence of these microcosms of democracy constitutes a potential threat they dare not ignore, undermining the absolute obedience which they insist citizens owe to the state. Hence joiners are among the earliest casualties of the totalitarian system. But under a reign of freedom self-constituted bodies are a constructive influence without which government could not respond to shifting human hopes and needs. Reaching out with interlocking membership to all parts of the country, embracing all ages, classes, creeds and ethnic groups, they have constantly demonstrated the underlying unity that warrants diversity. They have served as a great cementing force for national integration.

3

American contributions to civilization

SINCE the United States has now become the leader of the free world, our allies are asking, and we ourselves should be asking, what this portends for the future of civilization. The key to the answer, I suggest, lies in America's seminal contributions of the past. In my view these have been at least ten.

THE RIGHT OF REVOLUTION

First and foremost stands the concept of the inherent and universal right of revolution proclaimed in the Declaration of Independence: the doctrine that "all men are created equal" possessing "unalienable rights" to "life, liberty, and the pursuit of happiness," with the corollary that governments derive "their just powers from the consent of the governed" and that therefore the people have the right to supplant a government "destructive of these ends" with one which they believe "most likely to effect their safety and happiness." True, the history of England provided precedents for the men of 1776, and the Age of Enlightenment supplied intellectual support; but the flaming pronouncement, followed by its vindication on the battlefield, made the doctrine ever afterward an irrepressible agency in "the course of human events."

Europe was the first to respond. In 1789 occurred the great French Revolution, the forerunner of two later ones of the French people during the nineteenth century; and neighboring countries were not slow to follow. A series of revolts, centering in 1830 and 1848, drove the Turks from Greece, overturned or strove to overturn illiberal governments through most of the rest of the Continent, and hastened political reforms in other lands to forestall popular upheavals.

These convulsions all had their internal causes, but in every instance the leaders derived inspiration from America's achievement of popular rule as well as from its freely expressed interest in their similar aspirations. Presidents, Congresses, and civic gatherings applauded the uprisings, and American volunteers actually fought in the Greek war of liberation. After Russia helped Austria to suppress the Hungarian rebellion, a United States warship late in 1851 carried the Magyar patriot Kossuth away from the scene, and in this country he received the honors of an American hero. The citizens of Springfield, Illinois, for example, rallied to his cause in words which have a fresh and poignant significance for us today. Affirming "the right of any people . . . to throw off . . . their existing form of government, and to establish such other in its stead as they may choose," they condemned the "interference of Russia in the Hungarian struggle" as "illegal and unwarrantable" and asserted that "to have resisted Russia . . . would have been no violation of our own cherished principles . . . but, on the contrary, would be ever meritorious, in us, or any independent nation." Abraham Lincoln, then in private life, was one of the authors of the resolutions.

The doctrine of revolution, however, had still broader implications. The European eruptions in most instances sought merely to replace domestic regimes; the American revolt, to cast off a distant yoke. It was the first of the great colonial insurrections, an example all the more potent because Washington's ill-trained soldiers defeated the mightiest nation in the world. The Spanish dependencies to the south took heed and early in the nineteenth century won their freedom. Then, oddly enough, came a setback to the trend as a large part of Asia and Africa and many islands of the Pacific fell under the sway of Old World powers. And after a time even the United States, forgetful of its own once colonial status, followed suit.

But in the twentieth century the two world wars radically changed the situation, recalling the United States to its historic heritage, crippling the military strength of the European imperialist countries, and awakening subject peoples everywhere to their right of self-determination. America led the way by relinquishing its Caribbean protectorates and granting independence to the Philippines, and soon the Old World governments fell into line, some voluntarily to anticipate the inevitable, as in the case of England, and others because they were unable to quell native rebellions, as in the cases of France and Holland.

Although more than a century and a half has elapsed since America proclaimed the right of revolution, these events of our own day evidence its continuing vitality. Lest I be accused of claiming too much for a precedent so far in the past, consider the words of President Sukarno of Indonesia several years ago in his address of welcome to the Bandung Conference. This Asian-African gathering, the first of its kind in history, brought together delegates from twenty-nine nations, most of them newly free.

"The battle against colonialism [Sukarno declared] has been a long one, and do you know that today is a famous anniversary in that battle? On the eighteenth day of April, one thousand seven hundred and seventy-five, just one hundred and eighty years ago, Paul Revere rode at midnight through the New England countryside, warning of the approach of British troops and of the opening of the American War of Independence, the first successful anticolonial war in history. About this midnight ride the poet Longfellow wrote:

> A cry of defiance and not of fear,
> A voice in the darkness, a knock at the door,
> And a word that shall echo for evermore. . . .

Yes [he concluded], it shall echo for evermore . . . until we can survey this our own world, and can say that colonialism is dead."

THE PRINCIPLE OF FEDERALISM

Because of the difficulties experienced under the Articles of Confederation, the Constitution of 1787 established a partnership of self-governing commonwealths with an over-all elective government powerful enough to protect and promote their joint concerns and — what was no less important — with a provision for admitting later states on a plane of full equality. This was something new in history; Tocqueville called it "a great discovery in modern political science," for no other people had ever devised a federal structure over so large an area or with a central government chosen by popular vote or on such generous terms for future members. It offered mankind a key to the age-old problem of reconciling legitimate local interests with the general good.

Mexico, Argentina, and other Latin American countries adopted variants of the plan, and so did Germany and Austria-Hungary. Britain applied it to two of its largest colonies, Canada and Australia, and in the twentieth century recast most of its empire into a Commonwealth of Nations on the same basis. More dramatically, the principle caused men to conceive of some sort of federation of the world, first in the League of Nations and then in the United Nations, both sponsored by American Presidents; and in the not too distant future it promises to bring about a United States of Western Europe.

THE CONSENT OF THE GOVERNED

Neither the doctrine of revolution nor the principle of federalism necessarily ensured that the government so established would rest on the consent of the governed. This was an entirely different matter, as the history of Latin American dictatorships as well as that of other nations proves. But, as we have seen, it was a basic tenet of the founders of the United States and may well be regarded as America's third contribution to humanity.

The framers of the Constitution spurned European tradition by rejecting a monarchy, a nobility, or a hereditary legislative chamber, placing their trust in a government of the people, by the people, and for the people, one which should rule by counting heads instead of breaking them. Starting with a somewhat limited number of voters but in better proportion than in any other country, the suffrage was broadened generation by generation until it came to include all adults of both sexes; and at every point America set the pace for the Old World. The underlying philosophy was not that the common man is all-wise, but only that he can govern himself better than anyone else can do it for him.

THE ROLE OF WOMEN

Women played a man's part as well as a woman's in taming the wilderness, and until very recently, moreover, they were fewer in number than the opposite sex and hence received a consideration unknown abroad. From early times foreign observers marveled at the unusual educational opportunities open to women, their immunity from molestation when traveling alone, their freedom to go out of the home to agitate for temperance, antislavery, and other reforms. "From the captain of a western steamboat to the roughest miner in California," wrote one visitor, "from north, south, east, and west, we hear but one voice. Women are to be protected, respected, supported, and petted."

The organized feminist movement arose earlier in the United States than in any other nation not because American women enjoyed so few privileges but because they had so many that they demanded more — in short, all those exercised by their husbands and brothers, including that of suffrage. The famous women's rights convention at Seneca Falls, New York, in 1848, the first in the history of the world, turned the Declaration of Independence to account by proclaiming "all men and women are created equal," with the same unalienable rights to "life, liberty, and the pursuit of happiness." It took the women many years to achieve that goal, but in time they succeeded, and every victory spurred their sisters in other lands to similar endeavors.

THE MELTING-POT CONCEPT

A fifth contribution of the United States has been the fusing of many different nationalities in a single society. America has been in the best sense of the term a melting pot, every ingredient adding its particular element of strength. The constant infusion of new blood has enriched our cultural life, speeded our material growth, and produced some of our ablest statesmen. Over seventeen million immigrants arrived in the single period from the Civil War to World War I — more than America's total population in 1840 — and today English and Scottish blood, the principal strains in colonial times, constitutes considerably less than half the whole.

Many other peoples, it is true, are also of mixed origin; but the American achievement stands alone in the scale, thoroughness and rapidity of the process and, above all, in the fact that it has been the outcome not of forcible incorporation but of peaceful absorption. Significantly, the very nationalities which had habitually warred with one another in the Old World have lived together in harmony in the New. America has demonstrated for everyone with eyes to see that those things which unite peoples are greater than those which divide them, that war is not the inevitable fate of mankind.

Our most tragic failure has involved our Negro citizens, now a tenth of our number. Taken forcibly from Africa, trammeled in slavery for two and a half centuries, denied their constitutional rights after emancipation in the states where most of them lived, this ill-used race has been a standing reproach to our professions of democracy and has enabled Communist spokesmen as well as other foreign critics to impugn the very principle of human equality on which the Republic was founded. Nevertheless, even these injured people have not been unwilling Americans, as the Irish before winning their freedom were unwilling Britons: they have only been unwilling to be halfway Americans or second-class citizens. Hence they have unhesitatingly rejected the blandishments of Soviet propaganda. Fortunately they can now at long last look forward to the final rectification of the wrongs they have so patiently endured.

FREEDOM OF WORSHIP

The recognition that the relations between man and his Creator are a private affair into which government must not intrude contravened the age-long European practice of uniting church and state and imposing harsh restrictions on dissenters. The American system was a legacy of colonial times, when the theological motive for settlement was intense and the multiplicity of denominations suggested the need for mutual forbearance. Rhode Island, Maryland and Pennsylvania in the persons of Roger Williams, Lord Baltimore and William Penn set the pattern to which the Bill of Rights of the federal Constitution gave nation-wide sanction. Religion by choice was the natural counterpart of government by consent, and, contrary to Old World belief, the separation of church and state did not in fact weaken either but strengthened both.

THE PUBLIC SCHOOL

The principle of government by consent made it imperative that the people be literate and well informed if they were to vote intelligently. To ensure this essential condition, statesmen agreed that society must at its own initiative and expense supply the means of schooling. This, too, broke drastically with the Old World concept that education should be a privately financed undertaking for the upper classes, the rank and file supposedly having little need for any in what was deemed to be their permanently inferior station.

New England inaugurated the practice in colonial days; then, with the swift extension of the franchise during the first half of the nineteenth century, it was adopted throughout the North and later in the South. Free public education thus became the article of American faith it has continued to be ever since. From the United States the plan spread in modified form around the world. Japan, for example, in 1872 made it the cornerstone of its program of modernization. Probably America has conferred no greater boon on mankind, for popular education is the seedbed of virtually all other human aspirations. And akin to this system was the tax-supported free public library, in which America has also led the world.

THE SPIRIT OF PHILANTHROPY

Foreigners have always criticized the American for his pursuit of the Almighty Dollar, but have seldom gone on to note that he has in unparalleled degree returned the fruits of his labors to society. If he has been hardheaded about making money, he has,

so to speak, been softhearted about spending it. This constitutes
the American version of the Old World concept of *noblesse oblige*
carried to a point the Old World has never approached. Even
long before Carnegie and Rockefeller amassed their colossal fortunes, men and women of modest means gave freely to schools,
churches, foreign missions, colleges, hospitals, charities and other
projects for social betterment.

In the twentieth century this same concern has led men
of wealth to set up some four thousand philanthropic foundations staffed with experts to administer the funds with maximum
usefulness and for nearly every conceivable object of human
benefit. Their programs, exceeding all earlier bounds, include
the control of epidemic diseases and far-reaching researches in
the natural and social sciences. Even so, the lion's share of the
more than 7.8 billion dollars devoted to altruistic purposes in
1959 still derived from other than foundation sources.

And, increasingly, Americans have extended their beneficence
to foreign peoples. Over a century ago popular subscriptions
helped relieve Irish suffering during the terrible potato famines of
the 1840's and later aided with equal generosity the victims of
natural catastrophes in other lands. And, besides the work of
the Red Cross in peace and war, the great foundations have in
our own day improved health, educational and agricultural conditions in many countries. In the same tradition the private organization known as CARE has, since World War II, channeled
gifts of food, clothing, medicine and the like to the needy of Europe, Asia, Africa and Latin America. Thanks to this ingrained
trait of the national character, the government found it easy to
mobilize our people behind the Marshall Plan, a tax-supported
program for repairing the war-stricken economies of Western
Europe, and later behind economic aid for backward countries
all over the world. Though these official undertakings were in
part designed to halt the spread of Communism, they arose from
deeper springs of human compassion and have no parallel in
history.

MECHANICAL INGENUITY

Mechanical ingenuity, or what today is called technological
know-how, is, contrary to common belief, by no means a late de-

velopment. From the mid-eighteenth. century on, the people, confronted with a chronic shortage of labor and the problems arising from formidable distances and poor communications, devised means to overcome these handicaps as well as to ameliorate other conditions of life. The record is truly remarkable. Before the end of the nineteenth century Benjamin Franklin, Eli Whitney and their successors produced such epochal inventions as the lightning rod, the cotton gin, the steamboat, the metal plow, the harvester, vulcanized rubber, the sewing machine, the telegraph, the telephone and the electric light, among others. In still other instances they greatly improved on what had come to them from abroad.

The outcome was not only to transform American life but that of peoples everywhere. For the most part the machines, techniques and products made their way round the world by reason of their superiority to anything before known. As early as 1838 American locomotive builders were shipping their engines abroad, a few years later the Russian government employed American engineers to construct and equip a railroad between Moscow and St. Petersburg, and shortly Prussia sent a delegation to the United States to study this country's methods before launching her own rail system. At the international exposition in London in 1851 our inventors won so many awards as to amaze even informed Europeans. The Colt revolver, for example, was hailed by the British press as a weapon that would revolutionize the conduct of war as greatly as had the introduction of gunpowder, while a precision instrument for observing the stars earned the encomium of "the most wonderful achievement since the days of Newton." Thus, even before the era of great industrial expansion after the Civil War, American technology was well embarked on its international career.

Occasionally official United States missions lent a hand for diplomatic reasons. A notable instance occurred in the case of Japan after it abandoned its long isolation, while others involved taking the new discoveries and products to unprogressive Latin American countries. President Truman therefore was not occupying wholly new ground when in 1949 he proposed his Point Four Program to make "the benefits of our scientific advances and industrial progress available for the improvement and growth of underdeveloped areas" and thus "help them realize their aspirations for a better life." Under this program the United States has sent experts in industry, engineering and agriculture to many lands; built roads and bridges in Iran, irrigation works in India and fertilizer plants in Korea; and endeavored in countless other ways to remove the obstacles that have barred less enterprising countries from the advantages of modern civilization. Just as the government has made our philanthropic impulse a vital instrument of foreign policy, so also it has done with our technological skill.

EVOLUTIONARY PROGRESS

Our tenth contribution has been our way of meeting internal crises by bending without breaking our free institutions. The spirit of America has been empirical and pragmatic, dedicated to equalitarian ends but willing to realize them by flexible means. In the European sense of the term, America's major political parties are not parties at all, because they do not divide over basic ideologies. Neither wishes to overturn or replace the existing political and economic order; they merely desire to alter it at slower or faster rates of speed.

One of our proudest achievements has been the creation of a system of controlled capitalism that yields the highest living standards on earth and has made possible a society as nearly classless as man has ever known. The profit system as it has developed in America is a multiprofit system, sharing its benefits with all segments of society: capital, labor and the consuming masses. Yet even this was not due to a preconceived blueprint; it too was the result of trial and error. Unprincipled businessmen had first to be brought to heel by government restraints and the growing power of organized labor before they came to learn that they must serve the general good in pursuing their selfish interests. Now labor is in turn feeling the restraint.

Even our creed of democracy is no fixed and immutable dogma. Thus the statesmen of the early republic, though they were stalwart champions of private enterprise, chose to make the post office a government monopoly and to confide the schools to public ownership. Since then, by fits and starts, and most recently under the New Deal, the United States has taken on many of the characteristics of a welfare state. This has occurred, however, not under the banner of socialism or of any other "ism," but simply because the Americans hold with Lincoln that "the legitimate object of government is to do for a community of people whatever they need to have done but cannot do at all, or cannot do so well for themselves, in their separate and individual capacities."

Viewed as a whole, the contributions of America to civilization will be seen to have been for the most part in the nature of methods or processes. They have aimed to release men from political and religious disabilities, from ignorance and poverty, from backbreaking toil. They have struck at the fetters which from time immemorial the Old World has fastened on human beings. They have opened the doors of opportunity for the many while still assuring them to the few, in the belief that everyone should have an equal chance to be as unequal as he can without denying the same right to others. In brief, they have sought to substitute fluidity for rigid class distinctions as the vital principle of social well-being. And the consequence has been a general leveling of society upward instead of downward.

But what of the future? I recall what a thoughtful Hollander said to me a few years after World War II. Observing that Europe's age of greatness was now over and that Americans must henceforth take the lead in the advancement of civilization, he wondered whether they would be equal to the task. Plainly he had grave doubts, for like most foreigners he thought of us as having been only beneficiaries of the bounty of the Old World without making any creative returns in kind. But for an American historian the answer is clear. The true measure of our past contributions lies in the very fact that they have become so woven into the life of mankind that my Dutch friend was unaware of them. If we can only preserve our free institutions and our faith in the untrammeled human spirit, we shall triumphantly meet the challenge now before us.

4

The role of the immigrant

This happened longer ago than I like to think.

"Daddy," I said with a quaver in my voice, "the boys at school say I am not as good an American as they are. They say I can't be because you were born in Europe and their folks have been here hundreds of years."

I can still hear my father laugh.

"You tell them, son, that when their parents came to America they brought nothing but their bare skins, while I had clothes on my back at least. Tell them, too, that their parents had no choice about coming, but I came because I wanted to — because I thought the United States the best country on earth."

Ever since then I have thought of immigrants as voluntary Americans, not a chosen people but a choosing people; and as I have grown older, I have come increasingly to appreciate how heroic a decision it was to quit one's native soil for a land of strange ways, alien speech and uncertain fortunes.

A. M. S.

THE New World was discovered by a man who was seeking an older world than the one he left behind. Had Columbus known he had missed the fabled Orient, he would have died bitterly disillusioned. Yet in the eyes of history this egregious blunder established his greatness, for in failing to reach his goal he and those who followed him opened up to the European masses a means of escape from poverty and oppression for ages to come. The ratio between man and land was altered for the entire civilized world, and humanity, to its own great wonder, was enabled to make a new start. Because of political turmoil in Europe and the perils and cost of ocean travel the full possibilities of this epochal change appeared only gradually; the effects have been distributed through four and a half centuries. But the event itself stands as one of the tremendous facts of all time.

The great *Völkerwanderungen* set in motion by the unveiling of the Western Hemisphere differed from earlier migrations of mankind. Not only were they vaster in size, but they involved civilized beings instead of barbarians and, for the most part, proceeded peaceably rather than by marauding and conquest. They inaugurated, as Carl Schurz, one of the nineteenth-century migrants, remarked, "a new era in the history of the world, without first destroying the results of past periods; undertaking to found a cosmopolitan nation without marching over the dead bodies of slain millions." In essence all American history has been the outcome. Since the Indian played mostly a negative role in the nation's evolution, the history of the United States is in considerable part the story of these successive waves of humanity, their adaptation to a new environment and the adjustment of the older population to their presence.

I

Columbus's shipmates in his four voyages strangely presaged the future make-up of the American people, for they came from many lands. Acting under Spanish authority, this Italian navigator took with him not only subjects of Ferdinand and Isabella, but also a sprinkling of Italians, Portuguese, Englishmen, Irishmen and Jews, all elements that were later to enter fully into the heritage which his daring made possible. In the next two and a half centuries the rulers of the Old World vied with one another to stake out colonial claims within the present United States. Though balked in their expectations of permanent dominion, they laid cultural foundations still traceable in the legal systems and ways of life of different states and regions. A familiar example of a non-English influence is Louisiana, where Continental civil law rather than English common law underlies domestic relations and transfers of property as a reminder of the former sway of the Spanish and French.

Long before 1776 the people of England's thirteen colonies had become an amalgam of national and racial strains. Indeed, on the eve of Independence, they formed the most composite breed in the world. As the recently arrived Tom Paine put it in *Common Sense,* "Europe, and not England, is the parent country of America." In fact, the admixture was even greater. It was due partly to the forcible absorption in the seventeenth century of colonies planted by the Netherlands and Sweden, partly to the importation of African slaves, but mostly to immigration from various countries after the original settlements were started. If genealogy were the sole criterion, a Colonial Dame or a Daughter of the American Revolution might have nothing but French or German blood, or even pure Negro blood, in her veins.

The religious motive bulked large with the earliest comers, notably in the case of New England, Maryland and Pennsylvania, but the economic urge, operating independently or as a stiffening to religious or political conviction, was responsible for most of the adventurers. The colonial settler, in fact, who was never called an immigrant, differed not at all from the millions who in after years were so known. The term "settler," Theodore Roosevelt remarks in his *Autobiography,* was the "euphemistic name for an immigrant who came over in the steerage of a sailing ship in the seventeenth century instead of the steerage of a steamer in the nineteenth century." In both cases the poor rather than the rich were involved — the day laborer, peasant, artisan and shopkeeper rather than the nobleman, squire or great merchant. Occasionally religious or political persecution or unusual chances of acquiring wealth enlisted members of the upper middle class, but, broadly speaking, America was peopled by the underprivileged.

Colonizers like William Penn deliberately solicited persons to develop the country and enhance real-estate values. By means of pamphlets and paid agents Penn drummed up trade not only in the British Isles but also in the Rhineland and the Netherlands, offering land at nominal prices together with the advantages of living under a liberal regime. But the major means of populating the colonies was the practice which enabled migrants to pay their ocean passage by selling their services to an employer. These "redemptioners" or "free-willers," proceeding from Britain or the Continent, were auctioned off on arrival by the ship captain to the highest bidder for a term of from two to seven years. Many of them were recruited by English merchants who specialized in the traffic, and fraudulent practices were common. With the voyagers packed aboard like sardines in a can, a mortality of more than 50 per cent was not unusual. No other group of settlers showed greater resolution and endurance. Unsung by posterity, they composed almost half the total white immigration before 1776. This early labor-contract system lingered on in Pennsylvania and Maryland till the third decade of the nineteenth century. *1830*

Two other groups of immigrants, fewer in number, made the journey against their will. One consisted of English convicts sentenced to labor for a period of years under a colonial master. No less than 50,000 individuals were involved. In Benjamin Franklin's view the practice was "an insult and contempt, the cruellest, that ever one people offered another." Allowance, however, must be made for a criminal code which demanded death for stealing more than a shilling's worth of meat. The musty archives of Newgate and Old Bailey would undoubtedly clear up questions as to the genesis of many a present-day family of ancient American lineage. The other contingent comprised Negroes, who were immigrants only by dint of the superior force and cunning of the slave trader. Originating in a barely known continent and separated from their neighbors by color and the stigma of perpetual bondage, they composed the one element in the population which saw no hope of bettering its lot. As the Revolution approached, men of African blood approximated a fifth of the inhabitants.

The preponderance of the English in the seventeenth century served to fix governmental institutions and political ideals in an English mold and to make English speech the common language. The principal Continental infusions — the Hollanders, who founded New Netherland, and the French Huguenots, who filtered into many colonies after the Edict of Nantes was revoked in 1685 — left their mark chiefly on commerce. Such names as Roosevelt and Schuyler in New York suggest the Dutch influence, while the Huguenots account for such families as Faneuil and Revere in Massachusetts, De Lancey and Bayard in New York and Laurens and Manigault in South Carolina. In the next century the non-English additions increased rapidly, notably in the case of the Scotch-Irish from Ulster and the Germans. By contrast with the "great" migration of 20,000 English Puritans into early New England, more than 150,000 Scotch-Irish Presbyterians arrived in the eighteenth century, settling in nearly five hundred scattered communities. The Germans congregated in the new sections of New York and in the Pennsylvania back country, where they gave rise to the strain called the "Pennsylvania Dutch." At the outbreak of the War for Independence they numbered over 200,000. By that time fully half the population outside New England was of non-English background.

Men of older colonial stock viewed the more recent arrivals with an alarm which each new generation of the American people would repeat. The Germans aroused particular disfavor because of their strange speech and ways. Franklin called them "generally the most stupid of their own nation," adding that "as few of the English understand the German language, and so cannot address them either from the press or the pulpit, 'tis almost impossible to remove any prejudices they may entertain." At one time a bill to restrict their entry into Pennsylvania would have become law but for the governor's veto. Jefferson, too, warned against foreigners deluded by "maxims of absolute monarchies," though he endorsed the "importation of useful artificers." The familiar objections to immigration on grounds of political backwardness, religious differences, pauperism and criminality all had their rise in these early days, leaving to later and more congested times arguments based upon fear of economic competition.

The more characteristic colonial attitude, however, was one of welcome. In a new country there was room for everybody and manpower was at a premium. Jonathan Mayhew in Boston envied Pennsylvania her German laborers, declaring in an election sermon in 1754 that in a few short years they had made the Quaker province one of the most prosperous in British America. Likewise George Washington, seeking settlers for his frontier lands, considered obtaining a "parcel of these people." As pioneers in the backwoods the Scotch-Irish generally outpaced the Germans, but both groups proved remarkably successful farmers and, by their presence behind the coastal communities, acted frequently as buffers against Indian forays. As other signs of the times, intermarriage between the different stocks began early foreign words crept into the American vocabulary, and the people quietly adjusted themselves to religious creeds, social customs, architectural practices and dietary habits reflecting varied national origins.

Despite the apprehensions of men like Franklin and Jefferson the non-English elements actually strengthened democratic tendencies in the colonies. One of the German-born, John Peter Zenger, struck the first major blow for freedom of the press as editor of a New York newspaper in 1735. Against absentee landlords the immigrants fought for squatters' rights, and against grasping creditors they contended for relief from debt. Uniting with the native-born in the back country, they insisted on a due voice in the provincial legislatures and on equal access to the courts. Eventually their efforts helped to establish the principles of representation on the basis of numbers and of equality before the law. As the break with Great Britain approached, these self-reliant folk in the interior lent great propulsion to the movement for independence. They were probably the pivotal factors in Pennsylvania and South Carolina, where the tidewater inhabitants were sharply divided on the issue. The Scotch-Irish in particular burned with a fierce passion for liberty. Of the fifty-six signers of the Declaration of Independence, eighteen were of non-English descent, eight being first-generation immigrants. Franklin and Jefferson, making amends for their earlier doubts regarding the outlanders, joined with John Adams in proposing that the official seal of the United States bear the national emblems of England, Scotland, Ireland, France, Germany and Holland, thus "pointing out the countries from which these States have been peopled"; but other counsels prevailed. In the armed struggle, if the Pennsylvania loyalist Joseph Galloway is to be believed, the patriot army contained "scarcely one-fourth natives of America — about one-half Irish, the other fourth were English and Scotch." Be that as it may, there can be no doubt that colonists of immigrant origin contributed significantly to the winning of independence.

II

The Federal Convention, meeting in 1787, likewise embraced men of varied national strains, including four born in Ireland, two in England, one in Scotland and another (of Scotch-French Huguenot parentage) in the British West Indies. The Constitution as a matter of course sanctioned the process which had given the country its cosmopolitan character. It forbade Congress to bar the immigration or importation of aliens prior to 1808 (a disguised way of referring to the slave trade) while empowering the legislators to establish a uniform method of naturalization. It further provided that foreigners who had been citizens for seven years should, if of the designated age, be eligible for the House of Representatives and, after two years more, for the Senate. If citizens when the Constitution went into effect, they might aspire even to the presidency, though thereafter the incumbent must be a "natural born citizen." It was thought unnecessary to put any restrictions of birth or citizenship upon appointment to the Supreme Court.

The first Congress fixed two years as the period for naturalization. "Whether subjects of Kings, or citizens of free States wish to reside in the United States," declared a member, "they will find it in their interest to be good citizens, and neither their religious nor political opinions can injure us, if we have good laws, well executed." A little later, in 1795, the time was lengthened to five years, still an extraordinarily liberal provision and one which the dominant Federalists repented as it became clear that most of the outsiders, especially those from Ireland and France, favored Jefferson's party. "The greater part of the abuse leveled at the Government is from foreigners," exploded President John Adams's wife. Pricked beyond endurance, the Federalists in 1798 authorized the expulsion of aliens "dangerous to the peace and safety of the United States" and extended to fourteen years the residence requirement for naturalization. They had overreached themselves, and with Jefferson's accession in 1801 the Alien Act came to an end and the five-year span for citizenship was restored.

Congress's only actual move in this period to curb alien arrivals was in response to the constitutional provision regarding the "importation" of human beings. Starting with 1808, it banned the introduction of African slaves. This action, unhappily, came too late to halt the train of events leading to the Civil War. Toward European newcomers Federalist hostility continued to smolder, with the result that the Hartford Convention, held in 1814 to air the party's wartime grievances against the Madison administration, demanded among other things that the Constitution exclude naturalized citizens from federal office. Yet during these infant years of the Republic two of the foremost statesmen were immigrants: Alexander Hamilton, Washington's Secretary of the Treasury, born in the Leeward Islands, and Albert Gallatin, Jefferson's Secretary of the Treasury, a native Swiss. It is difficult to see how the country could have survived the financial shoals of this critical era but for their hands on the tiller.

III

In the twenty-five years from the ratification of the Constitution to the close of the War of 1812 the entire inflow from Europe probably did not exceed two hundred and fifty thousand. The Napoleonic wars abroad, combined with America's difficulties as a neutral and then a belligerent, served to restrict the numbers. But with the return of peace the totals began to shoot up, reaching half a million in the 1830's, over a million and a half in the forties and two and a half in the fifties. "There has been nothing like it in appearance since the encampment of the Roman empire, or the tents of the Crusaders," said the *Democratic Review*, little dreaming what the next generation would see. The bulk of the immigrants consisted of Germans and Irish, but appreciable contingents of English, French, Scots, Swiss and Scandinavians accompanied them. These stocks, though now mixed in altered proportions, were still pretty much the same as in earlier times.

The Germans, fleeing from bad crops and avaricious landlords, furnished one and a half million in the period 1830–1860. The so-called Forty-eighters, refugees from the revolution of that year in the fatherland, have received more attention than they deserved, for they comprised only a small fraction of the whole. The majority of the Germans settled in the Middle West. They gave Cincinnati its Teutonic character and pioneered in the newer parts of Ohio; they took up the hardwood lands of Wisconsin along Lake Michigan, making a capital of Milwaukee; they went in sizable bands to Indiana, Michigan, Illinois, Mis-

70   PATHS TO THE PRESENT

souri and the river towns of Iowa; some even colonized in Texas. The group contained a high percentage of educated and forceful leaders, who contributed signally to the spiritual and educational progress of their communities. In face of the general disapproval of the native-born the Germans also introduced a saving element of sociability with their singing societies, gymnastic clubs and beer gardens.

The Irish arrived in even greater numbers, totaling nearly two million in the three decades. Over half migrated after the potato famine in 1846 and later years. Originating in the central and southern parts of the island, they were peasants by occupation and Catholics by religion. In the unfamiliar surroundings they preferred urban jobs to farming both in order to flock with their kith and kin and to be near their priests. Many, hard pressed for cash, went forth temporarily into construction camps. These were years when new modes of transportation were being hurriedly built to meet the expanding needs of industry and trade. "Every American acknowledges," wrote Harriet Martineau in the 1830's, "that few or no canals or railroads would be in existence now, in the United States, but for the Irish labour by which they have been completed." One such migrant, from County Cavan, settled at Somerset in Ohio, where his son, General "Phil" Sheridan of Civil War fame, grew up. The congested life in the Irish quarters of Eastern cities excited both the pity and dismay of the older residents. A Boston municipal committee in 1849 attested to the "wretched, dirty and unhealthy" surroundings, with each room from cellar to garret apt to contain one or more families. Such conditions lent impetus to the many humanitarian movements that marked the times: temperance, public education, labor reform and others.

"The Irish emigrants," noted the *Emigrant's Guide* (London, 1816), "carry with them all their national prejudices and a bitter hatred to the British government" and "serve greatly to inflame the minds of native Americans against her." Though other groups might nurse Old World enmities, the Irish kept theirs alive longer and with greater political effect. As a British visitor observed in 1846, "Unscrupulous politicians fan the flames for their own purposes," constantly heaping on new fuel. Sometimes, however, freshly acquired American prejudices overcame time-honored ones. Thus the Repeal Association, formed in 1843 by the Irish of Charleston, South Carolina, to aid Daniel O'Connell's efforts for independence from England, promptly disbanded upon learning that the great man had uttered a "base and malignant libel upon the people of the South" for slaveholding.

Thanks also to the unscrupulous politician, fraud came for the first time to figure importantly in municipal politics. Forged naturalization papers and vote buying were used to corrupt the Irish and other foreign-born new to the franchise. A Senate committee in 1845 cited instances of indigent immigrants being marched directly from almshouses to the polls. By such methods Tammany, which had originated many years before as a patriotic and charitable society, climbed to dominance in New York City. It was the cynical view of "Boss" Tweed, whose brazen stealings brought him to heel shortly after the Civil War, that "This population is too hopelessly split into races and factions to govern it under universal suffrage, except by bribery of patronage, or corruption." Miss Martineau believed, however, that "the second and third generations of Irish are among the most valuable citizens of the republic."

The mounting influx of workingmen found ready employment in the factories that were beginning to dot the East. The economist Henry C. Carey in his *Essay on the Rate of Wages* (1835) argued that immigration not only benefited the employer, but that native wage earners also gained by reason of the increased demand for their handiwork. Labor, however, saw only the debasing effects on pay and hours. "If Congress have the power to protect the owners against foreign competition in the shape of goods," cried Seth Luther to a New England gathering, "they have the same right to protect the operative from foreign competition in the shape of foreign mechanics and labourers."

The ill-feeling engendered by such causes was intensified by religious antipathies. The old American stock, overwhelmingly Protestant, felt increasing alarm at the swift spread of Catholicism with its panoply of churches, convents and parochial schools. Mobs attacked religious edifices. Rumors circulated of plots to subvert the public schools and even the government itself. Alongside Ralph Waldo Emerson's complacence in 1844 at the "heterogeneous population crowding on all ships from all corners of the world to the great gates of North America" should be put his caustic comment to Thomas Carlyle twenty years later about "the wild Irish element, imported in the last twenty-five years into this country, and led by Romanish Priests, who sympathize, of course, with despotism." Though Emerson vented his feelings in private, Samuel F. B. Morse, eminent both as inventor and portrait painter, denounced in print the *Foreign Conspiracy against the Liberties of the United States.*

Out of these fears and antagonisms arose a passionate nativist movement demanding exclusion of the foreign-born and Catholics from public office and twenty-one years' residence for voting (as in the case of the American-born). Operating for a time through various oath-bound lodges, the nativists in the 1850's organized the American or Know-Nothing party as the political arm of the Order of the Star-Spangled Banner, the most militant of the secret societies. The Know-Nothings — so called because to outsiders they professed ignorance of their own existence — profited by the disruption of old party ties resulting from the Kansas-Nebraska Act in 1854. Attracting countless persons shocked by this revival of the slavery question, they captured Massachusetts, Pennsylvania and Delaware in the fall elections and elected about seventy-five Congressmen, adding a half-dozen or more states in 1855. Oddly enough, they even gained some foreign-born support, notably among the Swedes, whose ingrained Lutheranism occasioned dislike of the Sabbath-breaking Germans and horror at the growth of Catholicism. Though the party offered a presidential ticket in 1856, the sectional issue split its own ranks, and it soon passed into oblivion.

How potent a force the Know-Nothing crusade might have become but for the neutralizing effect of the slavery controversy, it is hard to say. Such flare-ups have always quickly burned themselves out in America. Moreover, the frenzy had made little headway in the West, where the need for population caused some commonwealths to go to the opposite extreme and, like William Penn, send literature and agents abroad to recruit settlers. Know-Nothingism in the South rested not on direct knowledge of the outlanders, for they numbered less than 3 per cent of the population as late as 1860, but on dread of the political strength accruing to the free states from the European accessions. "The great mass of foreigners who come to our shores are laborers, and consequently come into competition with slave labor," observed the Morehouse (Louisiana) *Advocate*. "It is to their interest to abolish slavery."

Immigrant guidebooks helped to keep aliens away from the South by emphasizing the dearth of jobs there and the necessity of initial capital for plantation production. The result of this abstention was to cause that section to accentuate its differences from the rest of the country and increasingly to stew in its own juice. Deprived of a plentiful supply of imported cheap labor, it proved more difficult for the South to diversify its agriculture or start manufactures. Its political as well as its economic life fell more and more under the sway of King Cotton and his vicegerents, the great planters. Moreover, the native white stock, left to itself, continually interbred, with the consequence that the bulk of the people were robbed of the liberalizing influences of contact with persons and ideas from other parts of the world. Proslavery apologists, however, made a virtue of this exclusiveness, citing the Frenchman Gobineau's writings on the danger of debauching the purity of the old Anglo-Saxon blood with inferior strains.

The immigrants massed in the North were not, however, as single-minded against slavery as the Louisiana editor supposed. Wherever their true interests lay, many were drawn into the proslavery Democratic party by the magic of its name. The Irish, indeed, remained incurably Democratic, partly because of concentration in the urban strongholds of the party, and partly because as Catholics they, like the minority of Germans who belonged to that faith, mistrusted the presence of former Know-Nothings in the Republican fold. The Republican party, organized in 1854 in protest against the Kansas-Nebraska Act for opening additional territory to the possibility of slavery, made a special point of wooing the foreign vote, particularly in the Midwest. While that measure was still before Congress, the antislavery leaders had joined in condemning it as "an atrocious plot to exclude from a vast unoccupied region immigrants from the Old World and free laborers from our own States." Eighty out of eighty-eight German newspapers promptly echoed the charge.

Carl Schurz, a Forty-eighter, was one of the midwives of the new party, addressing American as well as German audiences. To dispel suspicions of Know-Nothing infiltration, he persuaded the Republican national convention in 1860 to declare against any stiffening of naturalization requirements or abridging in any way the rights of foreign-born citizens. As another inducement to the immigrant voter the platform pledged free homesteads in the public domain. Abraham Lincoln, rounding up support for his candidacy, bought the *Illinois Staats-Anzeiger* for the duration of the campaign, thus helping to offset the *Staats-Zeitung's* advocacy of William H. Seward as the nominee as well as securing a vigorous Teutonic organ in the postconvention battle. As President he rewarded the editor with a consulate in Samoa. Many historians believe that the German vote, though some of it went to Stephen A. Douglas, one of Lincoln's two Democratic competitors, determined the Republican victory in the Northwest and hence in the nation. The smaller contingent of Scandinavians gave Lincoln almost undivided support.

Southern secession following the election dissipated most remaining doubts in the minds of the Northern foreign-born. Those who had refused to weep over the plight of the Negroes or tremble over the fate of the Western territories nevertheless viewed with consternation the threat to the Union. As Ole Munch Raeder, a Norwegian visitor, had discerned some years before, the patriotism of the immigrants was the "more concentrated and therefore stronger" than if they, like so many native sons, had "bestowed their affection upon some particular state or community." Coming from numerous lands they wanted the land of their choice to remain one land. They were Unionists even when not antislavery men.

"Now, in the hour of our peril," wrote the New Yorker Charles Loring Brace shortly after the war broke out, "when the Southern demagogue counted on treason from the poor foreigner . . . we find the foreign-born rising, if possible, with more enthusiasm and patriotic self-devotion to defend the Republic than our own citizens." Some formed their own companies and regiments, the Irish oftentimes flying the green flag alongside the Red, White and Blue. According to a statistical analysis made soon after the peace, the Germans and Irish appear to have furnished proportionately more troops to the Union army than did the native Americans.

IV

Between the Civil War and the first war with Germany the incoming stream became a torrent and certain basic changes occurred in its composition. "During the last ten years," wrote Josiah Strong in 1891, "we have suffered a peaceful invasion by an army four times as vast as the estimated numbers of Goths and Vandals that swept over Southern Europe and overwhelmed Rome." In all, nearly twenty-seven and a third millions migrated to the United States in the years 1865–1917, considerably more than the entire population in 1850. A million a year was not uncommon in the early twentieth century. Professor William Z. Ripley pointed out in the *Atlantic Monthly* in 1908 that those arriving since 1900 alone would, if settled in the newer parts of the country, people nineteen states.

The older immigrant elements, principally the German, Irish, English and Scandinavian in that order, predominated at first. Thanks to the increasing numbers of Norwegians, Swedes and Danes, the upper Mississippi Valley seemed about to become a new Scandinavia. Industrious and thrifty farmers, law-abiding and highly literate citizens, these descendants of the Vikings added materially to the well-being of their commonwealths. It was at this time, too, that the French-Canadians entered New England in force. Though fewer than the newcomers from Europe, these folk — actually more French than Canadian — thronged into the mill towns and augmented the Catholic character of what had once been a Puritan citadel.

In the eighties, however, the current from the Atlantic side of Europe began to wane before a rising flood from Eastern and Southern Europe, and in the nineties the new strains submerged the old. Overcrowded conditions at home and the persecution of Jews, Poles, Czechs and other minorities, together with the fabled attractions of the United States, explain a movement that was stimulated further by the advertising of steamship and railroad companies and by American industrialists who prepaid the passage of laborers agreeing to work for a pittance.

These expatriates, like the Irish before them, hived in the towns and cities, where their biceps were in demand and they could dwell in colonies. A metropolis like Chicago soon contained within itself a Greek city, a Slovak city, a Hungarian city, a Sicilian city, a Lithuanian city, a Russian city. In these densely packed communities the people cherished their native languages, institutions and folkways. Another bar to assimilation was the fact that about one in three stayed in the land of milk and honey just long enough to lay aside sufficient cash with which to go back home and live in ease. Meanwhile, their willingness to work on any terms impeded organized labor's effort to improve conditions. The great majority of the foreigners, however, regarded America as a new and better fatherland, and along with the birds of passage they supplied most of the backbreaking toil that went into the enormous expansion of factories, mines and railroads. The United States Steel Corporation, for example, drew its labor force almost wholly from their ranks.

The newcomers complicated the problems of sanitation, policing and housing in the cities. The rise of scientific charity, social settlements, public-health agencies and playgrounds was prompted largely by their presence. As had been their predecessors, they were preyed upon by corrupt politicians, with this difference, however, that the corruptionist himself was also likely to smell of the steerage. In New York, where this illicit traffic was best organized, Tammany Hall, formerly ruled by William M. Tweed of colonial ancestry, fell to a succession of bosses of Irish parentage or birth. The time lay ahead when an Italian-American should be mayor of New York or a native Czech mayor of Chicago. The astounding graft and waste that discredited municipalities in these years was generally laid at the door of the foreign-born, but James Bryce dryly noted a disposition "to use the immigrants, and especially the Irish, much as the cat is used in the kitchen to account for broken plates and the food which disappears."

The Scandinavian additions gave Lutheranism a new importance in the family of American religions, while the Russian and Polish influx did the same for Judaism. But the Catholic faith, which was recruited from many lands, proved the chief gainer, provoking a brief revival of Know-Nothingism in the late eighties and early nineties under the name of the American Protective Association. The rising sentiment for immigration restriction stemmed mainly, however, from other sources: distrust of the exotic ways and speech of the newer comers, alarm at the social and political problems they occasioned, and the desire to reserve the remaining frontier lands for the native-born. The numerous ancestor-worshiping societies, formed in the wake of the Revolutionary centennials, demanded, "Who shall respect a people who do not respect their own blood?" while organized labor clamored against the admission of workers who undercut wages and scabbed in strikes.

Nevertheless, the old pride in America as a haven for Europe's unfortunate and oppressed prevented any sudden or drastic action. Instead, Congress gradually worked out a policy of selection on the basis of individual fitness without regard to nationality or the total numbers involved. The law of 1875 barred convicts and prostitutes. Later legislation added potential paupers, contract laborers, the mentally and physically handicapped, contagious cases, polygamists, anarchists, moral delinquents, alcoholics, even "persons of constitutional psychopathic inferiority."

Total exclusion, however, befell the destitute strangers who since the mid-nineteenth century had been swarming across the Pacific from China. They constituted a species unlike the white race and presented a seemingly insoluble problem of assimilation. In California the agitation against the "yellow peril" was led largely by labor elements under Denis Kearney, an Irish immigrant. As Robert Louis Stevenson, sojourning there, astutely observed, "Hungry Europe and hungry China, each pouring from their gates in search of provender, had here come face to face." Congress responded in 1882 with the first of a series of laws stopping future coolie immigration (slightly modified in 1943). This precedent also determined the nation's course toward the Japanese early in the next century.

Immigration, while increasingly an object of national legislation, became also increasingly a force in national politics. Battle cries echoing the sectional controversy and the Civil War meant little to the newly naturalized voter. To this fact was due in no small part the Republicans' gradual abandonment of "waving the bloody shirt." On the other hand, both parties began deliberately to court the foreign vote, particularly that of the English-hating Irish. "Twisting the lion's tail" became a standard

device at a time when Irish-Americans were rushing into such organizations as the Irish National League and the Irish National
Federation. In 1884 the Republican presidential nominee,
James G. Blaine, whose mother was of Irish Catholic stock, lost
whatever chances he had of winning the support of her coreligionists when an indiscreet Protestant clergyman hailed him as
a foe of "rum, Romanism and rebellion." In the next two elections the rival parties went so far as to insert in their platforms
forthright declarations in favor of home rule for Ireland.

The Germans rallied to the polls as a unit in state and local
elections whenever their treasured right to imbibe beer and wine
was threatened, but they did not mobilize nationally until the
question arose of America's siding against the fatherland in the
first world war of the twentieth century. Yet, despite the frantic efforts of the German-American Alliance aided by professional Irish Anglophobes, the rank and file of these folk never
hesitated when America took up arms and they were forced to
choose between the home of their ancestors and that of their
children. As the Provost Marshal General attested, "Men of foreign and of native origin alike responded to the call to arms
with a patriotic devotion that confounded the cynical plans of
our archenemy and surpassed our own highest expectations."
Once again diversity of blood proved a source of military
strength.

On domestic issues of national scope the immigrants generally
took a conservative stand. This is indicated, for example, by
the fact that in the free-silver election of 1896 all the Midwestern
states but Iowa supported Bryan in the ratio of their proportion
of persons of native parentage. Note also that the outlanders
actually provided more budding captains of industry than they
did labor leaders. Only a small if noisy minority tried to intro-
duce alien ideologies. Embittered by persecution in Europe,
such persons saw in America simply another police state callous
to human welfare. A handful of Germans organized the first Socialist parties in American cities after the Civil War, and the
short-lived anarchist movement had a similar origin in the
1880's. The I.W.W.'s early in the next century also drew mostly
upon foreign-born migratory laborers. The important point is
not that a few espoused such causes, but that the overwhelming

majority ignored or opposed them. Far more typical of their reform activities were the efforts of the English Jew Samuel Gompers for unionization, of the Dane Jacob Riis for slum clearance, of the Hungarian Joseph Pulitzer in crusading journalism, and of the Irish-born E. L. Godkin and the German Carl Schurz to abolish the spoils system. They strove to make the American capitalist democracy more workable, not to destroy it.

v

The fact that the United States was itself in make-up a league of nations did not stop the Republican Senate from rejecting the League of Nations fashioned by the Paris Peace Conference in 1919. Indeed, many German-Americans and Irish-Americans, believing that the League Covenant discriminated against the old countries, joined in the assault; and party politicians, even when friendly to the League, hesitated to antagonize these groups on the verge of a presidential campaign. Isolationism was in the saddle, and with the Republicans' capture of the government in 1920 it struck also at immigration.

The immediate occasion was fear that a deluge from war-stricken Europe would take bread from the mouths of native workers and, as businessmen believed, propagate radical and subversive ideas. This alarm merely confirmed a growing conviction that the arrivals in recent years from Southern and Eastern Europe had been too different and numerous to assimilate. Books appeared on the theme of "Nordic superiority," Kenneth Roberts, for example, insisting that "if a few million members of the Alpine, Mediterranean and Semitic races are poured among us, the result must inevitably be a hybrid race of people as worthless and futile as the good-for-nothing mongrels of Central America and Southeastern Europe." A new upsurge of Know-Nothingism, borrowing the name and terrorist methods of the post-Civil War Ku Klux Klan, attained considerable political strength in the South and Middle West. Inciting hatred against Catholics, Jews, the foreign-born and Negroes, the Klan at its crest in 1925 claimed four million or more members.

Responsive to popular sentiment, Congress by successive acts weighted the scales against the "undesirables" from Southern

and Eastern Europe and, in addition, restricted the total volume
of immigration. As early as 1917 it had moved toward the first
goal by adopting a literacy test. In 1921 it fixed the yearly contingent from any European country at not more than 3 per cent
of the number of its immigrants in the United States in 1910.
Then in 1924 it cut the quota to 2 per cent and pushed the test
year back to 1890. The climax came in 1929 when, according to
the national-origins formula authorized by the act of 1924, the
ceiling for all Europe (and Africa) was lowered to 150,000 individuals (later adjusted to 153,879) who should be admitted
annually from the various countries in proportions that corresponded to the existing composition of the American population.
Henceforth the inflow from Southern and Eastern Europe was
reduced to a dribble. In the case of Great Britain, for example,
the yearly quota became 65,721 — almost a third higher than
the actual average before the war — while that of Italy dropped
to 5802, less than a sixteenth of the previous average. Among the
ardent proponents of the national-origins provision were the
Sons and the Daughters of the American Revolution, the Ladies
of the Grand Army of the Republic, the Sons of the Confederacy, the United Spanish War Veterans, the American Legion
and some seventy other hereditary and commemorative bodies.

With widespread approval and bipartisan support the United
States thus recanted its historic policy. The Statue of Liberty's
brave invitation to the Old World,

> Give me your tired, your poor,
> Your huddled masses yearning to breathe free,

bespoke a past now to be honored in the breach rather than the
observance. The avowed object was to prevent any further di-
lution of the nation's blood, to maintain at all hazards the status
quo. That blood had become steadily less Anglo-Saxon and
more cosmopolitan since the adoption of the Constitution. In
fact, if the statisticians knew their business, British, Scotch-Irish
and Canadian strains now comprised less than half the white
stock, while German, Irish, Scandinavian, Polish, Italian, Czech
and smaller infusions made up the major portion.

Events quickly disclosed how difficult a task the country had undertaken. The hammer blows of the Great Depression, striking first in the autumn of 1929, not only beat down immigration below the permitted figures, but in the years 1932–1935 sent more persons back to Europe than arrived. From the mid-thirties on, the German persecution of the Jews and other minorities had a further distorting effect, crowding the quotas in Nazi-ruled countries to overflowing while those in many other lands remained unfilled. In Czechoslovakia in 1939 the United States consulates had enough applications for eleven years. Meanwhile, there appeared from Latin American nations — which lay outside the quota system — a far higher proportion of immigrants than their percentage of the United States population warranted. Nevertheless, in the decade as a whole, a smaller number of aliens entered the country than in any decade since the 1830's.

As the Axis war drew near, it thus happened that the babel of voices that had assailed the nation in the prelude to the last war was muted. Although stealthy bands, springing up here and there, genuflected before Hitler, sowed hatred of Jews and flayed British imperialism, they drew their tiny followings less from immigrants than from the native-born. The most strident group was led by Charles E. Coughlin, a Canadian-born Irish Catholic priest of Detroit who harangued vast audiences by radio; but when the Japanese attack on Pearl Harbor plunged America into the maelstrom, his influence, even among his coreligionists, proved negligible. There was grim irony in the fact that the forces against the European Axis were directed by such men as Dwight D. Eisenhower and Carl Spaatz, both of Pennsylvania German descent, and the Prussian-born Walter Krueger, while the American commanders on the other side of the globe included Chester W. Nimitz, grandson of a German immigrant, and George E. Stratemeyer of similar background. Other stocks made their full contribution as well. At the Japanese surrender ceremonies Admiral Nimitz proudly recalled that in the military cemetery on Guam near his headquarters the rows of white crosses bore such names as "Culpepper, Tomaino, Sweeney, Bromberg, Depew, Melloy, Ponziani — names that are a cross section of democracy."

On the home front the war effort had no stouter advocate than Wendell L. Willkie, the defeated Republican presidential nominee in 1940, whose every drop of blood was German, while many "enemy aliens," especially of the refugee group, rendered essential help through their inside knowledge of Axis countries and their special technical and scientific skills. One measure of immigrant patriotism was that in 1943 naturalization reached an all-time high, with a total of 435,500 new citizens, of whom about 43,000 were in the armed services. Between 1940 and 1944 the whole number of noncitizens shrank from 5,000,000 to 3,400,000.

Victory posed the question of what the United States should do to help relieve the plight of the war-uprooted peoples abroad. The tragic predicament of a million displaced persons in Western Europe appealed to the sympathies of a country which once had freely welcomed the penniless and discouraged of the Old World. The quota system, however, stood as a bar, as did also the dread of an inundation of Communists and other radicals — though, in fact, most of the unfortunates were homeless just because they would not return to Communist-ruled lands. The concrete proposal before Congress was to use a small part of past unfilled quotas in order to admit 100,000 annually for four years. The D.A.R., the American Legion and the Veterans of Foreign Wars opposed the bill, while the AFL and the CIO, discounting fears of an overcrowded labor market, favored it. After long delay the lawmakers in 1948 adopted a compromise measure admitting 205,000 in the next two years subject to conditions which President Truman on signing it protested as "flagrantly discriminatory."

VI

If the thirty-nine million emigrants to America between 1776 and 1940 had stayed in Europe, the history of their countries as well as that of the United States would have been different. This is a matter to which scholars have paid scant attention. It is clear, however, that the more democratic governments of the Old World generally tried to stanch the drain of blood by healing the causes. Emigration thus speeded political and economic reforms at home. Despotic regimes, on the other hand, usually welcomed the departure of potential or actual troublemakers. Those who migrated tended to be the most restless and

ambitious members of the community, men and women rebellious against grooves and restrictions. Such progeny a wise parent could ill afford to lose.

The student of German history, for example, may well ponder
the consequences to the fatherland — and to mankind — of the
hegira from that country. Wrote a German farmer in Missouri to
his kindred back home in 1834,

> If you wish to see our whole family living in . . . a country
> where freedom of speech obtains, where no spies are eaves-
> dropping, where no simpletons criticize your every word and
> seek to detect therein a venom that might endanger the life
> of the state, the church and the home, in short, if you wish to
> be really happy and independent, then come here.

At a more sophisticated political level Theodore Poesche, an
émigré of the Revolution of 1848, commented, "The 'dema-
gogues' of the last four years are in exile; the energetic portion
of their adherents have followed them, going to the republic
when the republic would not come to them. Those who remain
behind have lapsed into their former state of contented servi-
tude." In sum, he said, emigration by removing the explosive elements from Germany acted as a "safety-valve" to preserve the
status quo. Little wonder that the docility and political imma-
turity of the German masses became a byword throughout the
world, eventually plunging them through the machinations of
their rulers into two global wars.

When the native went back to his homeland, as some did, further effects were apt to be felt in the older society. "The returned Americans," reported an official Norwegian commission
in 1913,

> put their stamp upon it all; the rural districts are hardly
> recognizable. The farmers are not so burdened with debt as
> before; people live better, eat better, clothe themselves bet-
> ter, — thus the population itself improves. All those who
> come from America begin to till the soil better than it was
> tilled before. . . . Furthermore, they have a will to take
> hold, and have in America learned a rate of work, which is
> different from what people are accustomed to here.

What was the Old World's loss was necessarily America's gain. In the words of the Danish-American poet Adam Dan,

> We came not empty-handed here
> But brought a rich inheritance.

Immigration introduced new life, new ideas, new skills, new brawn. The waves of fugitives from the Communist, Fascist and Nazi revolutions in the twenty-five years after 1917 underscored what had been happening unobtrusively since colonial times, for until the twentieth century there had never in all history been so huge and ruthless an eviction of science, learning, literature and the fine arts. From Germany alone America received such world-famous persons as the physicists Albert Einstein and James Franck, the mathematician Herman Weyl, the classical philologist Werner Jaeger, the scholarly ex-Chancellor of the German Republic Heinrich Bruening, the novelist Thomas Mann, the architect Walter Gropius, the composer Kurt Weil and the symphony conductor Otto Klemperer. New York City and its environs in 1940 contained the highest concentration of Nobel Prize winners ever known anywhere, including, besides Einstein, Franck, Mann and American recipients, the authors Maurice Maeterlinck and Sigrid Undset from Nazi-seized countries. The whole number of exiles from the revolutionary convulsions and their aftermath approximated 245,000 for just the years 1933–1944.

From a longer perspective the immigrant's role in American civilization is suggested by the late Charles O. Paullin's unpublished study of the eighteenth- and nineteenth-century figures in the twenty-volume *Dictionary of American Biography*. Foreign birth accounts for 20 per cent of the businessmen, 20 per cent of the scholars and scientists, 23 per cent of the painters, 24 per cent of the engineers, 28 per cent of the architects, 29 per cent of the clergymen, 46 per cent of the musicians and 61 per cent of the actors. In other words, the expatriates provided leadership, not so much in politics or war or even in business, but chiefly in the realms of the mind and spirit: religion, learning, research and the fine arts. They reinforced those tendencies in American life which Americans, engaged with pressing immediate tasks, tended to neglect. Such names as John Jacob Astor, Andrew Carnegie and James J. Hill typify industrial achievement, while those of John J. Audubon, Alexander Graham Bell, Nikola Tesla, Michael Pupin, Hidego Noguchi, Lafcadio Hearn, O. E. Rölvaag, Augustus Saint-Gaudens, Karl Bitter, John Ericsson, John A. Roebling, James McCosh, John Ireland, Theodore Thomas, Victor Herbert and Maurice Barrymore indicate the quality and variety of attainment in other fields. If the descendants of the foreign-born be included, America's debt to her adopted sons becomes immeasurable.

Nevertheless, James Bryce correctly noted that "the intellectual and moral atmosphere into which the settlers from Europe come has more power to assimilate them than their race qualities have to change it." Imperceptibly they merged into the composite American type — Crèvecœur's "new man" — altering even in height and physique with the second and third generations. Attempts to keep alive Old World customs usually tapered off into something reminiscent of pressed flowers in the family album. The nativist outbursts coincided with sudden increases in immigrant landings, when the strangeness of the newcomer was most glaring. Nearly every non-English people became in turn a target, and unthinking descendants of these groups joined in similar demonstrations against later arrivals.

The deeper meaning of America lies in the eagerness of the immigrant to cast his lot with the new country and in America's desire to have him do so. The national purpose has been to create a democracy of diverse cultures which should embody the values and ideals, the arts, knowledge and techniques, of men of every European background. This is the New World's answer to the Old World's way of segregating humanity in nations with different governments, different languages, different hopes. The authors of the national-origins formula would have denied any departure from this aim, though they hedged it about with what they believed to be necessary safeguards.

In no other sense does "100-per-cent Americanism" have historical warrant. Efforts to crush out minority heritages violate the national purpose and set a dangerous example for the rest of the world. By the same token, manifestations of intolerance may start a chain reaction destructive of all American liberties.

As Archbishop Francis J. Spellman declared in 1944, incidentally rebuking anti-Semitic individuals of his own once persecuted group, "All fair-minded Americans must oppose bigotry not only from a sense of justice but also from a sense of safety, for, if tolerated, it can be directed at any race or religion and then may rebound against all of them." To be true to itself, the United States must ever uphold the tradition that has contributed so profoundly to its greatness.

GOVERNMENT
OF THE PEOPLE

5

The tides of
national politics

IF THERE is one subject on which the average American considers himself an expert, it is politics. He may be unable to predict the weather; he may mishandle his own business; he may be a failure as a parent; but, whether in the Pullman smoker or at the crossroads gas station, he expatiates confidently on the political outlook. To his help in recent years has come the numerous tribe of columnists and radio and television commentators and, to their help as well as his, the various straw-vote organizations. It seems as though everything possible is done to expose the throbbing pulse of popular opinion to universal gaze.

Nevertheless, such self-appointed authorities, whether professional or amateur, labor at an insuperable disadvantage. Sizing up the future by indications of the present, they retain their standing as prophets either through sheer luck or because of the public's forgetfulness of their past mistakes. Preoccupied with the scene at hand, they fail to realize that current history is history without a current. Little wonder that the columnists and Washington correspondents may foretell one turn of events while the Gallup or *Fortune* polls foretell another.

I

To understand the deeper forces in political life it is necessary to take a longer and cooler view, to observe the process at a focal distance. Yet historians themselves are not agreed as to the nature of these underlying factors. The writers of the older schoolbooks clocked off American history into four-year units and represented each presidential administration as making its separate contribution. Other historians, rejecting so simple a formula, have ascribed epochal shifts in governmental policy to dominant personalities in the White House, tagging such turning points as the "Jeffersonian System," the "Reign of Andrew Jackson," the "Cleveland Era," the "Roosevelt Revolution." Today, however, most students find the explanation in the rivalry of parties.

Not contemplated by the Constitution and arising contrary to President Washington's wishes, these alliances of voters have dominated the stage since the Republic's earliest days. They have developed long-continuing and intricate structures and have impressed their programs on the country. They have been the shoulders on which strong-willed Presidents mounted to their posts of command. Most American of American institutions, these parties baffle the understanding of the average intelligent foreigner. Indeed, what is their true nature? The biologist sees in them many of the attributes of an organism. The economist recognizes them as a special variety of Big Business. The student of religion observes in their emphasis on faith, orthodoxy and hereditary attachment an inescapable likeness to the church. Their very longevity entitles them to respect. The Democratic party is more than a century and a half old, and the Republicans have begun their second century.

None will deny the prominence of parties on the political terrain. But to assume that they have been the mainspring — the prime initiating force — of governmental policy implies that they have been cohesive bodies of voters espousing coherent and contrasting programs. One would hesitate to say that today. A recent English visitor, cogitating the situation, concluded wearily that about the only thing clear to him was that the Republicans did not oppose democracy and no Democrat wanted to abolish the Republic. He added, "These parties are not at all like the British, which have the people who want things done on one side and the people who don't on the other." Nicholas Murray Butler, writing as "probably the member of the Republican party organization longest in its continuous service," confessed in 1942, "The traditional names Democrat and Republican no longer reflect any accepted body of political principles and policies, nor is there anything approaching agreement among those who still continue to bear either of these party names." Only two years before, his own political clan had run an ex-Democrat (Wendell L. Willkie) for President, while the opposition had picked a former Republican (Henry A. Wallace) as Franklin D. Roosevelt's running mate. In Congress it was the New Deal elements of both parties that lined up against the anti-New Dealers within the same camps.

What we forget is that this condition of affairs has always existed. Different from the English system, the two major parties have seldom advocated well-defined alternative programs and never for long. Faced with the problem of marshaling widespread geographic support, they have been coalitions of state and regional interests and local political machines, representing diverse tendencies of thought out of which pronouncements of policy emerged after much wrenching and compromise. Only minor parties have indulged the luxury of clear-cut convictions, with the result that they have nearly always stayed minor. Anticipating Nicholas Murray Butler, the political commentator Samuel Blythe in 1922 described the party designations of his time as "labels on empty bottles." James Bryce had used the same figure in the 1880's. Alexis de Tocqueville took a similar view more than a hundred years ago. Even Thomas Jefferson in his first Inaugural asserted of the then opposing groups, "We are all Republicans, we are all Federalists."

When a real clash of principle has divided the rival aggregations, it has been due to the temporary ascendancy of one faction over another in either party or in both. As a result of such internal tussles each party has pursued a zigzag course, often disowning its former dearly held tenets and sometimes even exchanging positions with its rival. Abraham Lincoln, commenting on the Democratic and Republican parties as the election of 1860 approached, said,

I remember being once much amused at seeing two partially intoxicated men engaged in a fight with their great-coats on, which fight, after a long and rather harmless contest, ended in each having fought himself out of his own coat and into that of the other. If the two leading parties of this day are

really identical with the two in the days of Jefferson and
Adams, they have performed the same feat as the two
drunken men.

Lincoln rightly regarded the newly formed Republican party,
rather than the proslavery Democrats, as the true exponents of
Jefferson's doctrine of putting "the man before the dollar." Yet
within twenty years of Lincoln's assassination his own political brethren, having meanwhile entered into a partnership
with Big Business, reversed the emphasis between man and the
dollar. With such basic shifts of attitude it is not surprising that
erstwhile party leaders have chosen to repudiate their former
political bedfellows. Long before New Deal heresies prompted
Al Smith to "take a walk" out of the Democratic fold in 1936, Martin Van Buren, Grover Cleveland and Theodore Roosevelt had
turned against the parties which once had raised them to the
White House.

II

If neither presidential administrations nor masterful personalities nor parties are the prime movers in political life, whence
comes the motive power? Is some influence at work less obvious
to the eye? Jefferson hinted at the answer when he observed,
"Men, according to their constitutions, and the circumstances
in which they are placed, differ honestly in opinion." Some, he
said, "fear the people, and wish to transfer all power to the
higher classes of society"; the others "consider the people as the
safest depository of power in the last resort; they cherish them,
therefore, and wish to leave in them all the powers to the exercise
of which they are competent." He called these contrasting conceptions Tory and Whig, aristocratic and democratic, Federalist
and Republican. Historians have called them Hamiltonian and
Jeffersonian. Today we would call them conservative and liberal.
A Gallup poll taken in 1939, when conservatism was on the up-
grade, revealed that the voters were about equally divided between the two schools, 52 per cent describing themselves as conservatives and 48 as liberals. Probably the balance has always
been much the same, a small shift from one side to the other determining the dominant mood.

Any scrutiny of American history discloses the alternation of these attitudes. A period of concern for the rights of the few has been followed by one of concern for the wrongs of the many. Emphasis on the welfare of property has given way to emphasis on human welfare in the belief, as Theodore Roosevelt put it, that "every man holds his property subject to the general right of the community to regulate its use to whatever degree the public welfare may require it." An era of quietude has been succeeded by one of rapid movement. Mere motion, however, is no proof of liberalism: it may be forward or backward or even in circles. The test is whether the object is to increase or lessen democracy, and the achievement is evidenced not by words but by the resulting legislative and executive accomplishment. Such oscillations of sentiment, moreover, express themselves through changes of direction within a party as well as by displacement of one party by the other.

These shifts of mood can be plotted with reasonable precision. In some instances historians might quarrel as to the exact terminal dates, but such differences would involve only trifling alterations. The analysis cannot be pushed back of 1765 because before then nothing resembling national political movements existed in America. Thereafter the periods run:

* (1) 1765–1787	* (7) 1861–1869
(2) 1787–1801	(8) 1869–1901
* (3) 1801–1816	* (9) 1901–1919
(4) 1816–1829	(10) 1919–1931
* (5) 1829–1841	* (11) 1931–1947
(6) 1841–1861	

The asterisks indicate the liberal dispensations.

The first period, dating from the Stamp Act Congress of 1765, was marked by the colonists' resistance to English imperialism, the setting up of the Republic and the "excess of democracy" under the Articles of Confederation. Then in 1787 the Constitutional Convention opened a new era with a frame of government based on the principle of safety-first for the conservative elements, thereby paving the way for the political dominance of the commercial classes. Jefferson's accession in 1801 restored the accent on popular rights, including a long-sustained effort for peace at any price in a world rent by war. After 1816 conservative ideals reasserted themselves in the form of higher tariff protection, the federal financing of roads and canals and the establishment of the Second United States Bank. But with Jackson's elevation in 1829 the plain people romped into power, rejected the program of federal aid to business and gave politics a democratic impulse to which even the conservative Whigs paid lip service in their log-cabin campaign of 1840. Under John Tyler in 1841 the tide again turned against liberalism, involving the nation in a land-grabbing war with Mexico and in a series of measures for strengthening and extending the institution of slavery.

The year 1861 marked the next *volte-face,* precipitating the disruption of the Union, during which the North initiated the policy of free farms for settlers, emancipated the four million slaves, and strove to safeguard their rights against white encroachment before readmitting the Southern states. The current, however, reversed in 1869 when President Grant entered office. For the rest of the century the government under conservative auspices devoted itself mainly to the promotion of business enterprise — the "politics of acquisition and enjoyment" — through such devices as land grants to railroads, tariff increases, the maintenance of the gold standard and the bagging of insular dependencies.

In 1901, with the advent of Theodore Roosevelt, liberalism recaptured the field, concentrating its energies on curbing business and financial aggression in the public interest, and reaching its climax when Wilson led the country into a war to make the world safe for democracy. Even the intervening Taft regime, though supposedly out of step with the times, placed important progressive measures on the statute books. But with President Wilson's loss of Congress at the close of the war conservatism and "rugged individualism" once more held the stage, reigning almost unchallenged from 1919 till the middle of the Hoover administration when the opposition party took over the House of Representatives. Beginning in 1931, the Democrats inaugurated a program of reform, culminating in the second Roosevelt's New Deal, which invoked the might of government on behalf of wage earner, farmer and the "forgotten man." This tide of liberalism ended in 1947 when the Republicans, having won both houses of Congress in the mid-term elections, proceeded to reorient the country in a conservative direction.

It should be underlined that the labels conservative and liberal as here used describe the effective tendencies in government; they may or may not denote a change of parties. With this in mind, Lincoln's story of the two befuddled wrestlers becomes intelligible. A party in one climate of opinion may move to the right and in another shift to the left, yet proclaim to a forgetful electorate that it is still the same residuary of immortal truth. American parties have been symbolized by such animals as the elephant and the donkey, but not by the leopard, which never changes its spots. Whether to gain or retain office they have to be responsive to the prevailing national temper. The Democratic rout in the autumn of 1946 did not ensure a prolonged sway by the Republicans unless in the years immediately ahead the victors should continue to convince the voter of their superior devotion to conservative policies. Nor do professed differences as to constitutional interpretation bear on the question, for conservatives and liberals have favored or opposed a strong national government according as it suited their immediate purposes. Broadly speaking, the group in power, whether of the one school or the other, has supported a vigorous exercise of federal authority.

Least of all is it true that popular sentiment is ever unanimous. Even in periods of transcendent crisis like that from 1765 to 1789 or from 1861 to 1869 dissident voices cried out against the dominant liberal leadership. To cite an instance of conservative supremacy, the years from 1869 to 1901 were constantly disturbed by the reform agitation of agrarian groups and labor elements. In a country of continental magnitude and great economic diversity, atmospheric conditions in politics may vary as widely as actual temperature and rainfall. Enclaves of conservatism survive in liberal epochs and vice versa.

Unlike the climate, however, the political trends arise from human causes. The alternation is no mere automatic process. Whichever attitude is uppermost, the existence of an insurgent minority fighting a rearguard action is essential if it is eventually to seize the offensive and rout the enemy. The government in exile must keep itself alive and stand ready to succeed. "The wintry blasts of reaction have swept the country, and liberalism has gone underground," declared the New Dealer Henry A. Wallace after the Republican landslide of 1946. "In times like these we must remember our proud heritage" and keep the "torch of liberty aflame." Change "wintry" to "fiery," "reaction" to "radicalism" and "liberalism" to "conservatism," and you have the rallying cry of the opposite sect when out of power.

III

Are these trends in American politics cyclical? Do they obey a rhythm which may afford a clue to the future as well as to the past? The average length of the eleven periods is 16.55 years; the actual duration has seldom varied far from the norm. Minor irregularities should be expected, since new directions of mass sentiment generally find effective expression at two-year and four-year intervals — at the mid-term and presidential elections. Major deviations occurred in two instances: the eight-year liberal span from 1861 to 1869 and the ensuing thirty-two-year reign of conservatism. It is reasonable to think, however, that the abnormal conditions of a country stricken with civil strife greatly hastened the tempo of reform in the one period, achieving results which otherwise would have taken a much longer time, while the prolongation of the countermovement in the next period was a form of compensation to restore the rhythm. In any event, the average length of the two epochs is twenty years, only three and a half years from the norm.

For purposes of prediction the analysis should be further refined. The five eras of conservative rule average 18.2 years; the six liberal dispensations, almost exactly 15 years. If the two atypical periods falling between 1861 and 1901 be omitted, however, the results are different. Conservative regimes would then seem to run their course in 14.8 years, liberal ones in 16.2. These figures afford a sounder basis for charting the years ahead, for the recurrence of a destructive sectional struggle like the Civil War is too improbable to be taken into account. On the other hand, if a form of totalitarianism should displace the democratic system sometime in the future, any forecast based upon trends in a free society would become invalid. On the assumption that no such catastrophe impended, the recession from liberalism which began in 1947 was due to end in 1962, with a possible margin of a year or two in either direction. On this basis the next conservative epoch will commence around 1978.

It is possible that in the future the activities of high-powered pressure groups may warp the pattern of alternation. Pressure groups, however, are not new to American history as anyone knows who recalls, for example, the part played by the Sons of Liberty and the committees of correspondence in fomenting the Revolution. Yet today they possess mighty new instruments in the radio and television. But if the thesis set forth in these pages is correct, these modern methods cannot materially affect the basic pulsations of opinion. The propaganda, to be effective, must harmonize with the national bent toward conservatism or liberalism, whichever happens to predominate. When in agreement with the bent, pressure tactics may goad the government into adopting extremer measures than it would otherwise have done. When not in agreement, the agitation merely serves the necessary purpose of keeping the opposition's "torch of liberty aflame." There is no evidence as yet that propaganda, however artful and heavily financed, can of itself reverse a fundamental drift of sentiment.

It is possible, too, that the increasing impingement of international urgencies upon domestic affairs may alter the trends. The effort begun during the Axis war to keep foreign relations on a bipartisan basis will, however, if successfully sustained, operate to the contrary. Furthermore, it should be recalled that there have been times in the past when the voter seemed more interested in the fortunes of other nations than of his own. A contemporary, alarmed by the ideological rifts in the 1790's, declared that everywhere he met "Francomen" and "Anglomen" but no Americans. John Adams, more conservatively, put a third of the people in each of these categories. On later occasions as well, the choices in domestic politics appeared to be influenced by events abroad. In the twentieth century, for example, the presidential campaigns of 1916 and 1940 saw the country at odds over the issue of isolationism versus interventionism. Since in all these instances the duration of the periods remained unaffected, it is far from clear that America's new role in the world will make any difference in the years ahead.

These periodic shifts of opinion, some say, suggest the action of a pendulum. The analogy is faulty, however, insofar as it implies that the oscillations occur between two fixed points. The conceptions, conservatism and liberalism, never stay put. "Time makes ancient good uncouth" for both sects, though for different reasons. Professor T. V. Smith has satirized the conservatives' accommodation to a reform trend by having them say,

First, we don't need improvement, for normalcy is enough. Then, we need some improvement, but what's proposed is wrong in principle. Then the principle's all right, but the way of working it out is all wrong. Then at last everything's all right (in about that tone of voice), but we Republicans can administer it better than you Democrats can — and, besides, we'll see to it that the thing doesn't go any further!

In other words, as the historical record makes clear, the chief liberal gains generally remain on the statute books when the conservatives recover power. They acquiesce in the new status quo, though they may try to sabotage it by halfhearted enforcement and reduced appropriations while advancing their own special ideals by such methods as are still available to them. As a case in point, the conservatives of the 1920's assented to principles of corporate control which their predecessors in the 1880's and 1890's would have railed at as populistic and socialistic. On the other hand, the liberals on regaining office discover both new abuses to cure and the need to plug up loopholes in past reform measures. Hence they push forward to fresh ground.

In fine, liberalism grows constantly more liberal and, by the same token, conservatism grows constantly less conservative. The process is not only periodic but progressive. For this reason a more appropriate figure than the pendulum is the spiral, in which the alternation proceeds at successively higher levels. Rubashov, a character in Arthur Koestler's novel *Darkness at Noon*, suggests a better analogy than either, that of a ship being hoisted by stages through a canal: "When it first enters a lock chamber, it is slowly lifted up until the water-level reaches its highest point. But this grandeur is illusory, the next lock is higher still, the leveling process has to start again."

IV

There remains the question of what generates these irresistible sweeps of sentiment. Is the alternation, to quote Jefferson, a response to what men desire "according to their constitutions," or does it arise from "the circumstances in which they are placed?" The modern disposition to identify politics with bread-and-butter motives suggests the economic explanation, but, in fact, no observable correlation exists between the political ups and downs and the peaks and valleys of the business cycle. Neither the three-and-a-half-year rhythm in industrial production, nor the nine-year rhythm in commodity and stock prices, nor the eighteen-year rhythm in real-estate construction, nor the fifty-four-year rhythm in wholesale prices, nor any combination of these and other economic rhythms provides an answer. There is an old saying that in hard times public opinion veers to the left. Yet two of the worst depressions in United States history fell within the period of 1869–1901 without stopping the ground swell of conservatism. On the other hand, the era of New Deal liberalism coincided with an interval of almost unrelieved bad times. The fact seems to be that the worsening of material conditions invariably disturbs the political waves, but, unless reinforced by other factors, does not affect the deeper waters.

Mr. Edgar Lawrence Smith, author of *Tides in the Affairs of Men* (1939), kindly offered to apply his hypothesis of solar-economic relationships to these reversals of political attitude, but for lack of adequate data or for other reasons he discovered no convincing connection. "It appears," he concluded, "that changes toward conservatism are predominantly (not exclusively) associated with years of Sun Spot Maxima, and changes toward liberalism, with Sun Spot Minima." To go even farther afield, the curious may wish to consider patterns of mutation as evidenced elsewhere: the fact that pneumonia and influenza reach peaks every three years; that field-mice plagues occur every four years; that there are nine-to-ten-year periods in the abundance of animal life; that the marriage rate conforms to an eighteen-year trend; that weather cycles repeat themselves every thirty-five years. Such data, however, merely emphasize the point that pulsations of change in different areas appear to take place independently of each other.

One would seem on firmer ground in looking to factors and events that bore upon the country's political development. Is there, for instance, a correlation between foreign wars and the mass drifts of sentiment? The answer is that these conflicts have taken place about equally in conservative and liberal periods, sometimes coming at the start, sometimes at the end and sometimes midway. Nor has the progressive enlargement of the electorate — from a relatively few white men to all white male adults, then to all black men and some male Indians and, finally, to all women and all Indians — left any perceptible trace on the timing of the currents.

Though it is true that a strong-willed President has inaugurated every liberal dispensation under the Constitution, other executives of this stripe — Polk, Cleveland and Wilson — invalidate any such generalization. The most that can be said is that the recurrent revolt against conservatism has found its initial outlet through the channel of a colorful or commanding personality. Moreover, contrary to what one might suppose, the physical growth of the country has not altered the duration of the cycles, and the same holds true of the immense changes resulting from improvements of transportation and communication, which, of course, helped to offset the effects of physical growth. Nor has the steady extension of popular education made any difference. If the year 1861 be taken as the dividing line, the evidence shows that, despite the higher momentum of American life since then, the average span of the later periods has been longer rather than shorter. The difference, though, is slight.

One might expect new directions of national policy to parallel similar tendencies in the states. Only an elaborate, comparative study could settle the point, but it is easy to test it by noting the moments of intense activity in state constitution making and revision. Down to 1902 seven such occasions had arisen, with an average interval of 18.7 years between them. By and large the changes adopted were liberal in character. Yet four of the seven periods fell in times of prevailing conservatism in the United

States in general. This showing, after all, should not excite surprise, for in a huge and diversified country local conditions are bound to foster local attitudes and policies at variance with the national mood.

No more rewarding is a comparison with like oscillations in the great Western European democracies. From data supplied by students of British and French history it appears that the movements of conservatism and liberalism in those countries observe their own timetables. The closest correspondence exists between the British average period of 16.2 years from 1760 to 1922 and the American average of 17 years in the comparable stretch from 1763 to 1919. In the case of France, where the analysis is harder to make, the normal duration is less than half as long as in the sister democracies.

v

The reason for the ebb and flow seems singularly elusive, but if perpetual fog veiled the moon from the earth, the secret of the ocean's tides might appear equally mysterious. Granted that the present discussion has until now reached only negative conclusions, there remains Jefferson's alternative suggestion of the reaction of men "according to their constitutions," the fact that human beings in the mass, unlike inanimate Nature, respond to psychological impulses.

The great Virginian himself worked out the concept in terms of successive generations. Using figures from M. de Buffon's table of mortality, he computed that half the population twenty-one years and older die off every 18.7 years, thus clearing the stage for a different set of men and measures. But this formula of a brand-new generation regularly replacing an old belies the facts. The biological process is actually one of continuous dissolution and renewal with no moment of time distinguishable from any other. Besides, since 1789, when he put forward the suggestion, the lifetime of a generation has greatly lengthened, thanks to improved diet and advances in medical and sanitary science. The accepted figure in 1934, for example, was 30 years. In neither instance, however, does the duration jibe with that of the political sweeps.

Changes in mass psychology evidently arise from some other source. Perhaps the truth may be arrived at by noticing the tendencies analogous to conservatism and liberalism that operate in fields where the confusing elements of the political drama are absent. Theology has in this manner seesawed between orthodoxy and heterodoxy. Imaginative literature has passed repeatedly through periods of classicism and revolt. The same freezing and thawing of the human mind has characterized the fine arts as well. It is reasonable to believe that American politics has undergone a similar interplay of subjective influences — influences springing from something basic in human nature. Apparently the electorate embarks upon conservative policies till it is disappointed or vexed or bored and then attaches itself to liberal policies till a like course is run.

As American history has shown time and again, there are concrete reasons why successive electorates react this way. Both conservatives and liberals take over the government in a spirit of zeal and dedication, convinced that truth crushed to earth has risen again. But neither group can stand more than a certain amount of success; thereafter the quality of their performance tends to deteriorate. The desire to continue in power encourages timidity and compromise; holding office as a means tapers off into holding office as an end. Is it not better, they argue, to be content with half a loaf of accomplishment than be reduced to the breadlessness of an impotent minority? The conservatives when in control encounter additional difficulty because their bond with the propertied classes exposes them to charges, not infrequently substantiated, of bribery and corruption. Thus both camps lose favor with the elements that elevated them and blindly dig their own graves.

VI

The alternating process of conservatism and liberalism casts a significant light on the workings of American democracy. Not preconceived theory but empiricism has been the guiding star. The ship of state has moved forward by fits and starts, choosing its course in obedience to the prevailing winds of opinion. Unlike the French, however, the American people have tried out each set of policies long enough to give them an honest test. On the whole, they have shown a greater tolerance of liberalism than of conservatism. In this respect they have differed from the British electorate, which has historically shown a somewhat greater preference for conservatism.

If this method of progress seems haphazard and wasteful, it has the merit of its defects, for it has enabled both groups to make their distinctive contributions to the public good. Macaulay to the contrary notwithstanding, the American political system has not been all sail and no anchor. Neither has it been all anchor and no sail. A period of imaginative leadership, of experimentalism and democratic innovation, has been followed by one of sober reflection, of digestion of the gains and renewed vigilance for the rights of property.

This two-way process has been born of the inner necessities of a political order which deems competition between opposing attitudes a positive virtue. Since each school is assured of an eventual lease of power, its adherents when out of office need not yield to despair or resort to revolutionary violence. They need only to talk and work and wait, knowing full well that ere long their own turn will come. No system could offer a better insurance policy against government by dictatorship or brute force. Only once did it fail to function — in 1861 — with consequences which the country has never ceased to lament. With democracy on trial throughout the world today, every citizen should mount guard to see that nothing is done to impair this balance wheel of orderly evolution. Neither conservatism nor liberalism, but a fair field for both, is the American ideal. Therein lies the crucial argument for the jealous preservation of the constitutional rights of free elections, free speech, free assemblage and a free press.

6

Rating
the Presidents

How good have America's Presidents been? Which ones have left an enduring mark? Who were the failures? Where do the others rank? Seventy-five students of American history, including two in English universities, have undertaken to answer these questions.

Had they been appraising the total careers of the men, the results in some cases might have been quite different. Madison, John Quincy Adams, Grant and Eisenhower, for instance, were certainly great Americans, though not, according to the panel, great Presidents. Their title to fame rests on contributions made before and after holding the office.

The present inquiry, however, has to do with a single point — achievement in the executive chair. Omitted from consideration — besides Kennedy, the chief magistrate then still in office — are two Presidents who were too briefly at the helm to permit a fair evaluation: William Henry Harrison, who died within a month of his inauguration, and James A. Garfield, who served little more than half a year.

Each participant in the poll applied his measuring rod in accordance with the relative importance he attached to the complex factors that helped make or break the particular administration. Did the President head the nation in sunny or stormy times? Did he exhibit a creative approach to the problems of statecraft? Was he the master or servant of events? Did he use the prestige and potentialities of the position to advance the public welfare? Did he effectively staff his key government posts? Did he properly safeguard the country's interest in relation to the rest of the world? How significantly did he affect the future destinies of the nation?

Admittedly, the judgment of the historians is not necessarily the judgment of history, but it is the best we can have without waiting for the sifting process of time. The members of the panel agreed with little dissent on the great and near-great Presidents and, at the opposite extreme, on those who made the poorest records. The principal differences involved the comparative ranking of the Presidents regarded as average and of those below average but not failures. Even in these cases, however, the preponderance of opinion was conclusive.

I

Results of the Poll

GREAT

1. Abraham Lincoln
2. George Washington
3. Franklin D. Roosevelt
4. Woodrow Wilson
5. Thomas Jefferson

NEAR GREAT

6. Andrew Jackson
7. Theodore Roosevelt
8. James K. Polk
9. Harry S. Truman
10. John Adams
11. Grover Cleveland

AVERAGE

12. James Madison
13. John Quincy Adams
14. Rutherford B. Hayes
15. William McKinley
16. William Howard Taft
17. Martin Van Buren
18. James Monroe
19. Herbert Hoover
20. Benjamin Harrison
21. Chester A. Arthur
22. Dwight D. Eisenhower
23. Andrew Johnson

BELOW THE AVERAGE

24. Zachary Taylor
25. John Tyler
26. Millard Fillmore
27. Calvin Coolidge
28. Franklin Pierce
29. James Buchanan

FAILURES

30. Ulysses S. Grant
31. Warren G. Harding

The reasons for the accolade of greatness will be examined later, but since the inclusion of Roosevelt may surprise persons still smarting from memories of New Deal times, it should be noted now that his place reaffirms the view of fifty-five historians, most of them overlapping on the present panel, whose findings were published in 1948. The longer perspective adds weight to the previous judgment.

After the top group stand the half-dozen figures who, while eclipsing the majority of White House residents, yet fail of the foremost rating. Jackson marked the coming of the common man to national power, and, in particular, Old Hickory distinguished himself by defeating South Carolina's attempt at nullification and by destroying the monopolistic second United States Bank. The 1948 poll, indeed, placed him among the great Presidents, but the present one, by a narrow margin, lowers him one degree. Theodore Roosevelt, responding to similar impulses, taught the electorate the danger to the public weal of consolidated business, and against entrenched opposition he instituted a program of federal regulation as well as of the conservation of natural resources.

Polk, for his part, extended the national borders until they embraced what is now the great Southwest and all the country lying between the Rocky Mountains and the Pacific Ocean. Added to Jefferson's acquisition of France's Louisiana territory, these accessions from Mexico and England gave the United States its continental breadth. Though Polk's conduct toward Mexico violated international ethics, it is noteworthy that his critics, neither then nor later, have ever proposed that the conquests be returned.

Truman, the only one in the near-great class still with us, discharged impressively the awesome obligations devolving on the United States as the leader of the free world upon the advent of the cold war with Soviet imperialism. The Truman Doctrine for the protection of Greece and Turkey, the Marshall Plan for the restoration of Western Europe, the Berlin airlift, the Point Four program for backward countries, NATO (our first peacetime military alliance) and the intervention in Korea in support of the United Nations — all these constituted landmarks in an assumption of global responsibilities undreamed of only a few years before.

Of the last two in the near-great group, the case for John Adams rests primarily on his successful resistance to his own party's demand for changing a limited conflict with France into an all-out war, while the inclusion of Cleveland recognizes his stubborn championship of tariff reform and of honesty and efficiency in the civil service.

II

Then follow the Presidents — more than a third of the whole number — who fall in the average or mediocre class. By and large these twelve, ranging from Madison to Johnson, believed in negative government, in self-subordination to the legislative power. They were content to let well enough alone or, when not, were unwilling to fight for their programs or inept at doing so. Johnson was the principal exception to a passive role, but his prolonged contest with Congress over Southern reconstruction brought him the ignominy of impeachment and a narrow escape from dismissal from office. Eisenhower, the most recent and, consequently, the hardest of the Presidents to evaluate, received a few votes in the near-great category but many more for beneath the average and failure. A two-thirds majority, however, placed him toward the bottom of the average incumbents.

Of the executives of still less stature, six of the eight qualify as below the average. Of these, Pierce and Buchanan by ill chance headed the government in the years of mounting crisis which precipitated the Civil War. Had more statesmanlike hands directed affairs, that tragic failure of the democratic process might have been avoided. A sizable number of the historians, indeed, rated the two as failures.

The verdict of total unfitness, however, was, by the overwhelming majority, reserved alone for Grant and Harding. Both were postwar Presidents who, by their moral obtuseness, promoted a low tone in official life, conducting administrations scarred with shame and corruption. Under Grant the wrongdoing reached as high as his private secretary, the Postmaster General and the Secretaries of War and the Treasury. In Harding's case, three members of the Cabinet were, for like reasons, forced out, one of them going to prison along with several other important executive officials. Harding, who could not plead Grant's political in-

experience, worked intimately with the notorious Ohio Gang,
which had accompanied him to Washington. His belated qualms
at betraying the public interest probably helped bring on his
death after two and a half years in the White House.

A comparison of the findings of the seventy-five historians in
1962 with those of the fifty-five in 1948 shows no significant
change except for the reduction of Jackson one notch to the rank
of near-great. Otherwise the choices in the five major classes
hold good, though the earlier survey, of course, necessarily
omitted Truman and Eisenhower. Within each of the intermediate categories — near-great, average and short of average — oc-
curs, however, some rearrangement of the order, notably the
lowering somewhat of the positions of Cleveland, Monroe and
Coolidge and the upgrading of Polk, Madison and McKinley.

III

Since ten of the thirty-five Vice-Presidents became President,
the poll sheds incidental light upon the capabilities of the heirs
apparent. Three of the number — John Adams, Jefferson and
Van Buren — fall into a special category because they were
elected to the higher position after serving full terms in the lower.
They qualify in the returns respectively as near-great, great and
average.

The seven who reached the presidency by deathbed succession
would seem more typical of the Throttlebottom tradition. All
had been put forward by their parties for reasons of sheer ex-
pediency — to placate disgruntled factions or to balance the
ticket geographically. No one of them, not even Theodore
Roosevelt, was in advance seriously considered for the major
nomination. Yet as Presidents they, too, court comparison with
the elected incumbents. Two (Roosevelt and Truman) qualify
as near-great, two (Johnson and Arthur) come out as average,
and the other three (Tyler, Fillmore and Coolidge) as poor without being failures. Of Roosevelt, Coolidge and Truman the
country thought well enough to extend their accidental terms by
election. To look at the matter from a different point of view, it
is probably not unfair to say that five of the group surpassed in
ability those whom they replaced, John Tyler being an im-

provement on William Henry Harrison, Fillmore on Taylor, Arthur on Garfield, Roosevelt on McKinley, and Coolidge on Harding.

Nevertheless, students of government rightly deplore the short-range considerations that determine the choice of the second man on the ticket. The results, to be sure, are reasonably good in the cases tested, but there is no way of knowing how representative the sampling is, and there remains the alarming fact that seven — more than a quarter — of the twenty-six individuals elected to the chief magistracy before the present administration have died in office. With democracy constantly being subjected to new trials and its basic concepts flouted in many parts of the world, both wisdom and safety require that no candidate should henceforth be named for the nation's second position unless he be also worthy of the first.

IV

What qualities and achievements elevated five Presidents over all their fellows? Was there a pattern of greatness which distinguished these men who otherwise varied so widely in education, personality and political style and who, moreover, faced problems special to their eras? The answer lies in the nature, direction and permanent effect of their accomplishments. A quick review will reveal the common elements.

Each held the stage at a critical moment in American history and by timely action attained timeless results. Washington converted the paper Constitution into a practical and enduring instrument of government. Jefferson expanded the original area of the United States to include the huge region stretching westward from the Mississippi to the Rockies. Lincoln saved the Union from internal destruction. Wilson tightened the restraints on big business and finance and carried the nation successfully through World War I. Franklin Roosevelt preserved the country in the face of its worst depression and marshaled its resources for victory in World War II. Lincoln excepted, all effected profound domestic changes peaceably within the democratic framework — revolutions by popular consent.

By the same token, each took the side of liberalism and the

general welfare against the status quo. Washington, to be sure, today seems a staid conservative to persons forgetful of his historical context. In truth, however, this director of a people's war of emancipation from colonialism devoted all his prestige and ability as their civilian head to justifying the daring new "republican model of government," the fate of which, he told his countrymen, was "*deeply*," yes, "*finally*, staked on the experiment intrusted to the hands of the American people."

Jefferson, standing on Washington's shoulders, widened the concept of popular rule by word and example, and in acquiring the vast trans-Mississippi domain he sought, among other things, to check the growing power of the Eastern business interests with an expanding agrarian West. Lincoln, given no choice in the matter, settled on the battlefield the question of "whether, in a free government, the minority have the right to break up the government whenever they choose," and while doing so he advanced the cause of human rights by outlawing the anachronism of slavery.

And in our own century the New Freedom of Wilson and the New Deal of Roosevelt have, in turn, enlarged momentously the government's responsibility for the social and economic well-being of the people.

v

These towering figures, moreover, acted masterfully and far-sightedly in foreign affairs. All cared profoundly about keeping the country out of war, though over the years circumstances beyond American control necessitated differences as to the means.

When the republic was young and craved time to build up its strength, Washington instituted, and Jefferson perfected, the policy of isolationism or neutralism toward the chronic power struggles embroiling Europe; and Lincoln, in the dark days of the Civil War, reversing the formula, averted, through consummate diplomacy, the calamity of British intervention on behalf of the South.

But with America's coming fully of age the situation changed. As Washington had foretold in his Farewell Address, the United States now could take "command of its own fortunes"; and the shrinkage of global distances plus the modern weaponry of destruction obliged a departure from the past. The goal of peace remained unaltered, but the method devised by Wilson and Roosevelt to achieve it was through an international structure for collective security. Under this sign Wilson pioneered the League of Nations; and Roosevelt, succeeding where Wilson had not in winning Senatorial approval, helped reshape that body into the more potent United Nations.

VI

The members of this group were not only constructive statesmen but realistic politicians. Washington apart, none of them waited for the office to seek the man; they pursued it with all their might and main. And upon winning it, they functioned as chiefs of their parties as well as chiefs of state. Washington, it is true, as the first to occupy the position, endeavored to shun political ties; he even appointed the contending party leaders, Jefferson and Hamilton, to his cabinet; but, taught by experience, he presently abandoned his nonpartisanship as "a sort of political Suicide." His successors unhesitatingly followed this course from the outset.

The arts of the politician were, of course, indispensable to gain the needed Congressional support for their policies. With unconvinced members they knew when to reason and to browbeat, to bargain and stand firm, to concede what was relatively unimportant in order to obtain what was essential. If occasion demanded, they used such means as bestowing or withholding federal patronage, employing or threatening to employ the veto and, when all else failed, they appealed over the heads of the lawmakers to the people.

Every one of these men left the executive branch stronger and more influential than he found it. As a matter of course they magnified the powers expressly granted them by the Constitution and assumed others not expressly denied by it. They acted on the conviction that when the framers of the document provided for a chief magistrate chosen periodically by and responsible to all the people they had intended that he should always be equal to the widening needs of society.

Inevitably, these Presidents encountered trouble with the Supreme Court, for its members, enjoying lifetime tenure and, moreover, restrained by the tribunal's past decisions, tended to speak for times gone by. Only Washington, the one President to name the entire body, escaped the dilemma.

Jefferson, alarmed lest the judiciary he had inherited from the political opposition would strike down "all the works of republicanism," got Congress to abolish a series of lower judgeships which the outgoing administration had prepared for its adherents, and he induced the House to impeach a grossly partisan member of the Supreme Court. Had the attempt at ouster succeeded, Chief Justice Marshall almost certainly would have been the next quarry.

Over and over again Lincoln, under plea of military necessity, ignored or defied judicial decrees. On one occasion he even disregarded a writ of habeas corpus of Chief Justice Taney himself. Wilson, though managing to avoid open strife, nonetheless viewed the Court's conservative bent as the nation's "most obvious and immediate danger."

And Franklin Roosevelt, when thwarted by the high bench in expanding his New Deal program, sought to correct its "horse-and-buggy" mentality by the addition of younger and more progressive Justices. Although Congress did not consent, the tribunal, in alarm, hastily changed its attitude.

In all these affairs, moreover, the verdict of time has upheld the Presidents' underlying purposes, if not always their methods.

Being strong executives, the five also offended vested economic interests and long-standing popular prejudices. Furthermore, their sins of commission and omission, though small in the backward view of history, looked enormous to critical contemporaries. Each, in turn, met with charges of subverting the Constitution, of lusting to be king or dictator, and of knuckling under on occasion to some foreign power.

The "arrows of malevolence" so wounded Washington that he exclaimed to a friend that he "had never repented but once having slipped the moment of resigning his office, and that was every moment since." Jefferson was pelted with such epithets as

"Mad Tom," "contemptible hypocrite," "a man without religion" and "a ravening wolf."

Lincoln suffered abuse, even from Northerners, as "the baboon in the White House," "a usurper" and "a perjured traitor." He said it was in his heart to pity Satan if "to be head of Hell is as hard as what I have to undergo." Wilson and Roosevelt, as many today will still remember, came off no better, both being reviled for wanton personal ambition and seeking to rule or ruin. In the case of each of the greats, the newspaper press added fuel to the flames when, indeed, it did not start them.

Yet, notwithstanding all the sound and fury, these Presidents were more deeply loved than they were hated. The rank and file of Americans re-elected every one of them to a second term and Roosevelt to a third and fourth.

VIII

Another factor marking the group was that, but for the self-made Lincoln, they came from an upper level of society (and, indeed, even Lincoln, before reaching the White House, had surmounted his humble beginnings to become a leader of the Illinois bar). This willingness of the voter to accept patrician leadership sheds an interesting light on the flexibility of United States democracy. Washington, Jefferson and Roosevelt, alike in being well-to-do landed proprietors, believed, as a matter of course, in the importance of preserving or recovering for the mass of people the kind of values and human advantages traditional to a rural way of life; and Wilson, growing up in a highly cultured but not affluent atmosphere, arrived at pretty much the same outlook on the basis of extensive reading.

But, superior though these personages were, only two, Washington and Wilson, excelled as administrators. The rest either lacked the ability or else believed the ends of public policy more important than the machinery for achieving them. On balance, moreover, their inattention served to unfreeze official routine and inject vitality and a readiness to innovate into the government ranks. Franklin Roosevelt in fact went so far as to declare, "The presidency is not merely an administrative office. That is the least of it." If he overstated the matter, all the others would have heartily endorsed his further view: "It is pre-eminently a place of moral leadership."

Moral leadership meant a commitment to maintain and transmit to future generations the liberal and humane ideals of the past. It involved the capacity to fit the national purpose to the constantly changing requirements of a dynamic people. In brief, the foremost Presidents possessed a profound sense of history, a rooted dedication to time-sanctioned principles which each, in his own day and way, succeeded in reinvigorating and extending. Essential as it was to win approval at the polls, they looked as well to the approval of posterity.

IX

James Bryce, assessing the United States chief magistrates down to 1900 in his book, *The American Commonwealth,* entitled a famous chapter "Why Great Men Are Not Chosen Presidents"; but he erred even for those years. Taking the entire span from Washington to the exit of Eisenhower, the historical consultants find that great men occupied the chair during forty of the 172 years and, if their near-great associates be added, the grand total approaches eighty years, or nearly half the lifetime of the Republic. Can any other nation display a better record?

Moreover, even the do-nothing stretches in the White House did not lack value, since, as a rule, they provided breathing spells for the country to digest the achievements of the forceful executives.

All in all, the historical picture fully justifies the present-day defenders of democracy against totalitarianism in relying on Jefferson's — and America's — trust in the people as "the safest depository of power."

7

Persisting problems of the presidency

OF ALL the contrivances of the framers of the Constitution none was more ingenious or more authentically American than the office of chief magistrate. The problem facing the infant Republic was to find a suitable alternative to a hereditary ruler, a democratic substitute for what Theodore Sedgwick called the "barbarous" system "by which executive power is to be transmitted through the organs of generation." The answer, in effect, was a succession of short-term kings.

To this "elective monarchy," as Chancellor Kent characterized it, was granted less authority than kings had known in the past, but far more, it turned out, than they were to know in the future. James Bryce, seeking a hundred years later in *The American Commonwealth* to explain the novel creation to puzzled Europeans, pointed out that the American President resembles neither the crowned head nor the Prime Minister in England, standing somewhere between. Nor is he like his namesake in France or Switzerland. In Latin America, Bryce could have added, the presidency is still different, notwithstanding that these countries avowedly modeled the office upon that of the United States.

The American arrangement, as judged in its workings by the seventy-five historians, has elevated from the mass of people a noteworthy series of rulers; yet, from the very beginning, there have been structural weaknesses in the institution, as well as others due to its exacting character and to the functioning of the party system. This essay treats these persisting problems.

I

Few voters stop to think that they cast their ballots not for a President but for electors to choose a President. According to the letter of the Constitution, their suffrages amount to a mere expression of preference, a public-opinion poll. Indeed, if the original intent had been respected, they would not necessarily have performed even this humble function. This fact is all the more significant because probably no question before the Convention absorbed so much time and thought as the method of selecting the chief executive, and Alexander Hamilton tells us in *The Federalist* that no feature of the great charter proved more acceptable to the public at large. At first the members had determined to allow Congress to pick the President; next they shifted to election by electors chosen by the state legislatures; then, after returning for a while to the scheme of letting Congress do it, they finally decided upon election by electors designated as each legislature might desire. Every state should name as many as it had United States Senators and Representatives.

While showing indecision as to the mechanics of the process, they never swerved as to the underlying aim, agreeing with George Mason of Virginia that "it were as unnatural to refer the choice of a proper character for chief magistrate to the people, as it would be to refer a trial of colours to a blind man." The electors should assemble every four years in the several states and out of their superior wisdom fix upon the republican king (and, of course, upon the crown prince or Vice-President). Since even Olympians might not always be of one mind, it was provided that, if nobody received a majority, the selection should fall to the House of Representatives, with each state delegation casting a single vote. As will be seen, the decision in two presidential contests — in 1800 and 1824 — did devolve upon the House, but not because the electors accidentally failed to agree. Events unforeseen at the time of the making of the Constitution had meanwhile robbed these worthies of their liberty of action.

What demoted the electoral college from a deliberative body to a puppet show was the rise of political parties. As people began taking sides on public questions, they were unwilling to leave the crucial choice of the chief of state to a sort of lottery. Instead, each party publicly announced its slate of electors and the candidate they would support. This usurpation of the electors' functions, though peaceably achieved, amounted to a *coup d'état*. It was an amendment of the written Constitution by the unwritten Constitution. The electors, while retaining their legal status of independence, became henceforth hardly more than men in livery taking orders from their parties.

A parallel change took place as the legislatures abdicated their function of electing the electors by transferring it to the voters. By 1824 three quarters had so acted, South Carolina alone refraining till after the Civil War. Andrew Jackson, among others, urged the next logical step — that the electoral college be abolished in favor of direct popular election. He himself had lost the White House in 1824, though polling more electoral and popular votes than John Quincy Adams, his nearest rival. With four entries in the race, however, neither of the top men mustered a majority in the electoral college, and the House of Representatives, acting under the constitutional proviso, seated Adams. Since six of the twenty-four states cast no popular votes, it is possible, if unlikely, that Jackson was not the country's preference. Old Hickory himself had no doubt about it, and after his triumphant campaign in 1828, personal pique reinforced his democratic urge to scrap the entire system. Insisting that "as few impediments as possible should exist to the free operation of the public will," he maintained that "a provision which does not secure to the people a direct choice . . . has a tendency to defeat their will." He pressed the issue in each of his eight annual messages to Congress but without result.

Nevertheless, the years since then have furnished indubitable evidence that the electors may thwart the "free operation of the public will." The Hayes-Tilden campaign affords one instance, though not the best, for the circumstances were unusual and not likely to happen again. In 1876 the country was still reaping the whirlwind of the Civil War. The voters in Florida and Louisiana, two of the three Southern states in which Northern-imposed Carpetbag governments survived, gave majorities to Tilden, the Democratic nominee, but the Carpetbag officials manipulated the results in such a way as to manufacture popular majorities for Hayes. Congress, faced with conflicting electoral returns from these states (and also with others from South Carolina and a single disputed vote from Oregon), set up a special commission to decide which were valid. Tilden needed but one of the twenty contested votes to win in the electoral college, while Hayes needed all. By strict party divisions the commission, composed of eight Republicans and seven Democrats, awarded the whole number, and therewith the presidency, to Hayes. It is known that one of the Republican members, Justice Joseph Bradley, intended to side with the Democrats in allotting Florida's four votes to Tilden, but was talked out of it by his wife and two Republican friends. It is also known that the outgoing Republican chief executive, Grant, considered Tilden the rightful victor. As it was, Hayes slipped into the presidency with one more electoral vote and 250,000 fewer popular votes than his Democratic competitor.

A better example is the 1888 election, for this took place under normal conditions and the outcome might at any time be duplicated. Benjamin Harrison secured an electoral majority of sixty-five — 233 to 168 — while Grover Cleveland, his Democratic opponent, carried the country by 5,540,329 to 5,439,853. The loser's margin of 100,000 popular votes was offset by his rival's success in garnering small pluralities in the pivotal large states — those counting most in the electoral college. A switch of 7000 out of the 1,284,500 votes cast for the two parties in New York State would have swung the electoral college to Cleveland, whereas his surplus of 146,000 in Texas proved sheer waste.

Harrison's victory was a self-evident case of what Jackson foretold — and nothing in Harrison's conduct in office tempered the result. (Cleveland had little trouble in overtopping him in both electoral and popular ballots four years later.) The fault, however, lay not so much with the Constitution as with the practice, which legislatures early adopted, of assigning a state's full electoral vote to the winning candidate. This scheme of the unit rule — of all or nothing — virtually disfranchises the members of the defeated party, however numerous they may be. To cure the difficulty it would, of course, be possible to go back to the once usual method of choosing electors by Congressional districts; another and better way, put forward by Senator Henry

Cabot Lodge, Jr., in 1948 in a proposed federal amendment, would be to divide each state's electoral vote according to the relative popular strength of the nominees. Why has nothing ever been done? The answer lies in the psychology of the party system. The minority hopes another time to be a majority and thus wield the same unfair advantage.

If the uncertain case of John Quincy Adams in 1824 be omitted, Hayes and Harrison have been the only nominees to succeed with a smaller popular support than their chief antagonists, but in many more instances men have triumphed with a minority of the ballots cast for all the aspirants. This held true of Polk, Taylor, Buchanan, Lincoln in 1860, Garfield, Cleveland in 1884 and 1892, Wilson in his two races, Truman and Kennedy in 1960. So, aside from Hayes and Harrison, ten of the twenty-nine elected to the office were demonstrably minority choices. It is far from clear, though, that this outcome violates Jackson's doctrine of the "free operation of the public will." If only two parties instead of three or more had competed in these campaigns, the plurality candidate might in every instance have been the majority choice. In any event he represented the most strongly expressed wish of the country. The alternative of a run-off election or some system of preferential voting has never been seriously discussed, probably because in practice the consequences of the present system have not been bad. On the contrary, five so selected — Polk, Lincoln, Cleveland, Wilson and Truman — rank in the category of great or near-great incumbents, with President Kennedy's record still in the making.

Recent doubts about the electoral college hinge largely upon other considerations. Though the unwritten Constitution has reduced the electors to rubber stamps, the written Constitution nevertheless still leaves them as free as the air. In early elections individuals occasionally resisted party dictation. In 1796, the first contested election, a Federalist elector in Pennsylvania voted for Thomas Jefferson instead of John Adams, his party's choice. In 1820 a New Hampshire elector threw his support to John Quincy Adams, who was not a candidate, thus depriving Monroe of a unanimous vote. (The motive was not, as legend asserts, to prevent the colorless Monroe from equaling Washington's record, but, rather, to protest against the increased expen-

ditures of Monroe's first term and to play up Adams's qualifications with an eye to the future.) Four years later three New
York electors who had been counted on to support Henry Clay
deserted to the enemy.

But thereafter signs of revolt died away. The crucial test
came in the Hayes-Tilden battle of 1876. Had one of the duly
chosen Republican electors been willing to declare for Tilden,
he would have assured him of the single vote needed for victory
and the action would have quieted the country's fears of civil
war because of the unprecedented situation. This course was,
in fact, urged upon James Russell Lowell, a Hayes elector in
Massachusetts, but such an act of independence was to him un-
thinkable. "My individual sympathies and preferences are beside the matter," he replied; "to refuse to comply with the mandate I received when I accepted my party's nomination would be
treacherous, dishonorable, and immoral."

So accurately did Lowell define the elector's role that sixty-
eight years later, in 1944, the public was shocked to learn that
some antiadministration Democrats running as electors in three
Southern states had announced they would not vote for President Franklin Roosevelt if he should be renominated. The national convention of the party ignored this attempt at political
blackmail, and in Louisiana and Mississippi the mutiny quickly
subsided. But in Texas the Democratic state convention found
it necessary to replace fifteen electors in order to assure the full
twenty-three votes to Roosevelt. Before the next quadrennial
election, Southern bitterness, now aflame against President Truman, caused the Virginia legislature to empower a state party
convention to direct the state's electors to vote otherwise than
for the national ticket; and a Democratic elector in Tennessee
also broke ranks. Similar insurgency has occasionally been displayed in Southern states in elections since.

This situation reveals in a new guise the latent danger of the
electoral system to the "free operation of the public will." A
method originally conceived to meet eighteenth-century ideas
of democracy has in the course of years become a kind of vermi-
form appendix, ordinarily harmless to the body politic but capable of poisoning its very blood stream. Only a few states bind
their electors by law to support the national party ticket. The

sensible remedy lies in a federal amendment either to make such a requirement universal, or else to abolish the electoral college entirely while retaining the electoral votes. In 1934 Senator George W. Norris proposed changing the Constitution for the latter purpose, and, more recently, Senator Lodge as part of his plan to divide the electoral votes in proportion to the popular vote in each state also included a provision to dispense with the archaic electoral machinery. His proposal was approved by the judiciary committees of both houses of Congress, but did not reach the floor.

A more drastic alternative would be direct election by the people across state lines without converting the popular results into electoral votes. But, however desirable from the standpoint of democratic principle, such an arrangement could not get far politically, since the smaller commonwealths would object to surrendering the advantage they now enjoy in the distribution of electoral votes. It is worth noting that not even Jackson's proposals for direct popular election involved a change in the relative weight of the states. Reform, should it come, will occur along less radical lines, and reform is essential, as the recent developments in the South render evident.

II

Difficulties and uncertainties lurk also in the mode provided by the Constitution for the presidential succession. The organic law as originally framed was silent as to what would happen if a prospective chief executive should die before being inaugurated. Since six Presidents have died early in their terms, Senator George F. Hoar correctly pointed out in his *Autobiography* (1903) that the contingency is "not an imaginary danger." The matter has most recently been brought to public attention by the attempted shooting of President-elect Franklin Roosevelt by a mentally deranged person at Miami, Florida, on February 15, 1933. Nine days before, however, the fault had been remedied. The newly adopted Twentieth Amendment specified that, if the President-to-be could not qualify, the Vice-President-to-be should take over the reins, and that Congress should designate the order of succession by legislation in case neither should be available. This step, however, Congress has not had to take.

The circumstances actually contemplated by the Constitution for filling a presidential vacancy are death in office (which has happened eight times), removal by impeachment (which Andrew Johnson narrowly escaped), resignation (which has never occurred, though a Vice-President, John C. Calhoun, resigned), and "inability to discharge the powers and duties of the said office." In every instance the Vice-President is to move up, and in all cases but the last the conditions of the succession are self-evident. As John Dickinson asked in the Federal Convention, "What is the extent of the term 'disability,' and who is to be the judge of it?"

This disturbing question has never been answered, even though in three administrations it has assumed an urgency. On July 2, 1881, President Garfield was shot by an assassin and lingered at death's door till the end came on September 19. During this interval of two and a half months he performed no official act except to sign an extradition paper. Luckily, the consequences for the nation did not prove serious since public affairs were relatively quiet, Congress was not in session, and Secretary of State Blaine looked after routine matters by conducting cabinet meetings, apparently with his chief's approval. Nevertheless the situation was fraught with needless hazard. As Chester A. Arthur told Congress upon succeeding Garfield, "Questions which concern the very existence of the Government and the liberties of the people were suggested by the prolonged illness of the late President and his consequent incapacity to perform the functions of the office."

The other two cases exhibit the perils still more gravely. President Wilson, stricken by cerebral thrombosis on September 26, 1919, lay helpless for almost three months during which his wife acted as his sole link with government affairs, deciding what he should know and how much and when. In everything but name Mrs. Wilson was America's first woman President. Meanwhile the country was passing through a crisis requiring the highest order of executive statesmanship. Strikes abounded, the battle in the Senate over the League of Nations was nearing a climax, and United States delegates in Paris were negotiating the minor peace settlements. As the President slowly improved, he gave increasing attention to public business, but it was not till April 13, 1920, six and a half months after his stroke, that he felt able to hold a cabinet meeting. Some light is thrown on the extent of Wilson's disability by the fact that twenty-eight bills became law without his signature because of failure to act within the specified ten-day period. He never completely recovered, and there can be little doubt that his frayed nerves and loss of mental resiliency had a profound bearing upon his failure to win the League fight.

President Eisenhower, the oldest man but one ever to assume the office, suffered three critical illnesses. The first, a coronary thrombosis on September 24, 1955, hospitalized him for two and a half months; the second, an ileitis attack on June 8, 1956, entailed a surgical operation which confined him to his bed for more than a week; and the third, a cerebral occlusion on November 24 of that year, impaired his speech for a time. As in Wilson's day, weighty problems plagued the nation, this time centering on menacing activities of the Soviet Union; but Eisenhower, unlike Wilson, managed to keep in touch with the operations of government, and he permitted Vice-President Nixon to hold meetings of the cabinet. (When Wilson learned that Secretary of State Lansing had occasionally called the cabinet together during his sickness, he curtly dismissed him for this "assumption of Presidential authority in such a matter.") After the third attack Eisenhower did what no predecessor had ever done: he put into writing what the role of his Vice-President should be in case of his chief's total disability. The Vice-President, at his request, should for the time serve as "Acting President"; if he was unable to make the request, the Vice-President should himself assume the functions "after such consultation as seems to him appropriate"; and in either contingency he (the President) should decide when to take back the office. President Kennedy, even before his inauguration, and President Johnson upon taking over from him adopted a like plan.

At best, however, these constitute strictly personal arrangements, not binding on future incumbents; and, even so, they ignore certain basic difficulties. Should a Vice-President be allowed to elevate himself after consultation with unspecified in-

dividuals? Should a President suffering from a mental afflic-
tion be permitted to determine when he has sufficiently recovered to resume the office? Obviously a more carefully considered
procedure is needed, and this requires action by Congress or possibly a constitutional amendment.

III

By contrast, Congress under express constitutional authority
proceeded early to specify the order of succession below the
vice-presidency. This matter might seem highly academic since
no occasion has ever arisen for such a provision. Yet it should
be remembered that not only have eight Presidents died in
office, but also seven Vice-Presidents, and that an eighth Vice-
President removed himself by resignation. It is sheer chance
that a vacancy in the one office has never coincided with a vacancy in the other. This, however, almost happened three times:
in 1844, when John Tyler, President Harrison's replacement, narrowly escaped death aboard a warship from the explosion of a
cannon; in 1865, when the plot to assassinate Lincoln involved
also the killing of Vice-President Johnson; and in 1868, when the
impeachment charges against President Johnson failed by a single vote.

The law of 1792 provided that, in case of simultaneous vacan-
cies, the President pro tem of the Senate (with the Speaker of the
House as alternate if the former were unavailable) should serve
as a stopgap until a new chief executive could be elected. The
party system was then still in the gristle, and it was not thought
incongruous that by this scheme the supreme office might temporarily fall to the political opposition. Subsequent years produced increasing discontent with the arrangement, and finally,
in 1886, a new law swung to the other extreme, by-passing Congress altogether and conferring the succession upon the Secretary of State (with the other cabinet officers following in the order of the creation of their posts), who presumably — the language is not explicit — should continue for the unexpired term.
This plan, of course, safeguarded the proprietary rights of the
party in power to the White House. Another reason for the
change was a doubt as to whether the head of either the Senate

or the House is an "officer" within the meaning of the Constitution and hence entitled to succeed.

Franklin Roosevelt's demise within three months after entering his fourth term prompted his successor, Harry S. Truman, to reopen the matter once more. Facing nearly four years without a second in command, and believing in any event that it was more democratic for the succession to fall to an elected official than to a presidential appointee, he recommended that the Speaker of the House (with the President pro tem of the Senate as alternate, followed by members of the cabinet) assume office for the time being until a new President and Vice-President should be chosen for the unexpired term in an emergency election. By way of explaining his preference for the House's presiding officer, he noted that "the members of the Senate are not as closely tied in by the elective process to the people," and also that the lower chamber is more likely to have the same political complexion as the administration.

In 1947 Congress adopted the proposal without the feature of a special election, thus providing that the newcomer should finish out the term for which his predecessor had been elected. Since both houses at the time were in Republican hands, the immediate effect was to put two of President Truman's principal political foes at the top of the list. This circumstance revealed that the law in sustaining one democratic principle might violate another. As the *Philadelphia Bulletin* remarked, "It would not be following the will of the voters if an accident to the President were to turn the White House over to the opposing party without consulting the electorate." Dissatisfaction with the law also arose because Speakers of the House in the past had seldom been considered of presidential caliber. Only one (James K. Polk) had ever been chosen to the office.

By and large, however, the counterproposals offered in Congress possessed no greater merit. One would have created two Vice-Presidents, which would merely double the existing difficulty of securing a man of presidential stature as the single Vice-President. Another would have authorized the Vice-President in the event of succession to appoint his own Vice-President, which does not differ greatly from the system which the act of 1947 supplanted. A third would have reassembled the electoral college to designate a new President and Vice-President, thus restoring to the electors some of the independence of action which custom had taken from them. Unlike these proposals, Truman's own original recommendation of an interim President, serving only "until the next Congressional election or until a special election called for the purpose of electing a new President and Vice-President," would not have entailed a constitutional amendment. This arrangement would, of course, have revived the underlying concept of the act of 1792. For reasons hard to understand it commanded little support in Congress. Had the suggestion prevailed, it would have avoided the obvious flaws of the law as passed and would have grounded the presidential succession solidly in the elective process.

Another defect of the act has received even less attention. The legislation was framed in bland disregard of the wartime hazards of an age of lightning mass destruction. A nuclear assault on the federal capital might wipe out overnight the President and all the officials earmarked to succeed him, thus paralyzing the government in the hour of its direst need. This contingency indicates a line of succession extending beyond the District of Columbia into the states, perhaps including the governors in some predetermined order. It renders all the more imperative some kind of provision for a caretaker executive until a new President be chosen in a special nation-wide election. Though a constitutional amendment would be required, considerations of national security plainly demand such action.

IV

Under the original Constitution the electors did not vote separately for President and Vice-President. The idea of the framers was that the person in whom the electors reposed the greatest trust would become head of the government and the one next in their confidence would serve as his understudy ready to succeed at a moment's notice. Both choices were expected to be of individuals eminently qualified for the more exalted office. In fact, however, the electors right from the beginning discriminated in their minds between the men they wanted for the two posts, with Washington everyone's favorite for the higher one in the first two elections. With Washington out of the running, the situation became further complicated by the rise of political parties. In 1796, the third election, John Adams, the chief of one party, was chosen President, and Thomas Jefferson, the chief of the other, Vice-President. The possibility of teamwork within the administration at once vanished. In 1800 an additional difficulty arose when Jefferson and Aaron Burr, candidates on the same ticket, received a majority of the electoral votes and an even number. Burr had been intended for the minor station, but the tie threw the decision into the House of Representatives, and there the Federalist opposition out of pique tried for thirty-five ballots to put the New Yorker in ahead. In the end Jefferson won out through the intervention of Alexander Hamilton who, though distrusting his long-time antagonist, nonetheless considered him the lesser of the evils.

As a result of these experiences the Twelfth Amendment, ratified in 1804, required the electors to state separately their choices for President and Vice-President. Senator Roger Griswold of Connecticut, opposing the change, predicted that the lesser post would "be carried to market to purchase the votes of particular States" or, in Senator Gouverneur Morris's words, be used "but as a bait to catch State gudgeons." What these critics overlooked was that the debasing process had begun even before the amendment was adopted. Starting with the first party contest in 1796, each of the rival aggregations had paired its candidates for President with less able men designed to appeal to voters in other sections. The Federalists preferred a Massachusetts-South Carolina combination; the Jeffersonian Republicans, an alliance between Virginia and New York. The Twelfth Amendment merely reduced the hazards of this strategy. Henceforth there was no possibility of the two supreme executive offices falling to opposing parties or of a Burr defeating a Jefferson.

The degradation of the vice-presidency has remained an unfortunate aspect of the American political system. Under the special circumstances existing before the Twelfth Amendment a Vice-President on two occasions — in 1796 and 1800 — was elected President after serving a full term in the minor capacity, but since then the only instance has been that of Martin Van Buren in 1836. The supposed necessity of geographical balance

on the ticket, combined often with the need to conciliate dissident factions in the party, has typically resulted in giving the
second place to relatively unknown or mediocre men, with no
thought of their qualifications for the higher position. Who but
a professional historian can even recall the names, say, of Daniel
D. Tompkins, Richard M. Johnson, William R. King, Schuyler
Colfax, Garret A. Hobart and James S. Sherman? Yet each of
these men stood for a time within a single heartbeat of the White
House.

The individual citizen, unfortunately, cannot effectively regis-
ter dissatisfaction with this practice. Through the system of
electors he must vote for both candidates of his party or for neither; like Siamese twins they must be taken together or not at
all. When John Quincy Adams learned of William Henry Harrison's death in office, he noted sourly in his diary that chance had
brought to the executive chair "a man never thought of for it by
anybody." Except for Theodore Roosevelt, Adams's remark regarding John Tyler holds just as true of all the others who succeeded in this manner: Fillmore, Johnson, Arthur, Coolidge and
Truman. It is beside the mark that some of the accidental Presidents acquitted themselves better than could rightly have been
expected.

From the adoption of the Twelfth Amendment in 1804 till the
end of the Civil War the decisive geographic combination
tended, as earlier, to consist in yoking candidates from a seaboard free state and a slave state. From 1872 through Coolidge's
election in 1924 the magic formula was to couple two Northern
states, one on the Atlantic with one in the interior. Since then,
however, the pattern has been confused. Hoover's victory four
years later offered for the first time two candidates from west of
the Mississippi. The New Yorker Franklin Roosevelt ran three
of his four times with candidates from Southern states. In Truman's case both the President and his running mate were from
Southern states. The New Yorker Eisenhower in his two races
had a teammate from the Pacific Coast. And the Kennedy ticket
in 1960 paired a citizen of Massachusetts with a Texan.

The result of this preoccupation with the map has been to restrict the two highest places in the government to residents of a
minority of the states. From the adoption of the Twelfth Amend-

ment through Eisenhower's two elections New York has scored twenty winning candidacies for the one office or the other; Ohio, seven; Virginia, Illinois, Indiana and Massachusetts, six each; Tennessee, four; New Jersey, three; and twelve other common-wealths, one or two apiece. (As regards the presidency alone the figures are: New York, seven; Ohio, seven; Virginia, five; Illinois, four; Indiana, one; Massachusetts, three; Tennessee, three; New Jersey, two, with the remaining states totaling five.) By a law of political physics the top places have usually gravitated to closely contested states with numerous votes in the party convention and the electoral college. To put it differently, twenty-eight commonwealths (not including the lately admitted Alaska and Hawaii) have been in an untouchable class. And a still larger number — nearly three quarters of the Union — have been denied the greater of these honors by either election or succession.

In other words, there has existed a great pool of potential talent which, because of politico-geographical considerations, has been left untapped. It is not a healthy condition for the body politic when its highest offices are available only to those who happen to live in favored places.

v

If regional credentials ordinarily determine the selection of candidates, other factors come into play when the victor enters the White House. What sort of training have Presidents had for the job? George Washington apart, the original common denom-inator was a knowledge of foreign affairs. For twenty-eight years following John Adams, who himself had served as minister abroad, the office was filled by men who had formerly been Secretary of State. This was an understandable preference in a period when the struggling young Republic was being buffeted about by great European wars, and diplomatic relations were a crucial consideration. Once the need ceased, however, revolt set in. "This artificial system of cabinet succession to the presi-dency," declared a Pennsylvania convention of Andrew Jackson's supporters in the campaign of 1824, "is little less dangerous and anti-Republican than the hereditary monarchies of Europe."

Unless the chain be broken, they warned, "then may we be fettered by it forever." Although they did not prevent the elevation of Secretary of State John Quincy Adams, he proved the last in an unbroken series to have this background. The only later ones were Van Buren and Buchanan, both before the Civil War, and they were elected for reasons other than their cabinet experience.

Jackson's eventual triumph in 1828 diverted the trend to warrior Presidents. Besides his martial career, however, he had served earlier in both houses of Congress as well as in a Tennessee judgeship, and nearly all the military chieftains who succeeded him had also had experience in elective posts. The sole exceptions, Taylor, Grant and Eisenhower, were professional soldiers; and Grant turned out to be one of the least successful of Presidents, while the other two rated respectively below average and average. Of the thirty individuals elected to the office, fourteen, most of them in the nineteenth century, had formerly held army commissions, nine as generals. Even more than the army, however, Congress has been the mother of Presidents. Of the elected incumbents seventeen had first served in the national legislature for periods of from two to seventeen years. As in Jackson's case, many of these had military records besides. The Senate and the House shared the parental honors about equally. With the emergence of modern America after the Civil War the dominance of Congress as well as of the army yielded gradually to that of the state gubernatorial chair. Woodrow Wilson suggested one reason for this in his *Congressional Government* (1885), written many years before he as New Jersey's governor aspired to the chief magistracy. The function of lawmakers, he stated, "is to pass bills, not to keep them in running order after they have become statutes. They spend their lives without having anything to do directly with administration." On the other hand, "the governorship of a State is very like a smaller Presidency; or, rather, the Presidency is very like a big governorship." There are involved comparable skills of leadership, of dealing with a co-ordinate branch of the government and of molding public opinion. From less disinterested motives party managers began to exhibit a like preference, seeing the advantages of running a popular governor, particularly of a pivotal state, who could be counted on to deliver its electoral votes to the national ticket. Even before the Civil War a few Presidents had incidentally been governors. During the rest of the century two of the incumbents, Hayes and McKinley, enjoyed the triple recommendation of previous military, Congressional and gubernatorial service. Grover Cleveland in 1884 really set the new pattern, having nothing to offer beyond his achievements as chief executive of New York. Since McKinley's time four of the eight Presidents have stepped from the governor's mansion into the White House, either directly or by way of the vice-presidency.

The background of the three latest elected incumbents presents an enigma. Eisenhower's elevation suggests a throwback to the time when the voters equated military success with fitness for civilian leadership. The victories of Truman and Kennedy, on the other hand, suggest that the Senate may be again a springboard to the White House, though only Kennedy won the office while a member of that body.

What other factors apart from innate ability enter into presidential performance it would be difficult to say. Nearly all the executives have been of British stock, with Van Buren and the two Roosevelts, however, revealing the Dutch strain. No woman has ever held the office though the Constitution at no time disqualified women. The successful aspirants except for Kennedy have invariably been Protestants, belonging to nine different denominations, with Episcopalians, Presbyterians and Unitarians heading the list. Two thirds have been college graduates, though among the ten lacking this advantage were such figures as Washington, Jackson, Lincoln and Cleveland. The legal profession has had the widest representation, and no captain of industry has ever been elected. In age the Presidents have ranged from Theodore Roosevelt, who at forty-two years and ten months succeeded McKinley, to William Henry Harrison, who took the oath when sixty-eight years and twenty-two days old. Up to Franklin Roosevelt's accession the average for the elected executives starting their first terms was fifty-four, nearly twenty years beyond the constitutional minimum.

On but two occasions have members of the same family in direct line of descent captured the prize. John Adams, the second President, was followed twenty-four years later during his lifetime by his son; and William Henry Harrison, who died soon after assuming power in 1841, was succeeded forty-eight years later by his grandson. Both families had participated in the founding of the nation, John Adams and Harrison's father having been signers of the Declaration of Independence. John Quincy Adams and Benjamin Harrison, the descendants, had records of public service in their own right before entering the executive mansion. Neither succeeded in obtaining a second term. Nevertheless, the itch to be President or, if that were impossible, the second in command lingered in the Adams family for two generations more. Henry Adams, grandson of John Quincy, relates in his autobiography that, when he visited the White House in 1850 at the age of twelve, he "half thought he owned it, and took for granted that he would some day live in it." Henry's father, Charles Francis, had run on the Free Soil ticket for Vice-President two years before and was to poll the highest vote for the presidency on the first ballot of the Liberal Republican convention in 1872. Although he lost this nomination to Horace Greeley, John Quincy the second, Charles Francis's son and Henry's brother, ran as vice-presidential candidate of the regular Democrats in that campaign.

It is natural for parties to seek to capitalize upon a famous name. Robert T. Lincoln, the only surviving son of the martyred President, joined Garfield's cabinet as Secretary of War and later had scattering support for the presidential nomination in the Republican conventions of 1884, 1888 and 1892. James R. Garfield, a son of President Garfield, served in Theodore Roosevelt's cabinet as Secretary of the Interior. In 1920 Franklin Roosevelt was named by the Democrats for the vice-presidency in the hope of detaching votes from his fifth cousin's party. (As late as 1932 it was alleged that some Rip van Winkles voted for him for President in the belief that "Teddy" was still running.) In 1924 the Democrats, seeking to offset the conservatism of their candidate, John W. Davis, the corporation lawyer, paired him with Charles W. Bryan, brother of their thrice defeated "Great Commoner"; and Hoover as chief executive returned an Adams to public life by appointing Charles Francis the younger, a great-great-grandson of the second President, to the headship of the navy. Nor has the end yet come. One need only recall the efforts of Senator Robert A. Taft, a President's son, to obtain the Republican presidential nomination in 1940 and his endeavors to retrieve his failure in 1948.

VI

One essential of successful performance in the presidency — a factor which has become more and more important — is a physique equal to the burdens and tensions of the office. These have increased partly because of the country's territorial growth, but even more because of the expanding functions of government and America's larger role in the world. As a result a President requires an enormous reserve of physical and nervous energy. He must not only conduct routine and ceremonial affairs, but rise to great emergencies; not only direct his party, but lead the nation as a whole; not only formulate domestic policies but supervise international relations in peace and war. No executive head of any other democracy is subject to so severe and unremitting a strain.

In the Republic's early history ex-Presidents lived to such advanced ages as ninety (John Adams), eighty-five (Madison), eighty-three (Jefferson), eighty (John Quincy Adams), seventy-nine (Van Buren), seventy-eight (Jackson) and seventy-seven (Buchanan). Or, to put it differently, the first Adams survived his incumbency by twenty-five years, Van Buren and Fillmore by twenty-one, Madison and the younger Adams by nineteen and Jefferson and Tyler by seventeen. But even in those days such personages as Washington, Jefferson and Jackson pleaded fatigue as a reason for not running again for office; and two executives — Harrison at sixty-eight and Taylor at sixty-five — died while in the White House.

Though medical science has greatly lengthened the life span of the American population since the Civil War, the showing made by the chief magistrates in this more recent period offers an alarming contrast to that of their predecessors. This has in no sense been due to their being older than their predecessors when inaugurated, for the contrary is true: they averaged five years younger. Most of these later ex-Presidents died between the ages of fifty-six and sixty-seven, and by the same sign most of them outlasted their official tenure by but one and a half to eight years.

Approaching the matter from another angle, statisticians of the Metropolitan Life Insurance Company in 1946 computed that, of the thirty deceased Presidents, only twelve surpassed their expectation of life at inauguration according to the mortality conditions then prevailing. The detailed analysis underlines the rapidly mounting occupational hazards of the office. (The study omitted the first Harrison, who served only a single month, and the three men who were assassinated.) Before the middle of the nineteenth century the incumbents exceeded their life expectancy by an average of three years. Between 1850 and 1900 they fell short of the normal span by nearly three years. In the twentieth century they dropped further back to eight years. The defeated aspirants, on the other hand, lived longer than the victors.

The great responsibilities of the office demand that the incumbent should be in the prime of his powers. Along with the usual qualifications for the presidency the country should therefore insist upon a properly attested medical certificate from each nominee. Such evidence, though not conclusive, would at least place all the relevant facts before the electorate and remove the question of health from the whispering gallery of rumor. Desirable as this would be for a first candidacy, it becomes indispensable for a second. Historical experience has erected a warning signal which political parties and the voters will ignore at their peril.

WAR AND
PEACE

8

America's stake in one world

In 1946 an American city became the capital of the United Nations, an organization founded a year before in another American city. Hardly more than a quarter-century earlier the United States Senate had spurned membership in a similar and weaker body. The decision of 1919–1920, though a narrow one and determined in some degree by maneuverings for party advantage on the eve of a presidential election, had rested more broadly upon three fundamental assumptions supposedly derived from the nation's history. These were that the founders of the Republic had counseled isolationism as an inflexible course for future generations; that thanks to this, the United States had always been master of its own fate; and, finally, that on going to war it had always speedily overwhelmed the enemy.

Now history should be an indispensable ally of statecraft, for its function is to extend the range of contemporary experience by showing how similar problems were handled at other times. In a sense it is true that history is always the same except that it happens to different people. Hence men, if they only will, can learn from the successes of their predecessors as well as profit by their mistakes. In short, the living generation is enabled to base its judgments upon a vertical as well as a horizontal view of tendencies and events. But history is a beacon light which in unskilled or self-interested hands may cast deceptive shadows, creating grotesque images and distorting actuality. It is relevant therefore to re-examine the evidence underlying the three presuppositions.

True, most Americans today are deeply committed to the

United Nations. They are fully aware that the technology of modern warfare in a world of rapidly shrinking distances exposes the United States — and every other country — to swift and probably unpreventable annihilation. They also realize as never before that the world's economic life is a seamless web. Yet, as long as there exists any possibility of a revival of former attitudes, it would be unwise to accept the present state of opinion as necessarily enduring. And history, properly read, shows that the major premises of the isolationists were always an illusion.

I

The founders of the Republic were isolationists only in the sense that they wished to shelter their unique democratic experiment in its infancy from foreign aggression. The very Declaration of Independence said that the now "free and independent States" had "full power" to "contract alliances, establish commerce, and to do all other acts and things which independent States may of right do." The Continental Congress gladly entered into commercial treaties whenever it could, and at the height of the Revolutionary War it even concluded a military alliance with monarchical and Catholic France. Many observers marveled at the spectacle of the United States grasping the Gallic hand wet with the blood of Americans in four colonial border wars. But these early statesmen were realists, seeking always to employ diplomacy as a flexible weapon for the country's advantage.

Independence having been won and the federal government organized under the Constitution, George Washington found himself the President of a nation which in population ranked not far above such minor powers as the Netherlands, Portugal and Sweden, while its whole occupied area, comprising a zone along the Atlantic Coast with outposts of settlement beyond the Appalachians, fell considerably short of the area of present Texas. Accordingly, he sought to steer the little ship of state in such a way as to avoid being sucked into the Old World's conflicts. "Europe," he reflected in his Farewell Address at the close of his second administration, "has a set of primary interests, which to us have none, or a very remote relation. . . . Hence, therefore, it must be unwise in us to implicate ourselves, by artificial ties, in the ordinary vicissitudes of her politics, or the ordinary combinations and collisions of her friendships or enmities." He pointed out, however, that "temporary alliances" might from time to time prove necessary, and he added, looking to the day when the people should be powerful enough to "defy material injury from external annoyance," that then "we may choose peace or war, as our interest, guided by our justice, shall counsel." Emphasizing the latter consideration as justifying America's neutrality in the then current strife between France and England, he declared, "With me a predominant motive has been to endeavour to gain time to our country to settle and mature its yet recent institutions, and to progress to that degree of strength and consistency, which is necessary to give it, humanly speaking, the command of its own fortunes."

Such sentiments obviously did not constitute a declaration of uncompromising isolation, but, rather, a practical judgment based upon existing needs without precluding a different policy in the future. Washington knew that the times would change because he had seen them change, so he left to posterity the question of what to do when the country should attain "the command of its own fortunes." Henry Cabot Lodge, biographer of the first President, put the matter accurately in a public address in 1916: "I do not believe that when Washington warned us against entangling alliances he meant for one moment that we should not join with other civilized nations of the world if a method could be found to diminish war and encourage peace." But this was before the Massachusetts Senator became involved in the bitter rancors of the battle over "Mr. Wilson's League of Nations." Then, the politician overcoming the student of history, he revised his opinion.

Actually, the expression "entangling alliances," which Lodge thus fathered on Washington, was not his at all but Jefferson's. In a mellifluous sentence of 239 words Jefferson listed in his first Inaugural the canons of his political creed, with the caveat: "I will compress them within the narrowest compass they will bear, stating the general principle, but not all its limitations." Included in this very considerable "constellation" was "peace, commerce, and honest friendship with all nations, entangling alliances with none." He did not enlarge upon the historic phrase and, no more than Washington, did he regard the concept as absolute.

On the contrary, when he learned in 1802 that Napoleon was scheming to acquire from Spain the mouth of the Mississippi, so essential to inland America's welfare and security, he wrote to the United States minister in Paris, "The day that France takes possession of New Orleans . . . seals the union of two nations, who, in conjunction, can maintain exclusive possession of the ocean. From that moment, we must marry ourselves to the British fleet and nation." Again in 1823, when in retirement, he favored making the Monroe Doctrine a joint Anglo-American pronouncement instead of a separate policy of the United States. "Great Britain is the nation which can do us the most harm of any one, or all on earth," he told President Monroe; "and with her on our side we need not fear the whole world. . . . Not that I would purchase even her amity at the price of taking part in her wars. But the war in which the present proposition might engage us, should that be the consequence, is not her war, but ours."

On such frail underpinnings rested the appeal to tradition which became the mainstay of the powerful isolationist school in after years. By a mythmaking process familiar in American history Jefferson's utterance against entangling alliances was put into the mouth of Washington, and a formula thereby arrived at which was represented as constituting a dogma applicable to all times and circumstances. Catch phrases, as history shows, may sum up truth or embalm error. The facts in the present case illuminate the adage that a little knowledge can indeed be a dangerous thing.

II

If narrow isolationism misrepresents the aims of the Founding Fathers, has not sheer physical isolation nevertheless shielded America, until recently at least, from the Old World's wars? Washington in the Farewell Address dwelt fondly on "our detached and distant situation," and Jefferson in his first Inaugural similarly rejoiced that the Republic was "kindly separated by nature and a wide ocean from the exterminating havoc of one quarter of the globe." In their day the Atlantic moat took a month or six weeks to cross; but even so, they were conjuring up an immunity which the New World had never actually enjoyed.

Professor Quincy Wright in his monumental *Study of War* lists fifteen wars since the founding of Jamestown in which, "with very few exceptions, all the great powers of the time participated" — an average of one world war about every twenty-one years. While the American people were still colonists, they became enmeshed in the four struggles of Britain and France for empire and trade. These two mighty antagonists drew to their standards many other European nations, and the hostilities extended beyond Europe to North America, India and, in the last clash, to Africa and the Philippines. America was most of the time merely a sideshow; what happened in Europe largely determined the final outcome. In histories of the United States these encounters are known as King William's War, Queen Anne's War, King George's War and the French and Indian War. Actually, they were the transatlantic phases of the War of the Second Coalition against Louis XIV, the War of the Spanish Succession, the War of the Austrian Succession and the Seven Years' War.

This record of repeated embroilment in the mother country's feuds loomed large in the minds of the patriot leaders as their thoughts turned to independence. John Adams eloquently rehearsed the dreary story on the floor of the Second Continental Congress, and Tom Paine in *Common Sense* early in 1776 aptly pointed the moral. "Any submission to, or dependence on, Great Britain," he wrote, "tends directly to involve this continent in European wars and quarrels, and set us at variance with nations . . . against whom we have neither anger nor complaint. . . . The blood of the slain, the weeping voice of nature cries, 'TIS TIME TO PART." Yet the Revolutionary War itself soon widened into a general international conflict, and this fifth world war of the American people was incited by none other than the United States with Paine's full approval. With cool calculation the Americans, having recently helped Britain drive France from North America, now persuaded France to join in driving out Britain. Spain and the Netherlands for their own reasons sided against England, while most of the rest of the Continent assumed

hostile array in the Armed Neutrality League. Again the fighting raged in Europe, North America, the West Indies and India.
It has been estimated that it cost France £50,000,000 to assist
the United States, while the latter, the principal beneficiary,
spent only £20,000,000.

But not even the war's successful issue won that exemption
from Europe's power politics which the patriot leaders had
hoped for. In the 1790's the French Revolution after destroying
the monarchy nurtured a militant nationalism which soon set
all Europe aflame and eventually drew America into her sixth
and seventh world wars. Once more France and England marshaled the contending hosts, and the theater of action embraced
remote parts of the globe. America became involved as a neutral
carrier of commerce on the Atlantic. In the first phase of the
titanic struggle the United States, despite every conceivable
effort to remain aloof, was provoked into naval hostilities with
France from 1798 to 1800. Then, after a short and uneasy peace
in 1802, the two gladiators resumed the contest with mounting violations of America's maritime rights. At last, in 1812, the
United States plunged into war again, this time with Britain.

On either occasion she might reasonably have fought the other
power, for both were at fault. As Nathaniel Macon declared in
the House discussions in 1812, "The Devil himself could not tell
which government, England or France, is the most wicked."
Probably the Madison administration made the wrong choice,
since Napoleon constituted the greater menace to world peace
and national security. What tilted the scales was that England
lay exposed to land attack in Canada whereas France was far
away. While the war was still on, ex-President Jefferson expressed alarm at Bonaparte's victorious advance into Russia,
with Britain almost certain to be his next victim. "Put all Europe into his hands," he told an intimate, "and he might spare
such a force, to be sent in British ships, as I would as leave not
have to encounter."

For the next hundred years Europe's power struggles left the
Atlantic undisturbed, and Britannia, constantly growing toward
greater democracy at home, ruled the waves without prejudice
to the United States. The principal foreign affrays were limited
ones, like the Crimean, the Austro-Prussian, the Franco-Prussian,

the Boer and the Russo-Japanese wars. A new age of international peace and good will seemed to have dawned for mankind. America, completing her continental boundaries, suppressing a great rebellion and developing her amazing natural resources and industrial potential, appeared at long last to have arrived at the point where she could stand on her own feet. In this climate of tranquillity and well-being isolationist sentiment naturally throve, heedless of a past marked by repeated involvements in other peoples' wars.

Meanwhile, however, the great European powers were scrambling for trade, raw materials and colonies on a scale undreamed of before, and human ingenuity was shortening all global distances by startling new applications of steam, gasoline and electricity. Though a smaller planet did not in itself enhance the dangers to peace, it ensured far greater destructiveness if a general war should come.

Then, like a bolt from the blue, a political murder in June, 1914, at Sarajevo in Bosnia, a dependency of the Austro-Hungarian Empire, showed how weak was the structure of international security. The incident lighted a fuse which set off explosions in every direction, propelling not only most of Europe into the conflict but also China, Japan and Europe's colonies encircling the globe. Britain and France captained the forces against imperial Germany and her allies, and as a century before, both sides disregarded America's maritime rights. England's acts, however, inflicted property losses only, while Germany's submarines destroyed lives as well. Moreover, the mounting effectiveness of Germany's undersea campaign spelled Britain's almost certain defeat and the placing of a feared and aggressive power, instead of a friendly one, in control of the Atlantic. Accordingly, the United States, forced to choose whether to forgo this indispensable condition of national security, in 1917 entered its eighth world war. This vital consideration underlay President Wilson's memorable appeal: "The world must be made safe for democracy."

Learning nothing from the past, the United States Senate after the military victory rejected the League of Nations as the best assurance for future peace; and in the 1930's Congress, with even greater naïveté, enacted a neutrality code virtually renouncing freedom of the seas in time of war and forbidding the financial and commercial transactions which allegedly had entangled the country in the recent contest. Though Mussolini and Hitler were already on the loose and the Japanese war lords had despoiled China of Manchuria, a Gallup poll in December, 1936, elicited the information that 60 per cent of the American people believed they could keep out of another general conflict, with only 36 per cent dissenting. Even a month after the lid blew off in September, 1939, 54 per cent still thought it possible to stay out.

The new hositilities, however, jarred Congress, despite isolationist objections, into repealing the neutrality code's embargo on munition sales to warring powers; and France's collapse before the Nazi juggernaut in June, 1940, leaving crippled England alone to guard the Atlantic, impelled the American government to prepare for what seemed almost inevitable involvement. Peacetime conscription was introduced, the administration transferred fifty destroyers to Britain in return for a chain of military bases off North America, and in the spring of 1941 Congress passed the Lend-Lease Act to outfit "any country whose defense the President deems vital to the defense of the United States." But open war, when it came, reached America from an unexpected quarter: the Pacific. The Japanese attack on Pearl Harbor on December 7 of that year demonstrated that future security requires that both oceans be in trusted hands. Notwithstanding the supposed magic of the neutrality code the United States was projected into this greatest of international collisions four months sooner than it had been into the preceding one.

This most recent global struggle has officially been designated World War II, and the history books will undoubtedly perpetuate the error. It would be far better to recognize it as World War IX, for then succeeding generations would know it for just what it was — not a fortuitous disaster, nor the sequel merely of its immediate predecessor, but one of a long series of general wars reaching back two hundred and fifty years and arising from substantially the same causes. President Washington, when the Republic was small and weak, foresaw the day when it should gain "command of its own fortunes," but though his country, as he hoped, became in time one of the most powerful on earth, it has never managed to avoid participation in any foreign

America's World Wars, 1689–1945

ABROAD	AT HOME
1. War of Second Coalition against Louis XIV (1689–1697)	King William's War (1689–1697)
2. War of Spanish Succession (1701–1714)	Queen Anne's War (1702–1713)
3. War of Austrian Succession (1744–1748)	King George's War (1744–1748)
4. Seven Years' War (1756–1763)	French and Indian War (1754–1763)
5. War of the American Revolution (1778–1783)	War for Independence (1775–1783)
6. French Revolutionary Wars (1792–1802)	Undeclared French War (1798–1800)
7. Napoleonic Wars (1803–1815)	War of 1812 (1812–1815)
8. World War "I" (1914–1918)	World War "I" (1917–1918)
9. World War "II" (1939–1945)	World War "II" (1941–1945)

conflict involving operations in the North Atlantic. Repeatedly it has been dragged into wars which other powers started for their own reasons. Geographic separation doubtless saved the United States from Europe's little fights but not her big ones. In the twentieth century these hostilities sent American soldiers to battle stations on every continent and strewed Europe, Africa, Asia and the islands of the Pacific with American blood. With the new weapons of mass demolition on hand World War X, should it come, will almost certainly ravage the homeland as well.

III

Nevertheless, most persons appear to think, Uncle Sam has always handily defeated the enemy when he once shouldered his musket. This too is a falsification of history. The fact is that the United States has never been ready for any of its major wars (and few of its minor ones). This habit of unpreparedness does not spring from a notably pacific disposition of the American people, as is sometimes said. Even during the century of general international peace following Waterloo we fought the Mexican War, the Civil War, the Spanish War and countless Indian campaigns.

Yet the country has never won a large-scale conflict without first losing it. In the struggle for independence General Washington bitterly complained of the untrained troops enlisted for short terms and subject to "shameful and scandalous desertions." After New York fell to the foe in September, 1776, he informed Congress, "To place any dependence upon militia is assuredly resting upon a broken staff." Even the means of warfare were wanting. Less than a tenth of the powder in the first two and a half years was produced at home, most of it coming clandestinely from France via the West Indies. A few weeks before the decisive battle of Saratoga in October, 1777, General Philip Schuyler reported that his men had "little ammunition and not a single piece of cannon." Luckily the British defeat on that occasion brought France openly into the fray, and, thanks to the resulting help in men, arms and ships, the American cause eventually triumphed.

The War of 1812, though presaged by five years of storm signals, found the United States with a feeble army and navy, incompetent heads of the War and Navy Departments and inefficient commanders in the field. Even on the brink of the hostilities Congress refused to appropriate money for additional warships or to levy new taxes. The attempts to invade Canada miscarried, and when British regulars, freed by Napoleon's abdication in April, 1814, arrived on the scene, they succeeded in sacking the national capital and forcing President Madison and his cabinet into ignominious flight. Unfortunately, Andrew Jackson's celebrated victory at New Orleans came after the peace was signed, too late to gain the objects for which the contest had been waged.

The Civil War proved a similar story. Though the South had been threatening secession for a decade or more, the federal authorities were utterly unready when the crisis broke. No steps had been taken to prevent arsenals, military posts and shipyards from falling into Confederate hands, most of the small regular army being stationed beyond the Mississippi. An even graver blow, for which, however, the government was hardly at fault, was the resignation of the ablest army officers to take enemy commands, thus obliging the Lincoln administration to find its military talent through the costly process of trial and error. Moreover, the forty naval vessels were scattered over the seven seas, and until April, 1861, no move was made to enlarge or even concentrate their slender strength. For two years the issue hung in the balance, with Washington constantly imperiled by the foe. And only after two years more did the North triumph.

In 1917 the nation was caught nearly as badly off guard. Despite the fact that Germany had for two and a half years been challenging America's neutral rights and security, it was not till the summer of 1916 that Congress reluctantly augmented the armed forces on a five-year plan and adopted a three-year naval construction program. Secretary of War Garrison, deeming the army increases too little and too late, resigned in protest; and though both political parties in the fall campaign pledged ampler preparedness, President Wilson won his narrow re-election largely on the strength of the slogan "He kept us out of war." When America entered the fray five months later, the armed forces were just beginning to expand; essential weapons, clothing and equipment were lacking; aircraft did not even exist; and the navy had no plans to combat the German submarine menace. According to Brigadier General John M. Palmer, U.S.A. (retired), writing nearly a quarter of a century afterward, "Our capacity for military intervention in Europe was negligible. In fact, we were not even organized to defend our own shores." It took a full year to place a substantial body of troops on the European front, and they had to fight with machine guns, heavy artillery and airplanes supplied mostly by the British and French.

President Franklin Roosevelt, learning from his experience as an official in Wilson's wartime regime, had the country on a better footing for the Axis war than it had been for any similar crisis before. By December, 1939, when America intervened, all types of armament were flowing from the factories, plane production was speeding up, new plants and factories were under way. In a few months, with the conscription law, a great army was in the making. Besides, the navy was the mightiest ever known in peacetime, and a working organization had been established in Washington out of which were to grow the principal war agencies.

Even this foresight, however, sadly underrated the magnitude of the task. "Approximately eight months," General George C. Marshall, America's chief of staff, later wrote, "were required by this country, acting in collaboration with its Allies, to accumulate the munitions, train the initial forces and transport them to where they could be employed in offensive action." In that grim interval the Japanese swept all before them in the Pacific, inflicting the most catastrophic series of defeats the United States has ever suffered. Not till the latter part of 1942 could America begin to fling her total strength into the contest, battling doggedly toward Japan island by island, and, with Allied assistance, expelling the European Axis the next spring from North Africa and presently from southern Italy. Fully girded by the summer of 1944, the nation, employing its combined military and material resources, turned the tide for victory, just as it had in the preceding struggle.

This unbroken record of waging war by declaring it without fully preparing for it reflects a deep-rooted aspect of the national psychology. Improvised or impromptu methods had generally worked well against the Indians, even against the British regulars at Lexington and Concord. The legend grew up of a million men ready to spring to arms — without regard to training, equipment or supplies. Patriotism was enough. The results had not been bad in fighting enemies close at hand, for they were commonly no better prepared; and as for distant foes, time always seemed available to assemble the necessary militia and volunteers. True, it usually required a Bunker Hill, a Bull Run or a Pearl Harbor to awaken the country to the real dimensions of the job, but the initial reverses were forgotten in the elation of final victory, and little account was taken of the needless cost in blood and treasure.

Behind such rationalizations, however, lay a more basic attitude: the instinctive reaction of a people who had left Europe because of their belief in human dignity and hatred of militarism. The Prussian Clausewitz's definition of war as "a continuation of politics by other means" seemed a shameful confession of the failure of rational democratic processes. Willing to fight if fight they must, they were unwilling to regard fighting as a normal occupation or a permanent profession. War, the exception in a land of the free, was the job of a citizen soldiery, not of a military establishment. Yet, even so, they feared that the excesses of the martial spirit might undermine elementary individual rights. Congressman Felix Grundy on the eve of the second encounter with England expressed the thought which others uttered time and again on like occasions. "We are about to ascertain by actual experiment," he said, "how far our republican institutions are calculated to stand the shock of war; and whether, after foreign danger has disappeared, we can again assume our peaceful attitude without endangering the liberties of the people."

The stacking of arms invariably brought precipitate demobilization, and Congress, seeking favor with the public, nearly always trimmed military appropriations to the bone, thus ensuring unpreparedness for the next war. The realist may rail at such suicidal improvidence, but the moralist perceives in this traditional attitude a sound instinct for preserving the humane values of civilization against the Moloch of destruction.

IV

From the historical record, therefore, three conclusions are inescapable. The doctrine of no entangling alliances, as conceived by its authors, did not rule out alliances, temporary or otherwise, redounding to America's own advantage. Geographic isolation has always been a fiction, for the American people have been drawn into every general European war jeopardizing the Atlantic safety zone. And a dread of militarism at home has transformed chronic unpreparedness into a national habit.

Against this historical background President Wilson, ex-President Taft and other public figures, appalled by the outbreak of the world war of 1914 following a long century of peace, urged the formation of an international organization for collective security to replace Europe's trouble-breeding balance-of-power system. As good may come out of evil, so the war might be made a war to end war. Using the Senate as a sounding board, Wilson in January, 1917, demanded that the belligerents provide in the peace settlement for a "definite concert of power which will make it virtually impossible that any such catastrophe should ever overwhelm us again." Then for his own countrymen he added, "There is no entangling alliance in a concert of power. When all unite to act in the same sense and with the same purpose all act in the common interest and are free to live their lives under a common protection." Returning to the theme a year later after the United States had joined the struggle, he climaxed the famous Fourteen Points of his program for peace by calling for a "general association of nations" to afford "mutual guarantees of political independence and territorial integrity to great and small nations alike."

Though at the peace table the Allies ignored many of the Fourteen Points, they agreed to the proposal for a League of Nations. Through this means Wilson hoped to repair the inadequacies of the Versailles treaty as well as to ensure future world stability. "Settlements may be temporary," he told the delegates, "but the actions of the nations in the interests of peace and justice must be permanent. We can set up permanent processes. We may not be able to set up permanent decisions."

At home public opinion seemed irresistibly behind him. The country's chambers of commerce had almost unanimously urged him to initiate the League. Thirty-two legislatures passed approving resolutions. So also did the American Bankers Association, the Associated Advertising Clubs and the American Federation of Labor, and a giant petition of seventeen thousand clergymen asked the Senate to ratify without material changes. A *Literary Digest* poll further indicated an overwhelming backing by newspaper editors, most of them unequivocally. Only 181 out of 1377 voiced all-out opposition.

Even a large majority of the Republican-controlled Senate favored the treaty. The battle as fought in the upper house was not over rejecting the League but over accepting it with or without reservations; only a handful were opposed to it root and branch. Personal dislike of Wilson, plus a Republican desire to gain credit in the approaching election for "improving" his brain child or to throw the blame on him if he wouldn't go along, motivated many of the critics; but as the weeks and months passed, the nation-wide debate revived much of the public's escapist psychology regarding international affairs. A contemporary suggested that the treaty's most formidable foes were two dead men, Washington and Jefferson, who, though unable to keep the nation out of the war, were now keeping it out of the peace. Wilson, seeking to stem the tide, made his ill-fated speaking tour through the Western states, asking the people to choose between the League substantially as he brought it back from the Peace Conference and a "great standing army," crushing taxes and a "militaristic organization of government." If sickness had not felled him on the journey, or if he had been able to appeal to the country by the then as yet unknown radio, he would probably have succeeded in securing ratification on terms he could approve.

Even so, the Senate, when the crucial balloting occurred on March 19, 1920, supported the treaty with the Lodge reservations by a vote of 49 to 35. A switch of seven nays would have provided the requisite two-thirds majority. Had the administration's thick-and-thin adherents sided with their reservationist colleagues instead of with their mortal enemies, the isolationists, the League would easily have passed. In retrospect the opposition to the Lodge reservations seems very much like straining at a gnat, for they differed in phraseology rather than in substance from the Hitchcock reservations which Wilson was prepared to accept. Most historical students will agree with Senator Borah's view five years after the event: "If we had gone into the League with the Lodge reservations, that would have been the last that would ever have been heard of the Lodge reservations."

Two months after the rejection, Senator Lodge, when weighing the Republican plans for the presidential campaign of 1920, confessed, "I think the bulk of the Convention and the mass of the people at the present moment are in favor of the treaty with the reservations which bear my name." Unhappily, the issue was never squarely submitted to the electorate. Though President Wilson asked that the election take "the form of a great and solemn referendum," the Republicans ran Senator Harding, a Lodge reservationist, on a platform that faced in all directions at once. The isolationists contended that it signified the League's utter repudiation, while a group of thirty-one eminent Republicans, including Charles E. Hughes, Herbert Hoover and Elihu Root, said that the question presented to the voters was "not between a league and no league," but whether the one Wilson proposed should be taken without conditions. Only after Harding's landslide did this quondam reservationist discover that the outcome meant the League "is now deceased."

It was of no use for ex-President Taft and Vice-President-elect Calvin Coolidge to deny his interpretation; nor did Harding's inclusion of Hughes and Hoover in his cabinet affect the situation. And subsequently, when Coolidge and Hoover in turn took over the presidency, they did nothing to resuscitate the corpse. Hoover, after solemnly affirming in his Inaugural in 1929 that "The United States fully accepts the profound truth that our own progress, prosperity and peace are interlocked with the progress, prosperity and peace of all humanity," added without change of pace, "Our people have determined that we should make no political engagements such as membership in the League of Nations."

If the decision had gone otherwise and the United States had joined the forty-two countries (later sixty) in the plan for mutual security, mankind might not have coasted into the new and greater war. As the only major power at a sufficient distance to view Old World controversies dispassionately, America could have used her influence both morally and materially to allay international tensions before they reached menacing proportions. This would have been far simpler to do in the 1920's than when the successor to the League was established, for Soviet Russia was still struggling for survival and, in fact, did not become a member till 1934 (and then, interestingly enough, she cast her full weight, though without avail, in favor of stern action against aggressors). In addition, the United States, by remaining aloof, impaired the League's principal coercive weapon: economic sanctions. Since America, the world's foremost trading nation, could not be counted upon to co-operate in economic measures against peacebreakers, the League can hardly be blamed for resorting increasingly to a policy of timidity and talk. Japan, Italy and Germany in turn defied the Geneva organization and then, having demonstrated its impotence, felt free to embark on yet greater imperialistic adventures.

Though Franklin D. Roosevelt, entering office meanwhile in 1933, disavowed any intention of taking America into the League,

he tried nonetheless to recover some of the lost ground by proposing parallel action by the United States whenever economic
sanctions should be imposed on aggressors. But a new upsurge of
isolationism in Congress and the country not only shattered his
hopes, but carried the government to the opposite pole of the
revised neutrality code.

With the onset of the Axis conflict in 1939, however, the atmosphere rapidly cleared. Twice in a single generation major tragedy had afflicted the world, and whether or not America was destined to become a victim again, the national conscience felt uneasy as to its own responsibility for the new cataclysm. By
shirking its duty toward collective security the country appeared
to have had as positive an influence for bad as it might otherwise
have had for good. The lesson was underscored by the flight of
the League's technical agencies to the United States, where most
of them appropriately found shelter in Princeton, Woodrow Wilson's former home. "The ghosts of William E. Borah and the elder
Henry Cabot Lodge, old Republican enemies of the League,"
reported George Gallup in July, 1942, "will shudder to hear not
only that the country as a whole is now in favor of American
participation in a postwar world league, but that in the Republican party the number approving such a step has increased from
four in every ten to seven in every ten in the short space of one
year."

Taking advantage of the chastened popular mood, President
Roosevelt, while the United States was still a neutral, joined with
Prime Minister Churchill in August, 1941, in drawing up the Atlantic Charter, which promised as one of the fruits of victory a
"permanent system of general security"; and upon America's
entry into the fight all the Axis-resisting countries pledged support. At Moscow in October, 1943, a declaration by the United
States, Britain, the Soviet Union and China dealt somewhat more
concretely with the proposal, and later conferences at Dumbar-
ton Oaks and Yalta gave the structure provisional outline.
Meanwhile at home the President, profiting by Wilson's blunders,
moved warily, keeping himself in the background of the discussions and seeing to it that Secretary of State Cordell Hull and
other high officials conferred frequently with Republican leaders
in Congress. As a result, both chambers voted overwhelmingly

in favor of the proposition, and both parties backed it in the presidential campaign of 1944. Among the ardent supporters in the Senate were George W. Norris of Nebraska and Arthur Capper of Kansas, aged survivors of the epic League fight which had seen them on the other side.

While the war was still raging around the globe, the fifty Axis-opposing countries met at San Francisco in April, 1945, to give the new world order final form. Roosevelt's sudden death denied him a part in the proceedings, but the able delegation he had appointed, including members of both parties and both houses of Congress, rendered effective service. After two months the Charter of the United Nations was evolved; and the United States Senate, in contrast to the stormy eight months' debate of 1919–1920, ratified it almost unanimously after only six days of discussion. America, moreover, outstripped all other countries in acting.

The Charter is obviously not a perfect document, nor is it a self-executing instrument. The new structure, however, is stronger than its predecessor, notably in the firmer commitments of the member governments, the numerous specialized agencies dealing with the economic and social conditions of global stability and the provision (not yet fully implemented) for an international police force. Besides, with the attainment of independence by many former African and Asian colonies, it has come to embrace more than a hundred different countries. Nor has the right of individual veto belonging to the four major powers and Formosan China in the Security Council seriously hampered the UN inasmuch as the General Assembly has succeeded in assuming more and more authority.

The Soviet Union's ambition to impose Communism on the rest of humanity has constituted the chief impediment to the achievement of the organization's purposes. Russia's course, indeed, has compelled America, contrary to her traditional postwar habit, to spend billions, as leader of the free world, on armaments on land, sea and in the air, as well as to conclude alliances with non-Communist nations encircling the earth and to maintain far-flung missile bases. This "balance of terror" has proved to be an unexpected and disappointing accompaniment of the new edifice of collective security.

Is the UN, then, the keystone of the arch of peace that had

been hoped for? Whatever its difficulties, it has removed many danger spots of misunderstanding; and, except for the armed intervention in Korea on behalf of its own authority, it has nurtured an atmosphere conducive to the pacific settlement of otherwise explosive disputes. In this fearful age of nuclear weaponry these services alone would justify its continued existence. Many problems lie ahead, but no one concerned with the survival of civilization can for a moment entertain the thought that the UN is not a permanent fixture. The object now is less to make the world safe for democracy than to make the world safe, for only if that is once accomplished can there be an opportunity for the growth and spread of free institutions.

9

World currents in American history

CIVILIZATION in the United States has arisen out of the interaction of three factors: the original introduction of Western European customs and institutions, the impact of the New World environment on the transplanted ways, and the continuing influence of the Old World. Historians have given considerable attention to the first of these factors, somewhat less to the second and very little to the third. Europe's persisting role has generally been disposed of by an account of diplomatic relations or of the foreign-born additions to the population. These topics, however, fall far short of exhausting the theme. Indeed, they omit the most essential aspect: the fact that America has all along shared in the principal pulsations of thought and accomplishment abroad. That the presence of immigrants facilitated the transfer there can be no doubt, but, had they stayed at home, United States history would still have been inextricably a branch of world history. No people bound to Western culture could, if it wished, have escaped the dynamic currents quickening the older civilization.

I

The neglect of this side of United States history is easy to understand. The Revolutionary leaders of 1776 built their case for separation upon the differences rather than the likenesses between the colonists and the mother country. The Declaration of Independence proclaimed what the patriots wished to discard, not what they treasured and intended to keep. This emphasis was indispensable in order to spur the people to take up arms on behalf of a nationality whose existence they themselves hardly yet recognized. Victory in the war with Britain established the new nation as a legal entity, and the Constitution both expressed and reinforced the sense of nationality by spurning the European institution of the monarchy and conferring all power upon the governed. Clearly the fledgling Republic could go its own way alone, setting at naught the precepts and example of its elders across the sea.

The nineteenth century fortified this conviction. Territorially the country came to stretch farther and farther away from the Atlantic Seaboard, directing eyes inward and predisposing men to forget the Old World except at times of diplomatic tension and war. Such occasions only heightened the belief that Europe, fearing comparison with the land of the free, wished to discredit the American experiment and delimit its place in the sun. The Civil War appeared to provide conclusive evidence, for the British and French governments, eager for the disruption of the Union, befriended the South to a point just short of actual intervention.

Little wonder that when the English historian Edward A. Freeman visited the United States in the 1880's he reported,

> Some people in America seem really to think that the United States, their constitution and all that belongs to them, did not come into being by the ordinary working of human causes, but sprang to life by some special creation or revelation. They think themselves wronged if it is implied . . . that their institutions did not spring at once from the ground, but that they were, like the institutions of other nations, gradually wrought out of a store common to them with some other branches of mankind.

As though anticipating Freeman's comment, Anthony Trollope, who had made his trip twenty years before, acutely remarked,

> This new people, when they had it in their power to change all their laws, to throw themselves upon any Utopian theory that the folly of a wild philanthropy could devise, to discard as abominable every vestige of English rule and English power, . . . did not do so, but preferred to cling to things English.

He explained the apparent paradox by pointing out that the colonists had "set themselves up as a separate people, not because the mother-country had refused to them by law sufficient liberty and sufficient self-control, but because the mother-country infringed the liberties and powers of self-control she herself had given."

History bears out this analysis. Mother country and colonies stemmed from the same institutional ancestry: Magna Carta and the common law, parliamentary rule and local self-government, the Puritan and the Glorious Revolutions. It was no coincidence that the provinces most solidly for the American Revolution, Virginia and the New England group, were those most English in composition, or that the American cause found warm defenders in Parliament. James Otis, Samuel Adams, Thomas Jefferson and other champions of colonial rights drew heavily on the arsenal of constitutional principles forged by John Locke, the great English philosopher of natural law, principles which they envisaged as the "fundamental rights of English subjects." The very Declaration of Independence was a Lockian treatise blazoning the sentiments of men who prided themselves on being better Englishmen than the English ruling class.

By the same token the Constitution and its annex, the bill of rights, drew heavily on British precedents either directly or through the colonial charters, and the very language was that of the English common law. The borrowed provisions greatly outnumbered the innovations. Even the novel division of the government into three co-ordinate departments was supposed by the framers to copy the mother country, since Montesquieu in his influential *L'Esprit des Lois* had so depicted the English system, and the people, moreover, had been used to something like it in their provincial governments. Similarly, the Republic's legislative practices derived from the parent land, the phrase "parliamentary law" surviving in a country where the name of no lawmaking body, state or national, warranted the adjective.

Equally noteworthy was the common law's persistence in the domain of private rights of person and property. Introduced without material change by the first settlers, this body of judge-made rules, though modified in some particulars by the Revolutionary generation, continued to undergird America's system of jurisprudence, even to the extent that decisions in English courts constituted valid precedents in United States tribunals. Only in the remnants of Spanish and French settlements in the South and Southwest was there a slight intrusion of Continental civil law. Probably no other institutional importation, not even the English language, has retained a more intimate connection with the older country.

In other words, the great decision of 1776 affected overseas governmental ties rather than English doctrines and usages consistent with colonial republican ideals. Appealing to this common intellectual legacy, John Greenleaf Whittier, poet laureate of the antislavery crusade, reminded the pro-Southern British ministry in 1861,

> We too are heirs of Runnymede,
> And Shakespeare's fame and Cromwell's deed.

As Freeman and Trollope suggested, the people could not have done otherwise. Not only had they lived one hundred and fifty years under British rule — nearly half of all American history down to the present — but for a long time thereafter the men who directed public affairs had spent their own formative years as British subjects. Indeed, Martin Van Buren, entering the White House in 1837, was the first President to be born a United States citizen. Granted these circumstances, a complete break with the past, however flattering to the national ego, would have been impossible and, from the standpoint of the orderly development of liberty, unwise.

II

Disliking to think of themselves as Englishmen even with a difference, the citizens of the early Republic wished nevertheless to feel that their bold undertaking accorded with the world stream of history. Youth, though disdaining age, always welcomes the moral support which comes from any signs of enlightenment it perceives in its seniors. In the 1790's many Americans found the evidence they desired in the French Revolution which, besides complementing their own, they viewed as indicating the irrepressible trend of mankind. They ardently manifested their approval by assuming Gallic republican ways, establishing counterparts of the Jacobin clubs, imitating French apparel and forms of address, and demanding that the United States help France in her war with England.

More significant because less transitory was this generation's penchant for classical antiquity, which had given the world its earliest examples of a republic. Pioneers driving their oxcarts westward through upstate New York strewed the landscape with rude communities flaunting such names as Utica, Rome and Syracuse; the New Englanders who planted Marietta on the Ohio had their Campus Martius; and the first seat of higher learning north of the river was located at Athens. In like spirit the disbanded officers of the Revolutionary War, exhilarated by the same backward view, founded a hereditary organization called the Society of the Cincinnati. Most striking of all was the vogue of Greek and Roman architecture, in which Jefferson was a leader. The new style sired many noble edifices and fixed on the rising federal capital its classical aspect, thereby setting a model for American public buildings for years to come.

In much more vital ways as well, the nation betrayed its kinship with the world it had professed to reject. The great transforming factors in Western European history, at least from the nineteenth century onward, have been democracy, nationalism, industrialism, imperialism and humanitarianism, operating either independently or in conjunction. The United States during this span of years faced its own special problems, yet, when local peculiarities are stripped away and attention is fixed on the underlying course of events, these factors emerge as also the central themes of American history. If historians have tended to slight this fact, it is because they, like their compatriots, have generally regarded America as sufficient unto herself, seeing their country in Ptolemaic terms as the center of the universe rather than as part of an interdependent Copernican system. These common processes will become clearer upon closer examination.

III

Consider the development of political democracy on the opposite sides of the Atlantic. In Britain during the nineteenth century the right to vote was extended by progressive stages in 1832, 1867 and 1884. Though the classes benefited were not the same as in the United States, the first of these advances corresponded with the crest of the American movement for white manhood suffrage, while the second and third almost exactly coincided with the granting of the franchise respectively to male Negroes and male Indians. And when Britain in 1918 conferred the ballot upon women (as did many other European governments about the same time), the United States took like action by federal constitutional amendment two years later. On the Continent, meanwhile, the Swiss obtained manhood suffrage in 1848, thirty-six years before the English arrived at a roughly equivalent status; and though the progress in other parts of Western Europe proved slower, nearly everywhere the tendency was the same.

American historians usually attribute the trend in their own country to the influence of the frontier, parroting the sentiment: "Democracy came out of the forest." But this is too parochial a view: the United States was part of the larger whole. What really came out of the forest was a special brand of democracy, one based on the notion that the best good of all was served by everybody looking out for himself. If the Pacific Ocean had washed the Appalachians, if no western zone of untapped natural resources had existed to relieve the growing tension between poor and rich, it is probable that the democracy which resulted would have been more of the European or welfare-state type. Then, as abroad, the discontented, unable to go forth to clear new lands, would have had to fight out the issue where they lived, and the concessions would have come at the expense of the possessing classes.

Americans at the time recognized that the democratic movement transcended national boundaries. Thus in 1843 John Greenleaf Whittier, the Quaker bard who "made his song a sword for truth," saluted the aspirations of the English Chartists:

> God bless ye, brothers! in the fight
>   Ye're waging now, ye cannot fail,
> Far better is your sense of right
>   Than king-craft's triple mail. . . .

The truths ye urge are borne abroad
    By every wind and every tide;
The voice of Nature and of God
    Speaks out upon your side.
The weapons which your hands have found
    Are those which Heaven itself has wrought,
Life, Truth, and Love; your battle-ground
    The free, broad field of Thought.

Thus, too, James Russell Lowell addressed King Louis Philippe when a popular uprising swept away his scepter in 1848:

Vain were thy bayonets against the foe
    Thou hadst to cope with; thou didst wage
War not with Frenchmen merely; — no,
    Thy strife was with the Spirit of the Age.

It was to the spirit of a later age that President Wilson appealed in 1918 when he demanded the equal-suffrage amendment. "We cannot isolate our thought or action in such a matter from the thought of the rest of the world," he told Congress. "We must either conform or deliberately reject what they propose and resign the leadership of liberal minds to others."

The United States took an almost proprietary interest in the recurrent democratic upheavals on the Continent. News of the overthrow of a monarch and the triumph of the people occasioned popular celebrations, banquets, parades, sometimes official holidays. Even the gentle Longfellow wrote, "So long as a king is left upon his throne there will be no justice on the earth." The Greek struggle in the 1820's to cast off the Ottoman yoke warmed Americans with a sense of contemporary antiquity, attracting both money and volunteer soldiers to the cause. John Adams, Jefferson and Madison — all the living ex-Presidents — praised the revolutionists, while the occupant of the White House, James Monroe, gave the undertaking his blessing in a message to Congress.

The French revolutions of 1830 and 1848 won similar acclaim from government and people. President Jackson, remarking the first of these occasions in a message to Congress, felicitated the French upon their "courage and wisdom," which "naturally elicits from the kindred feelings of this nation" a "spontaneous burst of applause." After the second uprising the House and Senate by joint resolution tendered "the congratulations of the American to the French people upon the success of their recent efforts to consolidate the principles of liberty in a republican form of government," while the Democratic national convention, surveying the convulsions in other lands as well, rejoiced that the "sovereignty of the people" was "prostrating thrones and erecting republics on the ruins of despotism in the Old World."

Despite the disappointing outcome of the "Year of Revolutions," Secretary of State Daniel Webster two years later, in 1850, dispatched his famous note to Austria regarding Hungary's fight for freedom. Reaffirming his countrymen's right "to cherish always a lively interest in the fortunes of nations struggling for institutions like their own," he declared grandiloquently that, compared with free America, "the possessions of the House of Hapsburg are but a patch on the earth's surface." When the defeated Magyar leader, Louis Kossuth, visited the United States a year later, huge ovations greeted him in the Eastern cities, and he was formally received by President Fillmore and honored with a congressional dinner.

The establishment of the third French Republic in 1870 finally vindicated America's unflagging confidence in that country's democratic disposition. Undeterred by having been the first to recognize the short-lived Republic of 1848, the United States again led the way, complimenting the people on instituting a government "unconnected with the dynastic traditions of Europe." The popular uprisings abroad, despite numerous setbacks, drew constant nourishment from the example and approval of the United States, while the American people were confirmed in their own liberal ideals by Europe's undismayed striving.

This striving aimed at nationalism as well as democracy, for since the French Revolution of the 1790's the two aspirations had been closely entwined. It was not till the mid-nineteenth century, however, that nationalism gained sufficient momentum in Central and Southern Europe to achieve significant results. Then, within a single decade, Italy and Germany took their places on the map, welding into strong political units peoples hitherto feeble because divided; and most of the Canadian provinces in

North America also joined in a federal system. Meanwhile the United States had been encountering the identical problem in a different guise, with the bonds of union constantly strained by the centrifugal pull of sectionalism. The solution came in the Civil War which, in harmony with the consolidating process elsewhere, established the indivisibility of the American people. Lincoln, from this point of view, did for his country what Cavour did for Italy and Bismarck for Germany. In the years that followed, nationalism in the United States, as elsewhere, strengthened the central organs of authority at the expense of local autonomy, causing government to exercise increasing control over economic life. And nationalism, as we shall see, became also a potent ingredient in imperialism.

IV

Industrialization, the third of the factors that ignored national frontiers, started with England's Industrial Revolution in the eighteenth century, spread to the United States and Continental Europe in the nineteenth and reached Asia in the twentieth. In America, the rise of the factory system, the introduction of improved methods of banking and investment, the expansion of markets by turnpikes, canals and railroads, all conformed to the British pattern. True, Parliament for some years tried by solemn prohibitions to keep the new machinery and processes a national secret, but by hook or crook Americans smuggled the knowledge across the ocean and set up their own mills and factories along the northern Atlantic seaboard. Soon they began to improve upon what they had filched; and aided by extraordinary natural advantages and a rapidly growing domestic demand, they presently outdistanced Britain in many branches.

The United States Patent Office bears witness to the growing aptitude for invention. With fewer than 62,000 patents issued prior to 1865, the number leaped to nearly 638,000 during the remainder of the century. The common impulse moving the American and foreign peoples is indicated by the many inventions made independently. France, Britain and the United States all claim credit for originating the steamboat, Britain and America for the steam locomotive, while William Kelly of Eddyville,

Kentucky, devised the air-blast process of refining molten iron several years before England's Sir Henry Bessemer did so. By 1860 America stood fourth as a manufacturing nation, and by 1900 first. At that date her production exceeded the combined output of Great Britain and Germany, her nearest rivals.

Industrialization emphasizes strikingly the interlocking of American and world history. Quite apart from the direct effects upon material progress, it injected into American politics the typical problems of the more mature European states. As the nineteenth century advanced and gave way to the twentieth, the country wrestled increasingly with such issues as the tariff, labor unrest, the dislocation of the farming population, currency regulation and the curbing of railroads, banking and business monopolies. The differences from the Old World were in time and degree rather than in kind.

Externally, the United States found its economic health jeopardized from time to time by conditions existing elsewhere on the globe. Every general industrial collapse at home coincided with a similar crisis abroad, the Great Depression of 1929 being simply the most recent case. So closely did business and finance weave their strands across mankind that a break at one point in the web unraveled the fabric everywhere. In time, America's growing economic resemblance to the Old World brought about the introduction of international political parties, groups committed to the Marxian dogma of the class struggle and the abolition of the capitalist system. Thanks to the abundant opportunities of American life, however, neither the Socialists nor the Communists were able to attract more than a negligible following.

Industrialism, moreover, abetted by nationalism, proved in considerable degree responsible also for the tidal wave of imperialism that inundated Europe and spilled over on the United States. Industry in the Old World constantly demanded fresh sources of raw materials as well as new markets for its surplus output; capital demanded openings for investment at exorbitant interest rates. If these perquisites could be obtained by annexing "backward" peoples, then businessmen would secure an advantage over their rivals in other countries, and the homeland would gratifyingly enhance its national prestige. In earlier times the white man's imperialism had generally involved the planting of colonies settled by whites; but urged on by the advancing industrialism, Europe after the middle of the nineteenth century embarked upon a course aimed primarily at exploiting the native populations. Between 1870 and 1900 the British Empire, exclusive of spheres of influence, amassed about five million square miles in scattered parts of the globe, France netted three and a half million and Germany a million.

Although the United States had steadily enlarged its territorial limits of 1783, the process consisted for many years in taking over border regions virtually uninhabited and therefore subject to American settlement. Land-seeking pioneers preceded actual annexation; the government then acquired the area by peaceful means — though sometimes with a gun behind the door — and in due course the acquisition gained political equality in the Union. In this manner Louisiana Territory, Florida, Texas and Oregon Territory shifted the Republic's original boundaries to the Gulf of Mexico and the Pacific Ocean. The Mexican War of 1846–1848, yielding California and the Southwest, constituted the only instance in this era of forcibly depriving another people of a slice of its homeland. In the nation's thinking, "manifest destiny," reinforced by the land hunger of a phenomenally expanding population, justified these additions, and the sectional quarrel over slavery probably did as much to hinder as to hasten the process.

But if little occasion existed in the early years for overseas dominion, the post-Civil War upthrust of industrialism, combined with Europe's example and America's fear of losing out in the race for investments and trade, changed the situation. Soon Washington was exploring the possibilities in the West Indies, Hawaii, Samoa. Then the "splendid little war" with Spain in 1898 pushed the government fully into the world current of imperialism. The United States not only annexed Spain's colonies of Puerto Rico, the Philippines and Guam in two oceans, but also, within a short stretch of time, Hawaii, American Samoa, Wake Island and the Panama Canal Zone, not counting a pendant of political and fiscal protectorates in the Caribbean. Since these additions were all separated from the mainland and inhabited by alien peoples, it was not intended that they should ever obtain statehood. Thus America, somewhat tardily, chose the path to empire, and the voters in the presidential election of 1900 cried a hearty amen.

By the same sign, America's later disillusion with imperialism paralleled a like tendency abroad. In the 1920's Great Britain, France and other European powers surrendered some of their special privileges in China, and Britain in addition set up the Irish Free State, conferred greater rights on India and Egypt, and presently transformed her ties with the self-governing dominions into the voluntary co-operation of the British Commonwealth of Nations. After the Axis war fueled nationalistic aspirations in colonial populations the trend became stronger. In the late forties and the fifties England gave dominion status to Ceylon and divested herself of India, Burma and Palestine (a mandate under the League of Nations), while France and the Netherlands emulated her example, with whatever ill-nature, in the case of their possessions.

Meanwhile the United States moved in the same direction. Beginning in the early thirties, America relinquished her protectorates in the Caribbean, provided for Philippine independence, and by admitting the twenty Latin American republics to full partnership in the Monroe Doctrine sought to reassure them against its future use as a weapon of Yankee aggression; then in the 1950's it granted commonwealth status to Puerto Rico as well as statehood to Alaska and Hawaii. Thus the United States not only shared in the rise of imperialism but also contributed to its decline.

v

Similarly, humanitarianism bridged the Atlantic. Early in the nineteenth century moral-reform movements, inspired largely by religious sentiments, sprang up in Britain and the United States. Whether in the one land or the other, the home missionary bodies, foreign missions, Sunday-school associations, Bible and tract organizations, Magdalene societies and the like had the same purpose: to combat vice among the unchurched by instilling Christian ideals of conduct. About the same time, in 1815, the peace movement arose in the two countries in the wake of the protracted anguish caused by twenty years of almost unrelieved world conflict. Soon the American and English peace groups joined hands, exchanging speakers, reissuing each other's pamphlets, and in time sponsoring international congresses which included like-minded Continental groups. Though rulers nevertheless continued to resort to war, this long-sustained effort helped to seed the ground for the attempts at global organization for peace in the twentieth century.

The agitation against intoxicating drink was solely American in origin, but so swiftly did it infect other countries that in 1841 the New Orleans Temperance Society exulted that even "in New Zealand, once noted for cannibalism, the temperance tree has taken root." Yankee tracts, widely reprinted in Europe in the thirties, brought about total-abstinence societies in the Scandinavian states, Germany and the British Isles. In Sweden the King headed one of the groups, while Prussia's monarch Frederick William III ordered that they be formed in every province. Soon James Silk Buckingham, an advocate of the cause in the British Parliament, was heartening American audiences with news of the progress made in his country, and Father Theobald Mathew, an Irish champion, toured the United States to win his many Celtic coreligionists to teetotalism. A World's Temperance Convention at London in 1846 formalized the cosmopolitan unity of endeavor.

If it were desirable to multiply instances, a moment's reflection would show that many other movements — such as those for penal reform, for married women's rights, for banning debt imprisonment, for the humane treatment of the insane — were in the same sense more international than national in character. Similarly, the multitude of Utopian communities hopefully begun in the period before the Civil War stemmed from the teachings of Robert Owen, a Scot, and Fourier and Cabet, two Frenchmen. Americans have been particularly blind in realizing the extent to which the drive to abolish slavery — the greatest blow ever aimed against inhumanity in the United States — was a world-wide campaign. Even historians generally treat Negro bondage as an exclusively domestic question, failing to note that it was American only in the sense that the United States lagged behind all other major countries in banishing the practice and that only in the United States did it provoke a bloody war.

Britain's impact on the American movement proved especially potent. In 1807 Parliament and Congress simultaneously took steps to bar further human importations from Africa; but then

England, unembarrassed by slavery in the homeland, outstripped the United States, adopting legislation in 1833 to extirpate the institution throughout the empire. The American leaders, uplifted by the glorious news, founded the American Anti-Slavery Society the same year, and William Lloyd Garrison hurried across the Atlantic to learn how the miracle had been accomplished. In the years that followed, he and other abolitionists repeatedly lectured there to collect funds for the cause, circulated English antislavery pamphlets widely through the United States and induced the British abolitionist George Thompson to take personal part in the crusade.

The closeness of the bond further appears in the fact that within a short space after the publication of *Uncle Tom's Cabin* that masterpiece of propaganda sold a million copies in the United Kingdom. On the mounting wave of pity excited by the novel, half a million British women addressed an appeal to their American sisters to right the terrible wrong. Southerners fully appreciated the importance of this transatlantic interest, one of them denouncing abolitionism as "a conspiracy of fanaticism originated in England and supplied with British gold." It was, of course, this communion of antislavery sympathy that so angered Northerners at the time of the Civil War when the British ministry hastily issued a proclamation of neutrality and planned to recognize Southern independence. As Whittier wrote,

> But yesterday you scarce could shake,
>   In slave-abhorring rigor,
> Our Northern palms for conscience' sake:
> To-day you clasp the hands that ache
>   With "walloping the nigger!"

America's indebtedness to British example deepened as the growing complexity of economic life created strains and maladjustments which the older country had earlier taken steps to solve. Most factory legislation in the United States had English precedents, while the American Federation of Labor, formed in the eighties under the leadership of London-born Samuel Gompers, consciously modeled its organization upon that of the British Trades Union Congress. To cope with the problem of poverty Americans borrowed the social settlement and the charity-organization system, and to groove religion to urban needs they imported the Y.M.C.A., the Salvation Army and the institutional church. Likewise, Christian Socialism, though making a more limited appeal, probably numbered as many adherents in the United States in the 1880's and 1890's as in the land of its birth.

VI

Democracy, nationalism, industrialism, imperialism, humanitarianism — these, then, were developments that transformed the United States as well as Europe. No less strong was the cultural nexus with the Old World. As the Bostonian Ezra S. Gannett remarked, every ship conveyed "the thought and feeling which prevail there, to be added to our stock of ideas and sentiments." His observation of 1840 held quite as true of 1740 or of 1940. America's religious faiths have had the most diverse ancestry. Our educational system sprang originally from English roots, to be later crossfertilized from German sources at both the kindergarten and graduate levels. Literature, though predominantly English in inspiration, came in time to mirror many other fashions, Occidental and Oriental. Painting passed successively through its British, German and French phases; sculpture after going to school to Italy reached manhood under Parisian tutelage, while architecture has recorded a myriad of alien styles, often simultaneously. Serious music has consisted largely of French, Italian, German and Russian compositions, and the simpler variety has found lasting expression in "America," an adaptation of the British national anthem, and in "Home, Sweet Home," written by a New Yorker in Paris, set to a Sicilian tune by an English musician and first sung in an operatic drama in London. Even America's abundant sports life has been in considerable degree an outgrowth of the great athletic revival in Britain in the mid-nineteenth century.

Scientific development merely underscores the point. At every stage of American life the progress of research elsewhere has conditioned our own thought and achievement. The American Association for the Advancement of Science, established in 1848, was the younger brother of the British Association of the same name, while the Smithsonian Institution, founded about the same time "for the increase and diffusion of knowledge among men," stemmed from the bequest of an English physicist who had never even seen the United States. Raymond B. Fosdick, referring to the international role of medical learning, has reminded his readers,

> Our children are guarded from diphtheria by what a Japanese and a German did; they are protected from smallpox by an Englishman's work; they are saved from rabies because of a Frenchman; they are cured of pellagra through the researches of an Austrian. From birth to death they are surrounded by an invisible host — the spirits of men who never thought in terms of flags or boundary lines and who never served a lesser loyalty than the welfare of mankind.

History as conventionally written stresses national differences — even when not genuinely such — to the neglect of national similarities. This emphasis, glossing over the fundamental interdependence of peoples, inevitably highlights the occasional misunderstandings and collisions, nourishes mutual distrust and contributes dangerously to national vainglory. In short, the scholars through whose writings the living generation learns of the past have compiled case studies of abnormal and exceptional behavior.

That is seeing truth through a distorting lens, and today, more than ever before, this is to be avoided. If international understanding is ever to be more than a vague aspiration or a matter of governments playing power politics in world organizations, we must have, as Archibald MacLeish has said, "a positive and creative recognition of the community of the human mind regardless of differences of race, nationality, language, ideology, or religious faith." "Since wars begin in the minds of men," declares the constitution of UNESCO, "it is in the minds of men that the defenses of peace must be constructed." Fortunately these defenses already exist; they need only to be given effect. If peoples will but stake their faith upon the things they have in common, if statesmen will emphasize the unifying instead of the divisive forces in civilization, then youth will gain fresh courage in facing the future, and age will revive its belief in man's capacity to establish enduring peace on earth.

10

The martial
spirit

AMERICAN nationality has been a plant of gradual growth. Many elements served to retard its development. The first century and a half under British rule forged emotional bonds with the old country difficult to break when the colonists struck for independence. Later, the expanding size of the nation nourished regional and state allegiances — usually reflecting economic attachments as well — which sometimes surpassed allegiance to the common flag. In addition, the varied origins of the population created danger of disloyalty in periods of international friction because of ancestral blood ties. Finally, in recent times, appeared divisive ideologies rooted in Marxian conceptions of the class struggle.

George Washington, who led his people in war before leading them in peace, was fully aware of the perils to domestic unity in the hopefully named *United* States. The Farewell Address summoned his fellow citizens to subordinate private interests to those of their new country and join in dismantling the "batteries of internal and external enemies." He cautioned them against sectional jealousies and ambitions, against the "insidious wiles of foreign influence" and even against political parties, which he regarded as breeding only mischief and discord. His successors in office, however, largely ignored these warnings. Parties, indeed, proved to be an indispensable means of adjusting contending interests and mapping an acceptable middle course of action, and as the country grew older, the other dangers seemed also less real. Statesmen believed that, as Washington himself anticipated, "time and habit" had now fixed the character of the government and attached the people unflinchingly to it. Partisan controversy, however fierce, signified a healthy state of the body politic; it would always stop short of jeopardizing the nation's very existence.

How well justified were these suppositions? An inquiry into the extent and reality of national unity in American history might take various forms, but clearly no other test is so decisive as the behavior of the country when confronted by an armed foe. Upon the outbreak of the struggle to preserve the Union, Stephen A. Douglas, who had divided the Northern vote with Lincoln in the election of 1860, told his followers, "There can be no neutrals in this war, only patriots — or traitors." With this as the criterion, how have the American people reacted in their major wars?

I

In an incandescent passage the historian George Bancroft, writing in 1858, declared of the War for Independence:

The hour of the American Revolution was come. The people of the continent with irresistible energy obeyed one general impulse, as the earth in spring listens to the command of nature, and without the appearance of effort bursts forth to life in perfect harmony. The change which Divine wisdom ordained, and which no human policy or force could hold back, proceeded as uniformly and majestically as the laws of being, and was as certain as the decrees of eternity.

The chroniclers of the winning side in a war always display a facility for glossing over past difficulties and divisions, and though the process is congenial to folklore, it does not make for good history.

Bancroft's view has, in fact, no support from people at the time. Jonathan Boucher, a Tory clergyman who fled Maryland for England after the initial hostilities, flatly denied in his *View of the Causes and Consequences of the American Revolution* (1797) "that the people of America, properly so called, were generally favourable to the revolt." Otherwise, he observed, the Whigs would not have resorted to the many harsh laws against those who refused to take the patriot oath of allegiance.

Lest such testimony be dismissed as grossly biased, let witnesses from the other side be called to the bar. John Adams, who in after years frequently reverted to the subject, stated that colonial unanimity steadily declined after the first troubles over the Stamp Act in 1765, when the issue was reform without thought of revolution. As the breach with the mother country widened, many upon sober second thought came to fear the consequences of the growing radicalism. Even the members of the First Continental Congress in 1774 were split in sentiment, being "one third tories, another whigs, and the rest mongrels." Adams estimated that after the die was cast a third of the people — approximately 800,000 out of 2,400,000 — still opposed the patriot cause, an opinion which led Thomas McKean, a cosigner of the Declaration of Independence, to rejoin that "more than a third of influential characters were against it." In addition to active antagonists there were the fence sitters, Adams's "mongrels" — persons who avoided a definite stand. Thomas McKean described them as "the timid and those who believed the colonies would be conquered, and that, of course, they would be safe in their persons and property from such conduct, and also have a probability of obtaining office and distinction." Others like John Ross of Philadelphia simply "loved ease and Madeira much better than liberty and strife."

The Tories according to their own lights were acting on principle. Their misfortune lay in being unwilling to take on a new loyalty fast enough. Included in their ranks was a considerable proportion of "influential characters": great landholders such as the De Lanceys and Philipses of New York, wealthy merchants like the Whartons of Philadelphia and the Chandlers of Boston, virtually all the crown officials in the colonies and many lawyers and other professional men. In South Carolina and Georgia they formed a majority, but they were also numerous elsewhere. "New York and Pennsylvania," said Adams in retrospect, "were so nearly divided, if their propensity was not against us, that if New England on one side and Virginia on the other had not kept them in awe, they would have joined the British." To quench this fire in the rear the patriots had recourse to mob violence and legal restraints, jailing or banishing the more prominent Tories and confiscating their property. Before the struggle was over, perhaps two hundred thousand suffered exile, voluntarily fled or died, a loss of substantial citizens comparable only to the flight of the Huguenots from France after the revocation of the Edict of Nantes or, more recently, of the Jews from Nazi Germany.

Disunity was inevitable in a contest which was by its very nature both a domestic and an international war. Further confusion arose from the fact that few of the colonial leaders had consciously aimed at separation. As late as four months after the bloodshed at Lexington and Concord, Thomas Jefferson, who was to pen the Declaration of Independence the next year, said that he "would rather be in dependence on Great Britain, properly limited, than on any nation on earth, or on no nation." And John Adams, echoing Jefferson, wrote some weeks afterward, "We cannot in this country conceive that there are men in England so infatuated as seriously to suspect the Congress, or people here, of a wish to erect ourselves into an independent state." Still later, in December, 1775, so ardent a partisan of freedom as Samuel Adams explained the slowness of the Second Continental Congress in taking action by saying, "We must be content to wait till the Fruit is ripe before we gather it." Even when the moment arrived, John Dickinson, whose *Farmer's Letters* a few years before had done so much to spur the movement of opposition, declined to sign the Declaration of Independence, though he subsequently sided with the revolutionists.

Probably in no later encounter with an external foe was so determined a body of opinion arrayed against the government. Valley Forge is rightly an imperishable symbol of American fortitude, but the sufferings of Washington's barefoot and hungry soldiers were uncalled-for. There was plenty of food on the countryside, and in Philadelphia not many miles away the redcoats were reveling on the fat of the land. Within the Continental army itself, as well as in seats of civil authority, actual disloyalty raised its head. Dr. Benjamin Church, director of the first military hospital, was in British pay. Chief Justice Metcalf Bowler of Rhode Island carried on a treasonable correspondence with the British commander, Sir Henry Clinton. The valiant and trusted General Benedict Arnold conspired to turn over West Point and its outlying forts to the enemy. A true understanding of the fight for freedom must take into account this hidden war as well as the open one. With independence at last won, however, the people

might well have expected that a united country would support
the government in any future conflict.

II

The first test came in the War of 1812. Though the number of
British-born Americans had by then greatly declined and loyalty
to the once loved flag was no longer a factor of importance, the
onset of the contest nevertheless revealed deep fissures in the
public. The peace sentiment centered in New England and the
Federalist party, bastions of the commercial and shipping interests mindful of their profitable prewar trade with Britain. John
Adams, unlike most of his party in favoring "Mr. Madison's war,"
believed that, as on the previous occasion, one out of three persons opposed the struggle. The *Connecticut Courant,* viewing
affairs with partisan bias, declared on March 7, 1815, after the
hostilities had ceased, that more than two thirds of the people
north of the Potomac had loathed it from the beginning and almost all of them at the end.

The war resolution passed the House 79 to 49 and the Senate
19 to 13, a majority of but three to two of the entire membership.
Nonetheless, as Mathew Carey pointed out at the time, "War then
became the law of the land. It was the paramount duty of all
good citizens to submit to it." The intransigent Federalist minority in the House, however, issued an address denouncing it as
"a party not a national war," undertaken by a "divided people."
In New York and Boston, news of the declaration brought forth
memorials and resolutions of protest, and the Massachusetts Senate pronounced the war "founded in falsehood" and "declared
without necessity."

Flags were hung at half-mast in the Bay State metropolis, and
both pulpit and press kept up the din. According to the Reverend John S. J. Gardiner, rector of Trinity Church, "It is a war unexampled in the history of the world, wantonly proclaimed on
the most frivolous and groundless pretences, against a nation
from whose friendship we might derive the most signal advantages," while the *Boston Gazette* shrieked, "Any man who lends
his money to the government, at the present time, will forfeit all
claim to common honesty and common courtesy among all true

friends to the country," and the *Connecticut Courant* at Hartford urged President Madison to resign forthwith. New Englanders, in fact, subscribed less than one out of every thirteen dollars that went into government loans.

As the conflict progressed, the peace party mounted in strength. New Englanders carried on a clandestine trade with the near-by Maritime Provinces for enemy manufactures, which they then marketed in other parts of the country. The Yankee governors uniformly declined to allow their militia to go into the field under federal command, and the Massachusetts Senate, hoping to check the growth of patriotic fervor, resolved that it was "not becoming a moral and religious people to express any approbation of military and naval exploits which are not immediately connected with the defence of our sea-coast and soil."

Talk of seceding from the Union became rife, and in October, 1814, when the nation's morale was dashed by the burning of Washington, the Bay State legislature sent out the call for the famous Hartford Convention to act on New England's grievances. With official delegates from Massachusetts, Connecticut and Rhode Island, the body, meeting for three weeks behind closed doors, disappointed the peace-at-any-price expectations. Instead, the cooler heads committed the rasher spirits to the view that "A severance of the Union by one or more States against the will of the rest, and especially in time of war, can only be justified by absolute necessity." But with the same breath the assemblage demanded certain amendments of the Constitution, one of which would have required a two-thirds majority of both houses of Congress for declaring war or engaging in other belligerent acts except to repel actual invasion. A second convention was to be held in case these proposals were ignored. This menacing movement quickly died, however, when the news arrived of Jackson's victory at New Orleans and of the peace treaty at Ghent.

III

Before the next armed strife occurred, a series of disputes over the slavery question created an atmosphere of tension between North and South amounting to a war of nerves. Although the greatest of these crises, that involving South Carolina nullification, was peaceably weathered in 1833, fresh difficulties developed within a few years over the question of acquiring slaveholding Texas, which had recently won independence from Mexico. In 1844 the Democrats elected James K. Polk on an annexation platform, and the new state was already admitted to the Union when he took office the following March determined to obtain additional Mexican soil extending westward from Texas to the Pacific. To that end he precipitated hostilities by marching troops into a strip of land claimed by both countries and, when the Mexicans resisted, blamed them for starting the fray. "War exists," he told Congress on May 11, 1846, "and, notwithstanding all our efforts to avoid it, exists by the act of Mexico herself."

At once a storm of anger blew up from the Whig Congressmen, who denounced the war as "treason against God" instigated by Southern politicians for more slave territory. Northern editors added to the uproar. "None of the aggressors of Europe or Asia ever resorted to justificatory reasons which were so false and hypocritical as those alleged for our aggressions on Mexico," asserted the *Kennebec Journal* of Augusta, Maine. The Mexicans, agreed the *Xenia Torch Light* in Ohio, "are in the right — we are in the wrong. They may appeal in confidence to the God of battles, but if we look for aid to any other than human power, it must be to the infernal machinations of hell." A convention of New England workingmen resolved that "we will not take up arms to sustain the Southern slaveholder in robbing one-fifth of our countrymen of labor."

Many of the Northern churches, notably of the Congregational, Unitarian and Quaker faiths, took as vociferous a stand. The Boston Unitarian clergyman William E. Channing declared that if he were to enlist it would be on the Mexican side. Three thousand Unitarians addressed an antiwar protest to Congress thirty-six yards long, only to be outdone by a Quaker remonstrance containing nine thousand signatures. Famous authors also spoke out. Thoreau spent a night in the Concord jail rather than pay a tax which might help the government wage the war. (The experience inspired him to write his flaming manifesto on "Civil Disobedience.") James Russell Lowell, choosing homespun satire as his weapon in the *Biglow Papers*, had Massachusetts cry to the South:

Call me coward, call me traiter,
    Jest ez suits your mean idees,—
Here I stand a tyrant-hater,
    An' the friend o' God an' Peace!

President Polk bitterly rebuked the divisionists in his message
to Congress in December, 1846, asserting, "The war has been
represented as unjust and unnecessary, and as one of aggression
on our part upon a weak and injured enemy. . . . A more ef-
fectual means could not have been devised to encourage the
enemy and protract the war." But his words had no effect. The
legislatures of Vermont, Rhode Island, Massachusetts and Maryland roundly condemned the "hateful" war, the Bay State body
calling upon "all good citizens to join in efforts to arrest" it "in
every just way."

After the Whigs carried the national House of Representatives
in the fall of 1846, petitions and editorials urged Congress to
stop the carnage by withholding appropriations. Though the
Whig members flinched from going that far, they intensified their
verbal barrage. Abraham Lincoln, a newcomer from Illinois in
the House, helped to press the attack, while Ohio's Thomas Corwin in the Senate declaimed, "Were I a Mexican, I would welcome these invaders with bloody hands to hospitable graves."
Little wonder that the *Washington Union,* the principal administration organ, fumed,

> The floor of Congress is another section of the field of con-
> flict. There the cause of Mexico is maintained with zeal and
> ability; . . . there the war is branded with every abusive
> epithet, and the President of our country, . . . before whose
> vigorous arm the invading enemy had fled into his strong-
> hold, is denounced as a bloody tyrant and murderer.

Finally, in January, 1848, after a year and a half of field operations, the House formally resolved by a vote of 85 to 81
(Lincoln siding with the majority) that the war had been "un-
necessarily and unconstitutionally begun by the President of the
United States." But peace was already in sight, and a month later
the Treaty of Guadalupe Hidalgo brought the obstructionism to
an end.

IV

"The Mexican War," asserted Abiel A. Livermore a few years later in his *War with Mexico Reviewed* (1850), "will be a standing topic of crimination and recrimination, through the present generation, if not during a longer time. It has sown our soil with dragons' teeth, and they will spring up armed men." He spoke no more than the truth, for the question of slavery in the former Mexican possessions deepened sectional animosities and started the train of events that culminated in 1861 in the South's attempt to dismember the Republic.

In the struggle to preserve the Union the North might have been expected to present a united front, but such was not the case. As the Southern states began to secede after Lincoln's election, many Northern spokesmen counseled a do-nothing policy. Horace Greeley's *New York Tribune*, the country's most influential paper, declared, "If the Cotton States shall become satisfied that they can do better out of the Union than in it, we shall insist on letting them go in peace." A national convention of workingmen at Philadelphia echoed, "Our Government never can be sustained by bloodshed but must live in the affections of the people." Other groups, though for different reasons, took a similar stand. Abolitionists like William Lloyd Garrison and Senator Charles Sumner welcomed secession as a means of cleansing the North of any guilt for slavery, while businessmen, anxious about the stoppage of trade and the collection of unpaid Southern debts, also favored peaceful dissolution. Mayor Fernando Wood even proposed that New York constitute itself a free city and continue relations with both the old Union and the new Confederacy.

But the firing on Fort Sumter in April, 1861, placed all these elements, including for a time Wood himself, squarely behind Lincoln's policy of armed coercion. There remained, however, a powerful pro-Confederate sentiment in the North, notably among the Democrats of the Ohio Valley states, where many of the inhabitants were of Southern birth or blood. As the war progressed, these irreconcilables or "Copperheads" carried on a defeatist propaganda in the press and on the stump, and a considerable number banded together in secret oath-bound societies such as the Knights of the Golden Circle, the Order of American Knights and the Sons of Liberty, groups which harbored military as well as political designs and sought to obstruct enlistments and the operation of the draft. One of their songs cruelly parodied a Northern recruiting song:

> We are coming, Abraham Lincoln,
>   From mountain, wood, and glen;
> We are coming, Abraham Lincoln,
>   With the ghosts of murdered men.
> Yes! we're coming, Abraham Lincoln,
>   With curses loud and deep,
> That will haunt you in your waking,
>   And disturb you in your sleep.

Clement L. Vallandigham, who later became "supreme commander" of these undercover bands, claimed in 1863 that they numbered half a million members — a figure undoubtedly inflated though accepted by the Judge Advocate General of the United States as approximately correct. "Judea," declared that official, "produced but one Judas Iscariot and Rome from the sinks of her demoralization but one Catiline; and yet, as events proved, there has arisen in our land an entire brood of such traitors all animated by the same patricidal spirit." Had the South not counted on their help, commented the *Dover* (New Hampshire) *Enquirer*, she would never have risked war with the Union.

The Copperheads wielded their greatest influence in 1863 when the fighting reached its most critical stage. In Indiana they kept the legislature from adopting any prowar measures, forcing the patriotic Republican governor to act as best he could on his own authority, while in the President's own state of Illinois the House of Representatives demanded an immediate armistice and a negotiated peace. In Ohio, Vallandigham's state, the ex-Congressman was arrested for publicly assailing the war as "wicked and cruel" and waged "for the purpose of crushing out liberty and erecting a despotism." A military tribunal sentenced him to prison for the duration of the hostilities; but Lincoln, perhaps recalling his own attitude during the Mexican War and wishing in no case to make Vallandigham a martyr, shrewdly altered the verdict to banishment to the Confederacy. While Vallandigham

was still on Southern soil, however, the Ohio Democrats nomi-
nated him for governor; and escaping through the federal blockade, he conducted his campaign from across the border in
Canada. Though defeated, he polled 187,000 votes — 40 per cent
of the total — an ominous showing in so important a state. He
might have won but for two things: 39,000 of the 41,000 soldier
ballots went against him, and the flagging morale of the civilian
voters had been revived by the recent Union successes at Vicks-
burg and Gettysburg.

Even as late as the national election of the next year the Copperheads continued active though with diminishing effect. The
Republicans themselves had doubts about running the President
again, and though they did so, Lincoln privately recorded his
opinion toward the end of the summer that "it seems exceedingly
probable that this Administration will not be reëlected." The
Democratic platform, influenced by Vallandigham, whose presence at the convention the federal authorities ignored, termed the
war "four years of failure" and called for immediate negotiations
to restore the Union. Their candidate, General George B.
McClellan, however, repudiated these sentiments, leaving the
country uncertain as to what course a Democratic regime, if
elected, would pursue. The outcome hung in the balance until
the victories of Sherman, Sheridan and Farragut in September
tilted the scales for the Republicans. Even so, Lincoln was returned by only 55 per cent of the popular vote, the Southern
states, of course, not participating. Five months later the Confederacy collapsed, and another chapter in wartime dissidence
came to a close.

v

The Civil War ended sectionalism as a danger to internal security; and in the years that followed, the unprecedented growth
of industry and agriculture, the occupation of the last frontier and
the tightening bonds of better means of conveyance and communication helped create an overarching unity which enabled
regional and class differences to be arbitrated at the ballot box
and in legislative halls. The English historian Edward A. Freeman, visiting America in the 1880's, observed that "where the

word 'federal' used to be used up to the time of the civil war, the word 'national' is now used all but invariably."

Peaceful relations with foreign powers buttressed the sense of national safety, fostering isolationist sentiments and the rise of an organized peace movement. The huge influx of immigrants introduced imponderables into the scene, but the newcomers adjusted quickly to their adopted country, and for a long time there occurred no war with their homelands to disturb their loyalty to the United States. With them also came the ideology of socialism directed against all wars as imperialistic adventures unless fought for the overthrow of capitalism. This half-century of peace after 1865 was only briefly interrupted by the Spanish War of 1898, an occasion which reminded old-stock Americans of how completely the former rift between North and South had closed. Confederate veterans rushed to enlist, and the nation happily sang, "He laid away a suit of gray to wear the Union blue."

Thus, when the World War of 1914 broke out, there were latent elements of domestic disunity but at first an almost universal agreement that the European strife was no business of the United States. "Peace-loving citizens of this country," asserted the *Chicago Herald,* "will now rise up and tender a hearty vote of thanks to Columbus for having discovered America." President Wilson early in his administration had resisted journalistic clamor to occupy Mexico by force in order to put down civil strife, and his Secretary of State, William Jennings Bryan, had long been preaching to Chautauqua audiences the gospel of international peace. Perceiving no questions at stake vital to America in the hostilities abroad, Wilson exhorted his countrymen to be "impartial in thought as well as in action," and a *Literary Digest* poll revealed the extent to which he mirrored the common view. Two hundred and forty-two newspaper editors professed indifference as to the outcome, one hundred and five others thought England and her allies had the juster cause and twenty expressed pro-German sympathies.

Isolationism plus an ardor for peace underlay this hands-off attitude. But as the contest went on, with America's maritime rights increasingly jeopardized and imperial Germany pressing dangerously toward victory, the public, while still averse to tak-

ing up arms, began to divide into camps. Concern for democratic
Britain and France came to predominate in the press and on the
platform, and both Congress and the administration leaned toward a policy of benevolent neutrality. But, as yet, only a tiny
minority, spearheaded by the bellicose Theodore Roosevelt,
wanted to use the mailed fist against the "Hun."

What George Washington had called the "insidious wiles of foreign influence" penetrated the country mostly in the shape of British propaganda, but these endeavors hardly did more than crys-
tallize long-held sentiments resting on common political ideals
and historic ties of language, literature and trade. Counterprop-
aganda, incited by the German and Austrian embassies and
consulates, made little impression, though Teutonic-inspired attempts to foment strikes and sabotage succeeded at some ship
docks and munition plants. The German-American Alliance's
efforts, however, attracted appreciable support from persons of
German extraction, as well as from professional Irishmen in
America, such as the Friends of Irish Freedom, who believed
that England's defeat would hasten Erin's independence. Yet,
even with strong backing from native pacifist groups, the Alliance could not induce Congress to ban munition shipments to the
Allies — an action which would have violated international usage
— nor could it dissuade the public from buying Allied war bonds.

Nevertheless President Wilson, fearing the possible consequences of importing foreign feuds into domestic affairs, told
Congress in December, 1915, that the "gravest threats" to American security were not from without, but from citizens "born under
other flags . . . who have poured the poison of disloyalty into
the very arteries of our national life." Let every American, he
admonished in the spirit of George Washington, "prove himself
a partisan of no nation but his own." He did not distinguish
between the two sets of belligerents, but in the popular mind his
condemnation helped fasten the stigma of "hyphenated Americans" on partisans of German and Irish stock.

Wilson himself continued to adhere to his original conception
of the nature of the war. The United States, he assured Congress,
had "no part or interest in the policies which seem to have
brought the conflict on." Six months later, addressing the League
to Enforce Peace, he repeated, "With its causes and its objects

we are not concerned." This belief mustered popular support behind him notably in the Middle West, the stronghold of pacifism and isolationism, and the Democratic campaign slogan, "He kept us out of war," weighted the balance in his favor in the election of 1916. As late as January 22, 1917, he still saw no ideological distinction between the rival coalitions, informing the Senate he hoped for an inconclusive outcome, "a peace without victory."

Within less than three months, however, he summoned the people to arms to preserve the principles of democracy against German militarized authoritarianism. "Neutrality," he now told Congress, "is no longer feasible or desirable where the peace of the world is involved and the freedom of its peoples, and the menace to that peace and freedom lies in the existence of autocratic governments backed by organized force which is controlled wholly by their will, not by the will of their people." In the interval, Germany, after having earlier yielded to America's protests, had resumed unrestricted submarine warfare, Wilson had learned of Berlin's scheme to draw Mexico into the struggle in case the United States entered, and a revolution in Russia had replaced the despotic czarist regime with Kerensky's popular government (though Japan, another antagonist of Germany, remained as undemocratic as before). The war resolution passed the House 373 to 50, and the Senate 82 to 6. Thirty-nine of the dissenting votes — 36 in the lower chamber — were cast by Midwesterners.

This about-face of the President and of a substantial body of American opinion, involving both military intervention and a changed view of the nature of the contest, incited fears of domestic discord. When the Socialist party promptly declared its "continuous, active and public opposition" to this "crime" of the capitalist class, something like hysteria gripped the nation, though the Socialists had polled only 3 per cent of the popular vote in 1916 and many members, including that year's presidential nominee, now bolted the party. Other cores of antiwar activity, even smaller and less representative, were the socialistic Industrial Workers of the World in a few Western mining towns and the pacifist Farmers' Nonpartisan League in the Dakotas.

Nevertheless, Congress in great alarm passed a series of drastic laws in 1917 and 1918 to stamp out disaffection and sedition, and the federal authorities conducted a widespread witch hunt. Eugene V. Debs, four times Socialist candidate for President, was among those sent to prison. As Professor Chafee has put it, "It became criminal to advocate heavier taxation instead of bond issues, to state that conscription was unconstitutional though the Supreme Court had not yet held it valid, to say that the sinking of merchant vessels was legal, to urge that a referendum should have preceded our declaration of war, to say that war was contrary to the teachings of Christ."

The Middle West, sloughing off its earlier pacifism, vied with other sections in patriotism, while the "hyphenates," from whom the most trouble might have been expected, afforded little or none. With rare exceptions their worst offense was a passive attitude. Nonetheless, local communities in an excess of zeal mobbed and persecuted former pro-Germans and even boycotted Teutonic music and musicians. The public displayed the extravagant emotions associated with sudden religious conversion. No doubt, too, memories of mass disloyalty, such as had complicated earlier wars, haunted the men's minds. In reality, such fears had slight basis. The war effort was at no time in danger. The people had never before been so united in a time of national peril.

VI

But disillusion quickly followed the triumph over Germany. Perhaps the martial spirit had been too revivalistic in character, too little impregnated with the ideological purposes which Wilson had at the last moment proclaimed. Perhaps, also, the military operations had ended too quickly to bring home complete realization of the threat of full-scale modern war to humanity. At any rate, the restoration of peace engendered bitterness toward the Allies, repudiation of the principles of the struggle, the disowning of America's own war statesmen and a resurgence of isolationism. Not only did the Senate reject the League of Nations and the World Court, but a Senate committee in the mid-1930's, headed by Gerald P. Nye of North Dakota, drew sinister conclusions from the facts it dug up concerning the huge profits which United States bankers, munition makers and other "mer-

chants of death" had reaped from relations with the Allies before
the intervention. An angry Congress proceeded to revamp the
neutrality regulations in order to preclude these and other possibilities of involvement for the future. In April, 1937, just twenty
years after America's entry, a Gallup poll indicated that 70 per
cent of the people believed the intervention to have been a mistake. A later survey recorded 34 per cent as blaming it on "propaganda and selfish interests," while only 26 per cent thought
"America had a just and unselfish cause."

This retreat from the world had somehow to be countermanded
if the country was to meet the situation created by the rise of new
predatory militarisms abroad. That such a reversal took place
was due partly to the frightening events themselves and partly to
the leadership of Franklin D. Roosevelt, who entered office in
1933, the year Hitler seized power in Germany. Over a period of
eight years Japan's aggressions on China, Italy's on Ethiopia and
Albania, and Germany's on her defenseless neighbors were impressed upon the mass of Americans by radio, news film
and press. They heard the Nazi Fuehrer scream his undying
hatred of "decadent democracy" over the air waves. They sent
money to rescue Jews and other refugees from totalitarian
savagery.

In October, 1937, Roosevelt pointed the moral in a speech at
Chicago, calling upon peace-loving countries to declare a "quar-
antine" against rulers who were breeding a "state of international
anarchy" before which "mere isolation or neutrality" stood helpless. "The peace, the freedom and the security of ninety per cent
of the world," he asserted, "is being jeopardized by the remaining
ten per cent, who are threatening a breakdown of all international
order and law." The nations he addressed proved unwilling to do
more, however, than administer a verbal rebuke to Japan, the
major culprit at the moment; but the American public gained a
new understanding of the ominous drift of affairs.

As the war drew closer, Roosevelt repeatedly tried to stave it
off by appeals to the aggressors to halt before it was too late. He
saw the impending struggle as a disaster for all mankind, his own
country as well as others, and unlike Wilson twenty-five years before, he had no uncertainty as to the ideological issues involved.
Increasingly the people shared his conviction. A Gallup survey

in February, 1939, indicated that more than two out of three favored any means "short of war" to support the Western democracies, if occasion demanded, against the Axis powers. When Britain and France at last declared hostilities against Germany on September 3 in defense of invaded Poland, Roosevelt that evening informed a nation-wide radio audience that the government would observe neutrality, "but I cannot ask that every American remain neutral in thought as well. . . . Even a neutral cannot be asked to close his mind or his conscience."

A Gallup poll several weeks later recorded 84 per cent of the country as wishing the Allies to win and but 2 per cent wanting a Nazi victory. Only 5 per cent, however, desired an immediate plunge into the fight, though 29 per cent were willing to intervene whenever the Allies should appear to be losing. This analysis probably disclosed with reasonable accuracy the varying shades of sentiment. Unlike the situation at the outbreak of the first German war, immigrant ties with the aggressive powers played little part. Not only had the quota legislation of the 1920's greatly reduced the inflow from Central and Southern Europe, but many of the arrivals were fugitives from Nazi and Fascist tyranny. As might be expected, the second and third generations tended to think like Americans of older stock, while the Irish-American hatred of England had softened since the setting up of the Irish Free State in 1922.

The Nazi authorities, nevertheless, did what they could to confuse American opinion and win support. But the Berlin government's attempt through underground channels to indoctrinate persons of Teutonic extraction with the idea that blood ties transcended allegiance to the United States met with response mainly from anti-Semitic bigots banded in chapters of the German-American Bund in some of the larger cities. They drilled and *heiled* in private and staged open meetings to castigate the Allies. A lunatic fringe of organizations of native background, such as the Silver Shirts, the Christian Front and the Christian Mobilizers, also denounced Jews and upheld totalitarian doctrines. Then after Mussolini entered the fray as Hitler's partner in June, 1940, his consulates added to the isolationist and appeasement propaganda, largely through the Italian-language press. Later that month an excited Congress, taking cognizance of these activities, passed a law requiring the registration and fingerprinting of all aliens, broadening the grounds for their deportation and severely restricting utterances and writings of a seditious tendency, even by the native-born.

A knottier problem while the Nazi-Soviet pact lasted was the plotting of American Communists who, though inconsiderable in number, instigated strikes and sabotage in order to obstruct the making of war materials. But their belief that the Western democracies were fighting an "imperialist war" vanished overnight when Hitler in June, 1941, launched a surprise assault upon Russia, their ideological fatherland. Henceforth the Communists and their fellow travelers became vociferous interventionists.

These schemes to cast public opinion in foreign molds had slight effect, however, on the main course of the controversy. This debate, which began with the opening shots of the contest and reached a white heat of intensity after the fall of France in June, 1940, revealed long-standing national attitudes. Extreme isolationists, headed by the well-financed America First Committee, of which Robert E. Wood, a brigadier general in the earlier war against Germany, was chairman, saw no issue at stake either of national security or of ideology and insisted on rigid neutrality. In Congress they had spokesmen in such men as Representative Hamilton Fish of New York and Senators Nye, Burton K. Wheeler of Montana and Robert A. Taft of Ohio; in the journalistic field, in such organs as the *Chicago Tribune*, the Hearst press and the *Saturday Evening Post*. At the opposite pole stood the interventionists who, judging the Axis dictators by both word and deed, considered the struggle a world revolution of totalitarianism against the free way of life. They demanded participation at once while resistance to Nazi might still continued in Europe rather than wait till America, fighting alone, should herself fall a victim. Strongest in the East, where the importance of preserving the Atlantic against predatory powers was keenly felt, the interventionists had adherents in many parts of the land, notably the South.

Midway between these extremes was the predominant sentiment of the country. Deeply convinced of the irrepressible conflict between the two systems of society, the bulk of the nation wanted to be as unneutral as possible without entering the fight.

This represented the administration's own attitude, and a militant Committee to Defend America by Aiding the Allies, led by William Allen White, widely known progressive Republican editor of Emporia, Kansas, strove to make certain that the popular support should be unwavering. As the government embarked upon successive measures short of war — repeal of the arms embargo, peacetime conscription, lend-lease, the convoying of ships to England, and the like — the public through opinion polls gave advance assurance of its backing. In the Democratic Congress more Republicans opposed than supported such steps; but it is clear that these did not speak for the rank and file, for in 1940 the party nominating convention shelved Taft and other isolationist aspirants in favor of Wendell Willkie, an ardent champion of aid to Britain, on a platform endorsing his stand. America therefore was one as to foreign policy in the campaign, and Roosevelt's third election in defiance of unbroken tradition meant simply that at so critical a time the voters preferred an experienced captain on the bridge.

By the autumn of 1941, according to a Gallup poll, two out of three citizens thought it more important to defeat Hitler than for America to stay out. Already the United States was waging undeclared hostilities against Nazi submarines in the North Atlantic, and an official break with Berlin was in sight when the Japanese war lords, angered by Roosevelt's stiffening attitude toward their aggressions in Asia, precipitated the crisis on December 7 by treacherously attacking Pearl Harbor. Congress with a single dissenting voice accepted the gage of battle, and when Germany and Italy declared war on America a few days later, the vote was unanimous.

Never before had the legislative branch acted so unitedly in the face of war or been so unitedly supported by the people back home. Such differences of opinion as had persisted up to Pearl Harbor disappeared overnight. Compared with 1917, America was prepared morally and mentally for the ordeal; there was no need to whip up eleventh-hour emotions, no occasion for flamboyant patriotism. It could not be contended that British propaganda had this time duped the nation, any more than it could be plausibly argued, in view of the neutrality regulations adopted since the last war, that Wall Street had tricked the country into fighting. The popular mood was sober, grim and unflinching. As the President told Congress a month after the intervention, "The Union was never more closely knit together and this country was never more deeply determined to face the solemn tasks before it."

With a state of national unity so unprecedented, the problem of disaffection or disloyalty scarcely existed. Even enemy aliens gave little trouble. Of over 300,000 unnaturalized Germans only 1715 had to be interned; of nearly 700,000 unnaturalized Italians, only 242. There was not a single important act of sabotage. The Japanese presented a special difficulty, not because of actual subversive conduct but because of the risks due to their concentration in the Pacific Coast military zone. Some 110,000, of whom two out of three were American citizens, were herded into relocation camps outside the prohibited area — an emergency action the harshness of which was later somewhat softened by allowing those of proved loyalty to remove to other parts of the country and even to join the armed forces. Such exceptions apart, public debate and criticism remained virtually unrestricted, no economic radicals were prosecuted for alleged un-American utterances, and there was a complete absence of rabid intolerance and mobbings of individuals suspected of Axis leanings. Contrasting conditions with those during the first German war, the American Civil Liberties Union (whose director had been imprisoned as a conscientious objector on the earlier occasion) happily reported, "Our democracy can fight even the greatest of all wars and still maintain the essentials of liberty."

VII

This comparative historical view of the times that tried men's souls casts significant light on the nature of the martial spirit under American conditions. Save for the Revolutionary War, when the nation was struggling for birth, an amazing latitude of public criticism and defeatist agitation prevailed in all the great crises down to the twentieth century. The country was not disposed to sacrifice the democratic values of the right of dissent even at times when domestic disunity endangered military success. There was indeed the hope that the welter of faultfinding might result in a more efficient conduct of the hostilities. As

Woodrow Wilson summarized the matter, "We do not need less criticism in time of war, but more. It is to be hoped that the criticism will be constructive, but better unfair criticism than autocratic suppression."

In a free society like that of the United States all citizens could hardly be expected to think alike or to submit meekly to the majority will even when facing a common military peril. What certain individuals or groups, rightly or wrongly, deemed a higher duty to their country impelled them to denounce what they considered a mistaken and dishonorable war. In some instances, in fact, time has vindicated the morality of their stand. James Russell Lowell, for example, who implacably opposed the conflict with Mexico, has fared well at the hands of posterity. Indeed, his own government subsequently honored him with diplomatic posts in Spain and England. Conscientious pacifism arising from religious or other convictions was another ingredient in the antiwar attitude, though it has never proved determining. It is to be noted, further, that the dissidents were hardly ever intentional agents of the enemy. The Revolution, which presents a unique case of the conflict of loyalties, affords the single instance of treasonable conduct, with or without enemy pay, on the part of high military and civil officials.

In an important degree, wartime disaffection sprang from the failure of statesmen to prepare the public mind for the ordeal and to clarify in advance the underlying questions of principle. The humane presuppositions of democracy tend to make both political leaders and people blink away the possibility of armed strife in the abiding hope that reason and mutual concession will prevail. Any other course subjects a President to the charge of warmongering and involves the danger of generating a popular hysteria which may actually prevent a peaceable adjustment. But Franklin Roosevelt succeeded at this difficult task of educating the electorate where Woodrow Wilson did not even attempt it. One can only surmise what would have been the effect on Northern unity if men of Lincoln's insight had been in the White House in the 1850's instead of time-serving politicians. Lincoln with all his superb gifts of exposition and persuasion came into office too late to undo the damage.

Dissension behind the lines has not only hindered a single-minded prosecution of hostilities, but it has fortified the enemy's hopes of achieving victory because of the internal differences. To that extent disunity has served to prolong the fighting and exacted a heavier toll in life and treasure. It has been merely America's good fortune that in her wars before the twentieth century the foe usually suffered from similar divisions.

In this as well as other ways our own century has given unprecedented importance to wartime unity of opinion. The enemy on each occasion consisted of a coalition of highly centralized, militaristic regimes which ruthlessly suppressed domestic dissent. A divided America would have been intolerably handicapped in the circumstances. Furthermore, success in the field no longer depends on the exertions of an armed fraction of the inhabitants but on a comprehensive and integrated effort of the whole people. "Under modern conditions," as Secretary of War Newton D. Baker pointed out in 1917, "wars are not made by soldiers only, but by nations. . . . The army is merely the point of the sword." This has required a general conscription, with every able-bodied man assigned to an allotted task whether in the fighting services or industry. Moreover, other citizens in their various walks of life must also make a maximum contribution to the effort. In order to win the shooting war it is essential to win the war of production.

This battle behind the lines has rendered an unquestioning loyalty indispensable. The enemy by secret means can strike damaging blows by crippling the output of defense industries and disrupting transportation. German agents and sympathizers so worked to promote strikes and sabotage in the neutral years 1914–1917, and the Socialist party and the I.W.W. apparently hoped to accomplish a like purpose after America's entry. With greater success the Communists, strongly entrenched in sectors of the labor movement, pursued similar tactics in the subsequent period of neutrality. It was only America's good fortune that the collapse of the Nazi-Soviet pact in June, 1941, reversed the party line and turned them into Hitler's furious antagonists. Had the alliance endured, the United States as a belligerent would have been confronted with a problem of national security exceedingly hard to solve. To this extent American solidarity in the war was a gift from Hitler himself.

The new face of events in the twentieth century prompted Congress to enact the restrictive legislation of 1917, 1918 and 1940, which exceeded in harshness the Alien and Sedition Acts of the 1790's. Repressive measures, however, cannot alone cure the evil. They may indeed render the opposition more dangerous by driving it underground, and in the hands of overzealous legislators and hysterical administrators may even curb legitimate discussion and criticism. The long-term remedy lies in maintaining a type of society which, if war ever comes again, will evoke the people's dynamic loyalty, a way of life which constantly demonstrates its superiority over any rival system, whether of the extreme right or the extreme left. Democracy, in other words, must unremittingly show its capacity to advance the general welfare without sacrifice of basic human freedoms. It is in this respect, above all others, that the nation in peace must prepare for war in the full knowledge that in so preparing for war the soundest foundations are also laid for the fruits of peace.

AMPERSAND

11

The city in American civilization

"THE true point of view in the history of this nation is not the Atlantic Coast," declared Frederick Jackson Turner in his famous essay of 1893, "it is the Great West." Professor Turner, writing in Wisconsin, had formed his ideas in an atmosphere of profound agrarian unrest, and the announcement of the Superintendent of the Census in 1890 that the frontier line could no longer be traced impelled him to the conclusion that "the first period of American history" had closed. His brilliant paper occasioned a fundamental reappraisal of the mainsprings of national development.

Today, however, it seems clear that in the zeal to correct older notions he overlooked another order of society which, rivaling the frontier even in the earliest days, eventually became the major force. The city marched westward with the outposts of settlement, always injecting exotic elements into pioneer existence, while in the older sections it steadily extended its dominion over politics, economics and all the other phases of life. The time came, in 1925, when Turner himself confessed the need of "an urban reinterpretation of our history." A true understanding of America's past demands this balanced view — an appreciation of the significance of both frontier and city. The broad outlines of the particular role of the city are here suggested.

I

The Atlantic shore constituted the original frontier. Though the great bulk of colonists took up farming, the immediate object of the first settlers was to found a village or town, partly for mutual protection and partly as a base for peopling the nearby country. Other advantages presently gave these places more lasting reasons for existence. There persons could enjoy friendly intercourse with their neighbors as in Europe and there, too, ply a variety of occupations. These communities, besides taking in farm produce for consumption and export, developed local manufactures, arts and crafts and carried on fisheries and an active overseas trade. Without the articles so provided — hardware, firearms, medicine, books and the like — the colonial standard of living would have greatly suffered.

In time the coastline became beaded with towns, many of them so well situated with respect to geographic and trading advantages as to grow into the great cities of today. The establishment of settlements like Albany in New York and Lancaster in Pennsylvania, moreover, foreshadowed the rise of urban communities inland. If colonial towns seem small by modern standards, it is well to remember that this was also true of contemporary English provincial towns, for industrialization had not yet concentrated populations in the homeland. Philadelphia with forty thousand people on the eve of Independence was one of the metropolises of the British Empire.

From the outset townsfolk were plagued with what would today be called urban problems. There were disadvantages as well as advantages in living close together, and as these disadvantages became flagrant, the citizens were moved to action. Though they seldom assumed community responsibilities willingly, their record compares favorably with that of provincial cities in the mother country. To combat the increase of crime the public-spirited in some places maintained night watches out of their own purses, while in others the city fathers required persons to take turns guarding the streets by night on pain of fines. Sooner or later, however, the taxpayers accepted such policing as a normal municipal charge. The fire hazard early prodded the authorities to regulate the construction of chimneys, license chimney sweeps and oblige householders to keep water buckets; and when these measures fell short of the requirements in the eighteenth century, the people formed volunteer companies which, long after the colonial period, continued to be the chief agency of fire fighting. The removal of garbage generally devolved upon roving swine and goats, while drainage remained pretty much an unsolved problem, though occasional individuals laid private sewers. The pressure of urban needs also fertilized American inventiveness, producing Franklin's lightning rod and the fireplace stove.

Thanks to the special conditions of town life, the inhabitants developed a sense of collective responsibility in their daily concerns that increasingly distinguished them from the individualistic denizens of the farm and frontier. Other circumstances served to widen the distance. As cities grew in size and substance, they engaged in economic rivalry with one another which tended to ignore the interests of the intervening countryside. Boston, New England's metropolis, possessed special mercantile advantages which enabled her for nearly a century to maintain a position of primacy in British America, with New York, Philadelphia and lesser centers hardly more than commercial satellites. These other ports, however, contended as best they could for their share of ocean-borne traffic and briskly cultivated their local trading areas.

New Yorkers, for example, successfully fought the proposal of the East New Jersey authorities to erect a competing port at Perth Amboy, and for a time prevailed upon the provincial legislature to tax and otherwise hinder Boston's commerce with eastern Long Island. The fur trade with the Iroquois brought Manhattan and Albany businessmen immense profits, but watchful of every advantage, the New Yorkers contested with Philadelphia for the trade of the Susquehanna region. Farther to the south, Charleston and Virginia merchants staged a similar struggle for the deerskins of the back country, with the South Carolinians emerging victorious. An unpremeditated result of this fierce competition for pelts was a notable stimulus to westward exploration and settlement.

As the eighteenth century advanced, Boston's rivals came to stand securely on their own feet, aided by their rapidly developing hinterlands. New York now completed its sway over western Connecticut and eastern New Jersey, while Philadelphia merchants annexed western Jersey, Delaware and northern Maryland. So eager was the pursuit of business that the chambers of commerce of New York and Charleston, formed respectively in

1768 and 1774, antedated all others in English-speaking lands. Meanwhile, in the tributary areas, these early indications of urban imperialism bred jealousies and resentments which were to reach critical intensity in later times. The metropolis of a given region became a symbol of deception and greed. "A Connecticut Farmer," venting his spleen against New York in the *New-London Gazette*, August 17, 1770, expressed the fervent hope that "the plumes of that domineering city may yet feather the nests of those whom they have long plucked."

Happily for America's future independence, Britain's new revenue policy after 1763 struck deep at the roots of urban prosperity. The business classes rallied promptly to the defense of their interests and, heedless of the dangers of playing with fire, secured the backing of the artisan and mechanic groups. Throughout the decade of controversy the seaports set the pace of resistance, supplying most of the militant leaders, conducting turbulent demonstrations at every crisis, and mobilizing farmer support when possible. Even in rural commonwealths like Virginia and Maryland the most effective steps of opposition were taken when the colonists consulted together at the provincial capitals while attending legislative sessions. Boston's foremost position in the proceedings may well have arisen from the fact that, having recently fallen behind Philadelphia and New York in the commercial race, she was resolved at any cost to stay the throttling hand of Parliament. With the assembling of the First Continental Congress the direction of the movement shifted to Philadelphia, the principal city, presently to become first capital of the new Republic.

The colonial town, however, was more than an embodiment of political and economic energies or a means of gratifying the gregarious instinct. Cities, then as now, were places where one found a whole gamut of satisfactions. Ports of entry for European settlers and goods, they were also ports of entry for European thought and standards of taste. At the same time their monopoly of printing presses, newspapers, bookstores and circulating libraries exposed the residents to a constant barrage of mental stimuli. Hence the spirit of innovation expressed itself quite as much in intellectual as in commercial undertakings. It was townsfolk who led in founding schools and colleges. The protracted battle to establish inoculation as a preventive against smallpox was fought out in the cities. The first great victory for freedom of the press was won by a Philadelphia lawyer defending a New York editor. Besides, mere numbers of people made it possible for the professions to become more clearly differentiated, so that a merchant need no longer plead cases before the courts nor a clergyman practice medicine. Before the colonial period ended, bar associations and medical societies were flourishing in New York, Boston and elsewhere, and medical schools were drawing students to Philadelphia and New York.

The man whom a biographer has called the "first civilized American" was the scion of not one but many cities. Boston, Philadelphia, London and Paris all contributed to Benjamin Franklin's intellectual growth and social understanding. Few elements of American culture but are indebted to his fostering care: printing, publishing, journalism, belles-lettres, education, the postal service, theoretical and applied science. All these achievements rested in final analysis on that interest, encouragement and financial support which a populous community alone could provide. How diligently Franklin utilized these advantages appears in his autobiography, which reveals, for instance, how he set about arousing his fellow Philadelphians to the need of such projects as a lending library, a hospital and the American Philosophical Society.

Yet Franklin with all his many-sidedness was less "civilized" than urban society as a whole: his ambit of interests did not embrace the theater, architecture or an active concern with art. In all these lines the pre-Revolutionary town, with the steady increase of wealth and leisure, showed a growing maturity. Cities, for example, vied with one another for the services of outstanding portraitists. Robert Feke, a Newport artist, painted also in Boston, New York and Philadelphia. John Singleton Copley of Boston found on a visit to New York "so many that are impatient to sit that I am never at a loss to fill up all my time." Like the Philadelphian Benjamin West, however, Copley eventually removed to London.

The city, both in its internal life and external relations, deeply affected colonial society politically, economically and culturally. Though in 1776 only about one in twenty-five Americans dwelt

in places of eight thousand or more, the urban influence, thanks
to its concentrated character, carried far greater weight than its
fractional representation in the population indicated. Moreover,
city residents evolved a pattern of life which not only diverged
from, but increasingly challenged, that of countryside and frontier. These restless, aspiring urban communities foreshadowed
the larger role that cities would play in the years ahead.

II

That role townsfolk began to assume in the struggle for a
strong central government following the Revolution. As a contemporary newspaper observed, "The citizens in the seaport
towns . . . live compact; their interests are one; there is a constant connection and intercourse between them; they can, on
any occasion, centre their votes where they please." Faced by
interstate trade restrictions, stay laws and growing social turmoil, the urban business and creditor classes feared for their
future welfare and the sanctity of property rights. The framing
and ratification of the Constitution represented in considerable
degree their triumph over the debtor groups and small farmers
of the interior. In the circumstances the first Congress under the
new instrument was greeted with petitions from Philadelphia,
New York, Boston and Baltimore for a tariff to protect American
manufactures.

The underlying strife between city and country led also to the
formation of the first national parties under the Constitution.
Hamilton's famous financial plan, intended to benefit urban capitalists and thus indirectly the nation, formed the rallying point
of the Federalists, while Jefferson, imbued with physiocratic
notions, organized the Republican opposition. The Virginia
planter, unlike the New York lawyer, dreaded the growth of a
powerful moneyed class, and in the spread of cities he foresaw
a repetition of the social miseries typical of the Old World. "For
the general operations of manufacture," he declared, "let our
work-shops remain in Europe." He could even regard calmly
the destructive yellow-fever epidemics in Philadelphia and other
ports in the 1790's, since the pestilence might teach people to
avoid populous centers.

The contrasting social ideals and economic motives reflected in this early alignment of parties evoked differing views of constitutional interpretation and of particular measures. From that day to this the chief business of American politics has been to reconcile these interests in furtherance of the national welfare. True, the relative purity of the original groupings gradually became diluted. With the multiplication of urban voters through the years, Jefferson's political progeny, confident of the agricultural South, sought also to appeal to city wage earners. By the same token, the opposition party tended to be a coalition of city businessmen and Northern farmers. Hence each party came in time to constitute a battleground of contending urban and rural elements within its own ranks, a situation which continues to characterize American politics.

III

The westward surge of population beginning shortly after the Revolution has obscured the fact that the leading Atlantic cities, though hard hit by the war, soon resumed their growth, and that with the coming of the nineteenth century the rate of urban development in the nation at large far surpassed that of rural development. Between 1800 and 1860 the number of townsfolk increased twenty-four times while the rural population merely quadrupled. By 1810 one out of every twenty Americans lived in communities of eight thousand or more, by 1840 one out of every twelve, and by 1860 nearly one in every six.

Paradoxically enough, westward migration itself helped to bring this about, for the trans-Appalachian region bred its own urban localities. Serving at first chiefly as distributing centers for commodities from the seaboard, these raw settlements quickly developed into marts where local manufacturer and farm dweller exchanged products. Pittsburgh early began to make glass, shoes, iron castings, nails and textiles, and already in 1814 the *Pittsburgh Gazette* was complaining of the sooty atmosphere. By that time Cincinnati, farther down the river, boasted of two woolen mills and a cotton factory, and its meat-packing business was winning it the sobriquet of Porkopolis. Emboldened by such achievements, apparently every cluster of log huts dreamed of equal or greater eminence. The Indiana pioneers, for example, hopefully named their forest hamlets Columbia City, Fountain City, Saline City, Oakland City and Union City or, setting their sights still higher, called them New Philadelphia, New Paris, Rome City and even New Pekin.

Meanwhile, in the East, scores of cities sprang into being, generally at the fall line of the rivers, where water power was available for manufacturing. As the budding industrialists looked about for new worlds to conquer, they, together with the Eastern merchants and bankers, perceived their El Dorado in the settling West. Soon New York, Philadelphia and Baltimore were racing for the trade of the trans-Appalachian country. This clash of urban imperialisms appeared most strikingly perhaps in the rivalry for transportation routes to the interior. The Baltimoreans led off by building a turnpike to tap the eastern terminus of the Cumberland Road, which the federal government by 1818 had completed as far as Wheeling on the Ohio. In order to counter this move, Pennsylvania promoted Philadelphia's wagon trade with the West by subsidizing a chain of roads to Pittsburgh. New York City, utilizing her natural advantages, now secured state backing for an all-water artery through upstate New York from the Hudson to Lake Erie.

The instant success of the Erie Canal, opened in 1825, forced a change of strategy on Manhattan's competitors. Philadelphia with legislative help promptly instituted a part-water, part-land route through the mountains, while Baltimore pushed the project of a Chesapeake and Ohio canal. Other citizens in the Maryland metropolis, however, conceived a bolder plan. Just as the canal had bested the turnpike, why should not the newly invented railroad best the canal? The construction of the Baltimore and Ohio Railroad, begun in 1828, once more altered the major weapons in the contest. In the next quarter of a century Baltimore and Philadelphia completed their rail connections with the West; New York acquired two lines; and Boston, which had lagged behind during the turnpike and canal eras, recovered some of the lost ground with a railroad linking up with the eastern extremity of the Erie Canal.

Middle Western towns, following the Eastern example, meanwhile entered upon a somewhat similar struggle, each seeking to

carve out its own economic dependencies and spheres of influence
and to profit from the new ties with the seaboard. By 1840 a network of artificial waterways joined Cleveland and Toledo on
Lake Erie with Portsmouth, Cincinnati and Evansville on the
Ohio. As in the East, however, the arrival of the steam locomotive changed the situation. Now every up-and-coming municipality strove by hook or crook to become a railroad center, sometimes plunging heavily in debt for the purpose. And looking to
the commercial possibilities of the remoter West, Chicago, St.
Louis, Memphis and New Orleans concocted rival plans for a
Pacific railroad — a maneuvering for position that had political
repercussions in Congress and contributed to the passage of
the Kansas-Nebraska Act in 1854, which it was thought would
facilitate the building of a transcontinental line from St. Louis.
This law, by authorizing slavery by "popular sovereignty" in a
region hitherto closed to it, helped to set the stage for the Civil
War.

The progress in transportation facilities, confined largely to the
North, spurred urban development throughout that part of the
country. The Erie Canal, reinforced by the rail arteries to the
West and the magnificent harbor at the mouth of the Hudson,
established conclusively New York's pre-eminence on the seaboard and in the nation. From only 60,000 inhabitants in 1800
its population (not counting Brooklyn) climbed to 800,000 by
1860, outdistancing Philadelphia and placing it next to London
and Paris in size, while Philadelphia with more than half a million in 1860 was larger than Berlin. Brooklyn, Baltimore and
Boston came next in size. Indicative of the westward movement
of the urban frontier was the fact that at the latter date all the
other centers of over a hundred thousand — New Orleans, Cincinnati, St. Louis and Chicago — were in the heart of the country.
Chicago, though the smallest of these in 1860, had already gathered the economic sinews which would make it New York's chief
rival before the century closed. Anthony Trollope, observing the
Midwest in 1861, remarked that except for a few river and lake
sites "settlers can hardly be said to have chosen their own localities. These have been chosen for them by the originators of the
different lines of railway." Urban communities greatly augmented the demand for farm products, accelerated the invention

of labor-saving implements like the steel plow and the reaper and thus furthered commercial agriculture, which in turn speeded city growth.

To master the new complexities of urban living demanded something more than the easygoing ways of colonial towns. Enlarged populations called for enlarged measures for the community safety and welfare, whether by government or otherwise. As might be expected, the bigger cities set the pace. After the lethal yellow-fever visitations of the 1790's frightened Philadelphia into installing a public waterworks, other places fell into line, so that more than a hundred systems came into existence before the Civil War. Unfortunately, ignorance of the yet-to-be-discovered germ theory of disease fastened attention on clear water instead of pure water, thus leaving the public health still inadequately protected. To cope with the growing lawlessness the leading cities now supplemented night watches with day police. In 1822 Boston instituted gas lighting and in 1823 set the example of a municipally owned sewerage system. About the same time regular omnibus service was started on the streets of New York, to be followed in the next decade by horsecars running on tracks.

Fire fighting, however, continued generally in the hands of volunteer companies. Though Boston organized a paid municipal department in 1837 and Cincinnati and other Western towns greatly improved the apparatus by introducing steam fire engines in the 1850's, New York and Philadelphia, thanks to the political pull of volunteer brigades, resisted changes in equipment and waited respectively till 1865 and 1871 to municipalize their systems. The cities did nothing at all to combat the evil of slums, an unexpected development due to the great inrush of foreign immigrants into the Atlantic ports in the forties and fifties. Even more serious for the ordinary citizen was the growth of political machines, rooted in the tenement-house population, the fire companies and the criminal classes, and trafficking in franchises for the new public utilities. Appointments to government office for partisan services, first practiced in Eastern cities, preceded and led directly to the introduction of the spoils system into state and national politics.

The "diversities of extreme poverty and extreme wealth," which Edwin H. Chapin etched so sharply in *Humanity in the City*

(1854), distressed the tenderhearted and gave rise to most of the reform crusades of the pre-Civil War generation. Compact living facilitated the banding together of such folk and also the collection of funds. Never before had America known so great an outpouring of effort to befriend the poor and the handicapped. Under urban stimulus arose the movement for free schools, for public libraries, for married women's property rights, for universal peace, for prison reform, for a better deal for the insane. The new conditions of city life begot a social conscience on the part of townsfolk which would be of lasting effect and which increasingly differentiated them from their brethren on the farm and frontier.

In these crowded centers, too, the labor movement took form, for the vaunted safety valve of the frontier failed to work for the mass of the wage earners. "The wilderness has receded," declared Orestes A. Brownson in 1840, "and already the new lands are beyond the reach of the mere laborer, and the employer has him at his mercy." Early in the preceding decade trade unions began to appear, first along the seaboard, then at such inland points as Buffalo, Pittsburgh, Cincinnati and St. Louis; and for a short time a national federation flourished. But the long economic slump following the Panic of 1837 shattered most of the organizations and turned the thoughts of men like George Henry Evans, a New York labor editor, to plans for siphoning excess urban inhabitants into the federal domain by means of free farms. During the discussions over the homestead bill of 1852, even an Alabama member urged Congress "to help the cities to disgorge their cellars and their garrets of a starving, haggard, and useless population." But the House measure failed in the Senate, and until the Civil War further attempts went awry because of Southern fears that antislavery Northerners would fill up the Western territories. In any event the farm population would have been the chief beneficiaries, for it is unlikely that urban workingmen could have been enticed to exchange known ills for the hazards and uncertainties of pioneering.

Besides, along with the known ills went cultural opportunities and advantages absent from the countryside. The fast-growing cities afforded the largest public America had yet known for the appreciation and patronage of letters and the arts, and greatly increased the chances for the discovery and recruitment of talent in all fields. Townsfolk, moreover, were the first to feel the bracing impact of new currents of European thought. A varied and vital intellectual life resulted which directly or indirectly affected all members of the community, including the children, for whom municipal authorities now began to provide free high schools.

Newspapers and magazines proliferated. The first modern publishing houses sprang up. The theater became firmly established, with native players like Charlotte Cushman and Edwin Booth winning additional laurels in England. Artists multiplied, being at last assured of adequate support at home, and the founding of the National Academy of Design in 1826 raised New York to the position of the country's chief art center. In literature also this richly creative period demonstrated urban superiority, with Boston, Cambridge and Concord largely responsible for the "flowering of New England," and New York and Philadelphia, even Cincinnati and St. Louis, making their own bids for fame. Only in architecture did the city botch the possibilities, for the mushroom growth of population forced new construction at a pace that ignored aesthetic considerations. The typical city, even in its wealthy residential sections, exhibited a fantastic patchwork of styles.

Whatever the attractions of town life, the elevenfold leap in urban population between 1820 and 1860 aroused increasing dismay and foreboding among rural folk who saw their own sons and daughters succumbing to the lure. "Adam and Eve were created and placed in a garden. Cities are the results of the fall," cried Joseph H. Ingraham, a popular religious novelist. Country preachers joined in denouncing these human agglomerations "cursed with immense accumulations of ignorance and error, vice and crime," while farm journals implored the young not to sacrifice their manly independence in order "to fetch and carry" and "cringe and flatter" for a miserable pittance. Political attitudes further mirrored the deepening distrust. Western opposition to the Second United States Bank sprang largely from alarm at the control of credit facilities by the "great cities of the Northeast, which," according to Missouri's Senator Thomas Hart Benton, "have been for forty years, and that by force of federal legislation, the lion's den of Southern and Western money — that den into which all the tracks point inward; from which the returning track of a solitary dollar has never yet been seen."

Since, however, the West was growing its own towns and cities, it was becoming steadily more like the Northeast, whereas the South, chained by Negro slavery to agriculture, contained few sizable cities and those mostly at its edges. The widening breach between North and South was in no small part due to these divergent tendencies. Every year sharpened the contrast between the urban spirit of progress animating the one section and the static, rural life of the other. Few important industries existed below the Mason and Dixon line. Though illiteracy prevailed among the mass of whites as well as blacks, little or nothing was done to further free schools, and the North's humanitarian crusades were derided as Yankee fanaticism. Moreover, the Southerners, lacking the nerve centers for creative cultural achievement, fell behind in arts, letters and science. "It would have been surprising had they not desired secession," remarked Anthony Trollope, in America shortly after Fort Sumter. "Secession of one kind, a very practical secession, had already been forced upon them by circumstances. They had become a separate people, dissevered from the North by habits, morals, institutions, pursuits and every conceivable difference in their modes of thought and action." Beyond the tie of language, he went on, "they had no bond but that of a meagre political union in their Congress at Washington."

In addition, their economic life lay under thrall to the Northern business community. "It is a hopeless task," affirmed the South Carolinian William Gregg, "to undertake to even approximate to the vast sums of wealth which have been transferred from the South to the North by allowing the Northern cities to import and export for us." For twenty years before the war, Southern commercial conventions sought ways and means to escape this bondage, but the hope of creating their own trading and financial centers was vain so long as lands and Negroes held a superior attraction for capital. It was no mere coincidence that Charleston, dropping rapidly behind the Northern ports, initiated every disunionist movement in the entire South from Jackson's time onward; and the *Charleston Mercury*'s bitter comment in 1858 that "Norfolk, Charleston, Savannah, Mobile, are suburbs of New York" suggests that other places shared the bitterness.

Withdrawal from the Union coupled with free trade with England seemed the answer, since then, it was believed, "Charleston
in the course of ten years will become a New York"; and other
localities nursed similar hopes. Under the circumstances the leading towns and cities strongly supported the movement for separation. Even New Orleans, despite its large infusion of Northerners
and foreign-born, chose twenty secessionists and only four unionists to the state convention summoned to take action. Not sur-
prisingly, the Confederate authorities on assuming power invali-
dated the private indebtedness — estimated variously at forty to
four hundred millions — owing to Northern merchants, bankers
and manufacturers. But the North's industrial might and greater
manpower overwhelmed the South in war as well as in peace.

IV

In the generation following the Civil War the city took supreme command. Between 1860 and 1900 the urban population
again quadrupled while the rural merely doubled. With one out
of every six people inhabiting communities of 8000 or over in
the earlier year, the proportion rose to nearly one out of four
in 1880 and to one out of three in 1900. Considerably more
than half of the urban-moving throng gravitated to places of
twenty-five thousand and upwards. Since every town dweller
added to his effectiveness by association with his fellows, even
these figures understate the city's new role in the nation. Nevertheless the sheer growth of particular localities is amazing. By
1890 New York (including Brooklyn) had about caught up with
Paris, while Chicago and Philadelphia, with over a million each
as compared with New York's two and a half million, then out-
ranked all but five cities in Europe. In the Far West, Los Angeles
jumped from fewer than 5000 in 1860 to more than 100,000 in
1900, and Denver from nothing at all to 134,000, while, in the
postwar South, Memphis with a bare 23,000 in the former year
surpassed 100,000 in the latter. "The youngest of the nations,"
wrote Samuel L. Loomis in 1887, "has already more large cities
than any except Great Britain and Germany." Thanks to the
progress of settlement in the West and the burgeoning of industry
in a South emancipated from slavery, the city had at last become
a national instead of a sectional institution.

As urban centers grew in size and wealth, they cast an ever stronger spell over the American mind. Walt Whitman, returning to Greater New York in September, 1870, after a short absence, gloried in the "splendor, picturesqueness, and oceanic amplitude of these great cities." Conceding that Nature excelled in her mountains, forests and seas, he rated man's achievement equally great "in these ingenuities, streets, goods, houses, ships — these hurrying, feverish, electric crowds of men." (More tersely, Dr. Oliver Wendell Holmes, weary of hearing Cowper's line, "God made the country and man made the town," retorted, "God made the *cavern* and man made the *house!*") Little wonder that the young and the ambitious yielded to the temptation. "We cannot all live in cities, yet nearly all seem determined to do so," commented Horace Greeley, adding that with "millions of acres" awaiting cultivation "hundreds of thousands reject this and rush into the cities."

The exodus from the older countryside proved especially striking. While the cities of Maine, Vermont, Massachusetts, Rhode Island, New York, Maryland and Illinois gained two and a half million people between 1880 and 1890, the rural districts of these states lost two hundred thousand. The drain of humanity from backwoods New England left mute witnesses in deserted hill villages and abandoned farms. In the nation as a whole, 10,063 townships out of 25,746 in thirty-nine states and territories shrank in population during the decade. Some of the rural decline was due to the shifting of agriculturalists from older regions to the free unworked lands of the trans-Mississippi West, but the phenomenon was so widespread — and, indeed, as characteristic of Europe during these years as of America — as to evidence the more potent and pervasive influence of the city. True, the 1880's merely climaxed a historic trend. In the century from 1790 to 1890 the total population had grown 16-fold while the urban segment grew 139-fold. Hence the celebrated announcement of the Superintendent of the Census in 1890 that a frontier line no longer existed can hardly be said to have marked the close of "the first period of American history." Rather it was a tardy admission that the second period was already under way.

The lusty urban growth created problems which taxed human resourcefulness to the utmost. Though European precedent helped solve some of the difficulties, American ingenuity in most respects outdistanced that of Old World cities. The record is extraordinary. Hardly had New York in 1870 opened the first elevated railway than San Francisco contrived the cable car, and hardly had the cable car begun to spread over the country than Richmond demonstrated the superiority of the electric trolley system, and Boston at the end of the century added the subway. The need for better lighting prompted the invention of Brush's outdoor arc lamp and Edison's incandescent bulb for indoors, and in another application of electric power the telephone brought townsfolk into instant communication. By means of the apartment house and the department store cities simplified problems of housing and shopping, while by means of the steel-framed skyscraper they saved further ground space by building their business districts upward. Density of population also led to more effective protection of the public health by turning to account the principles of the germ theory of disease just being discovered abroad. Before the century's close nearly every municipality of ten thousand or over had one or more officials charged with the duty of charting and checking communicable maladies. The bigger cities had become healthier places to live than many rural sections.

These civic advances, however, came at a price already beginning to be evident before the Civil War. Americans had developed their political institutions under simple rural conditions; they had yet to learn how to govern huddled populations. Preyed upon by unscrupulous men eager to exploit the expanding public utilities, municipal politics became a byword for venality. As Francis Parkman wrote, "Where the carcass is, the vultures gather together." New York's notorious Tweed Ring denoted a sickness that racked Philadelphia, Chicago, St. Louis, Minneapolis and San Francisco as well. "With very few exceptions," declared Andrew D. White, "the city governments of the United States are the worst in Christendom — the most expensive, the most inefficient, and the most corrupt."

Though an irate citizenry succeeded now and then in "turning the rascals out," the boss and the machine soon recovered control. Nevertheless, the good-government campaigns ventilated the abuses of municipal misrule and aroused the humane to the worsening plight of the urban poor. Under reform prodding, the

New York legislature from 1865 onward adopted a series of laws to combat the slum evil in America's metropolis, though with disappointing results. More fruitful were the steps taken by private groups in Manhattan and elsewhere to establish social settlements and playgrounds and to replace the indiscriminate almsgiving of earlier times with a more rational administration of charity. Religion, awakening to the social gospel, helped out with slum missions and institutional churches. In the city, too, trade unions made a new start, organizing the swelling army of urban workers on a nation-wide basis, joining with the reformers in securing factory legislation and gradually winning other concessions from the employing class. Occasional voices with a foreign accent advocated socialism or anarchism as the remedy for the city's gross disparities of wealth and want, while Edward Bellamy in *Looking Backward* offered a homemade version of communism in his fanciful account of Boston as it would be in the year 2000.

The increasing tension of living was evidenced in a variety of ways. Masses of people reared in a rustic environment had suddenly to adapt themselves to the frantic urban pace. One outcome was a startling growth of neurasthenia, a word coined by Dr. George M. Beard of New York in his work *American Nervousness* (1881), which traced the malady to the hurry and scurry, the din of the streets, the frenzied struggle for existence, the mental excitements and endless distractions. From the ranks of the high-strung, Mary Baker Eddy gathered most of her converts to the new religion of Christian Science, and for much the same reason townsfolk now gave enthusiastic support to organized sports. Flabby muscles unfitted most persons for direct participation, but they compromised by paying professional contestants to take their exercise for them. If, as a magazine writer said, nervousness had become the "national disease of America," baseball, partly as an antidote, became America's national game.

The stress of existence seemed only to enhance creative powers, however. The cities, re-enacting their role of the "fireplaces of civilization" — Theodore Parker's phrase — provided compelling incentives to cultural achievement, multiplying colleges, public libraries and publishing houses and founding art museums, art schools and conservatories of music. A Henry James might still find Europe an intellectually more congenial milieu, but William

Dean Howells, Mark Twain and Joel Chandler Harris discovered the needed stimulus at home; and the same held true of all or nearly all the leading painters, sculptors, architects, composers, playwrights and scholars. A statistical study showed that localities of eight thousand and more gave birth to almost twice as many men of note as their proportionate share, and that in fields like science, engineering, art and literature the ratio was far greater. But even such computations do less than justice to the city, for there, too, gifted newcomers from the countryside and foreign shores entered their Promised Land. Civic pride prompted the holding of two great expositions, one at Philadelphia in 1876 and the other at Chicago in 1893. That the second and grander took place in an inland metropolis revealed how decisively urbanization had altered the face of traditional America.

The new age of the city rested upon an application of business enterprise to the exploitation of natural resources such as mankind had never known. The city, as insatiable as an octopus, tended to draw all nutriment to itself. Railroads, industrial combinations, investment capital, legislative favors, comprised the means. There arose a complex of urban imperialisms, each striving for dominion, each battling with rivals and each perforce yielding tribute to the lord of them all. "Every produce market, every share market," observed James Bryce, "vibrates to the Produce Exchange and Stock Exchange of New York."

As the city forged ahead, imposing its fiat on less developed regions, the rift between country and town widened portentously. Historians speak of a new sectionalism aligning West and South against East in these years, but Charles B. Spahr in *The Distribution of Wealth in the United States* (1896) pointed out more acutely that the antagonism "only exists in so far as the East is the section of the cities, while the South and West are the sections containing the great body of the farmers." Everywhere rural life was in chains: "The people on the farms and in the villages in the East have shared no more in the advancing wealth of the past quarter of a century than the people on the farms and in the villages of the South and West." He estimated that city families possessed on the average almost three times as much as country families.

The passage of years heightened the husbandman's conviction

of being a second-class citizen, of losing out in the technological
and cultural progress that dowered townsfolk. He lacked the
telephone, electric lighting, central heating, plumbing, sewerage,
street cars, recreational facilities. Herbert Quick in after years
remembered the women as "pining for neighbors, for domestic
help, for pretty clothes, for schools, music, art, and the many
things tasted when the magazines came in." The drift of youth to
the cities emphasized the shortcomings, embittering those who
stayed behind, even though they loved the land and would not
have left if they could. The farmer, moreover, accepted too readily the urban estimate of his calling. Once acclaimed by orators
as the "embodiment of economic independence," now, remarked
a magazine writer, he was the butt of humorists: "The 'sturdy
yeoman' has become the 'hayseed.' "

This feeling of rural inferiority, this growing sense of frustra-
tion, underlay the political eruptions in the farming regions: the
Granger movement in the 1870's, the Farmers' Alliances of the
eighties and the Populist conflagration in the nineties. Each time
specific economic grievances like steep freight rates, high interest
charges and low crop prices stirred the smoldering embers into
blaze. These were tangible hardships which the farmers demanded the government remove by such measures as railroad
regulation and silver inflation. It fell to the greatest of the agrarian champions, addressing the Democratic national convention
in 1896, to hurl the ultimate challenge at urban imperialism.
"Burn down your cities and leave our farms, and your cities will
spring up again as if by magic," cried William Jennings Bryan of
Nebraska in a speech that won him the nomination, "but destroy
our farms and the grass will grow in the streets of every city in
the country." In the election that followed, the big cities of the
East and Midwest, including New York, which for the first time
went Republican, responded by casting decisive majorities
against the Democrats and free silver.

v

No one in 1900 could have foreseen the transformation which
the twentieth century was to effect in both town and country. In
the cities the reformers made steady progress in bridling the

predatory forces which, in James Bryce's familiar phrase, had
made municipal government "the one conspicuous failure of the
United States." Early in the century a crusading type of mayor
rode into power — men like "Golden Rule" Jones and Brand
Whitlock in Toledo, Tom Johnson in Cleveland and Emil Seidel
in Milwaukee — who aroused the citizens from their apathy and
showed that elected officials could zealously promote the public
good. Even more important was the introduction of the commis-
sion-manager plan of government, which by 1960 came to prevail
in nearly a thousand places. A radical departure from the
clumsy older form, which imitated the checks and balances of
state governments, the new system copied the streamlined structure of business corporations, with the commission corresponding
to the board of directors and the city manager resembling the
president or general manager named by the board to conduct detailed affairs. In nearly every case the reform quickly justified itself, though eternal vigilance by the voters continued to be the
price of ensuring the best results.

Alongside these improvements occurred the first sustained attempts at city planning. Instead of letting urban communities
evolve in hit-and-miss fashion, the endeavor now was to guide
their growth in the interests of sightliness and of the people's convenience, safety and health. By an extensive use of zoning ordi-
nances, appropriate locations were mapped for business and factory districts, residential neighborhoods, recreational facilities;
and the New York legislature's adoption of an effective tenement-
house code in 1901 inspired other states and municipalities to a
vigorous attack on the slum evil, though it was not till the 1930's
that the federal authorities took a hand in the matter. Already by
1922 a hundred and eighty-five towns and cities had set up official bodies to chart over-all programs of development, and by
1940 the number had risen to well over a thousand. City planning, moreover, stimulated interest in county planning and state
planning and helped create the atmosphere for the New Deal's
ventures in regional planning.

These advances went hand in hand with a further piling up of
townsfolk. By 1930 approximately half the nation dwelt in localities of eight thousand or more and nearly a third in centers of
one hundred thousand or more. Urban dominance was further

enhanced by the emergence of great metropolitan districts or regions. These "city states" had begun to form in the nineteenth century as swifter means of transportation and communication flung the inhabitants outward into the suburbs, but it was the coming of the automobile and motor truck and the extension of electricity and other conveniences into the surrounding territory that gave these supercommunities their unprecedented size and importance.

Each consisted of one or more core cities with satellite towns and dependent rural areas, the whole knit together by economic, social and cultural ties. The 133 metropolitan regions in 1930 grew to 140 by 1940, when they contained almost half the total population. New York's region overlapped four states, an irregular tract twice the area of Rhode Island, with 272 incorporated communities and intervening farm lands. Chicago's embraced 115 incorporated places, and San Francisco's 38. By 1960 the metropolitan areas numbered 212. Subdivided into independent municipalities, the people faced enormous difficulties in looking after such common governmental concerns as policing, sewage disposal, public health and schooling. Some students, despairing of any other solution, proposed separate statehood for the larger metropolitan regions. New and unanticipated strains have been placed on a federal system framed in the eighteenth century for a simple agrarian economy.

Of all the new trends in urban development, however, none had such profound effects as the altered relationship of country and city. Historians generally attribute the decline of the free-silver movement in the late nineties to the discovery of fresh sources of gold supply and an uptrend of crop prices, but probably the more fundamental cause was the amelioration of many of the social and psychological drawbacks of farm existence. The introduction of rural free delivery of mail after 1896, the extension of good roads due to the bicycle craze, the expanding network of interurban trolleys, the spread of party-line neighborhood telephones after the basic Bell patents expired in 1893, the increase of country schools — all these, coming shortly before 1900, helped dispel the aching isolation and loneliness, thereby making rustic life pleasanter.

Yet these mitigations seem trifling compared with the marvels which the twentieth century wrought. The automobile brought farm families within easy reach of each other and of the city; the motorbus facilitated the establishment of consolidated schools with vastly improved instruction and equipment; while the radio and television introduced new interests and pleasures into the homes themselves, shedding the benefits impartially on country and town. At the same time the mechanical energy used in agriculture grew enormously, thus lightening the husbandman's toil and adding to his opportunities for leisure. Moreover, the state and national governments increasingly employed their powers to improve the farmer's economic and social status. The Smith-Lever Act, passed by Congress in 1914, provided for agricultural-extension work in rural communities through county agents; the Federal Farm Loan Board, created in 1916, offered long-term loans at relatively low rates of interest; and the Smith-Hughes Act of 1917 appropriated public funds for teaching agriculture and home economics in country high schools. Such enactments reached a climax in the 1930's when the New Deal embarked upon far-reaching programs of rural betterment like the Tennessee Valley and Columbia River developments, farm-price supports, government-aided electrification and measures to boost farm tenants up the ladder to ownership. Though inequalities remained, the tiller of the soil had come to share many of the comforts and refinements once belonging only to townsfolk. He had attained a position in American society of which his Populist forebears could hardly have dreamed.

Just as rural life became more urbanized, so urban life became more ruralized. Wooded parks, tree-shaded boulevards, beautified waterfronts, municipal golf courses, athletic fields and children's playgrounds multiplied, while an increasing army of white-collar workers and wage earners piled into motorcars and buses each night to go farther and farther into the suburbs. Within the metropolitan regions population actually grew faster in the rustic outskirts than in the central cities, creating for the latter problems of deficient tax support and the need of concentrated efforts for public housing and like accommodations. Retail trade too felt the centrifugal tug, and even factories showed a tendency to move into outlying villages where taxes, rent and food cost less. The extension of giant power will doubtless speed the trend, affording more and more townsfolk a chance to live and work and bring up their children in country surroundings. The dread specter of nuclear attacks may operate to the same end in the interests of national military security.

Thus the twentieth century has been spinning a web in which city and country, no longer separate entities, have been brought ever closer together. When the city encroaches sufficiently on the country and the country on the city, America may hope to arrive at a way of life which will blend the best features of both the traditional ways. The people will have within grasp the realization of Plato's vision of a society in which "youth shall dwell in a land of health amid fair sights and sounds and imbibe good from every quarter; and beauty, the emanation of noble works, will flow into the eye and ear like an invigorating breeze from a purer region and imperceptibly woo the soul from infancy into harmony and sympathy with the beauty of reason."

From humble beginnings in the early seventeenth century the city thus traced a varied course. In Europe the modern urban community emerged by gradual stages out of the simple town economy of the Middle Ages; by comparison, the American city leaped into being with breath-taking speed. At first servant to an agricultural order, then a jealous contestant, then an oppressor, it now gives evidence of becoming a comrade and co-operator in a new national synthesis. Its economic function has been hardly more important than its cultural mission or its transforming influence upon rural conceptions of democracy. The city, no less than the frontier, has been a major factor in American civilization. Without an appreciation of the role of both the story is only half told.

12

Food in the making of America

THE history of American history is a history of the conflict of interpretations as to the causes of events. Nearly every generation has fitted its own special key to the lock. Wordy battles have raged over the religious factor, the great-man theory, the power of ideas and ideals, the geographic influence, the economic influence, the role of the masses. No single thesis has been able to occupy the field for very long, however, because in reality human motives are so complex — so subtly intermixed with the rational and irrational — that no one explanation by itself is sufficient. Yet, oddly, the continuing search has neglected one clue to the past that is the most basic of all. Men must have food if they are to think and act. Here is a want which precedes and conditions all other hopes, aims and achievements. How has this need affected the history of the American people?

I

The very discovery of the New World was the by-product of a dietary quest. Europe's upper classes in the Middle Ages relied upon imported spices to season their coarse and monotonous fare as well as to preserve food from putrefaction. Spices were so highly prized that sovereigns sometimes exchanged them as ceremonial gifts. The sole source of supply was the Orient whence the precious cargoes, supplemented with other rare commodities, moved slowly by boat and caravan to the Levant, constantly imperiled by both marauders and natural disasters. The Ottoman conquest of Asia Minor in the latter part of the fifteenth century put the Turks astride this route and, by endangering its continuance, turned Europe's thoughts to the possibility of establishing safer connections with the Far East. In particular, the ambitious monarchs bordering on the Atlantic perceived the chance of grabbing the lucrative trade. Soon Portuguese mariners were probing southward along the rim of Africa and eventually rounded the Cape of Good Hope, while Columbus, outfitted by Ferdinand and Isabella, set his prow boldly westward. Portugal succeeded in achieving the goal; Spain had to be content merely with finding a New World.

Though Columbus failed in his object, he and those who followed him made ample amends by laying bare a wealth of foodstuffs such as Europe had never imagined. Their enterprise effected a dietary revolution unparalleled in history save possibly for the first application of fire to the cooking of edibles. Picture the long centuries when the Old World existed without white and sweet potatoes, tomatoes, corn and the many varieties of beans, and you have some notion of the extraordinary gastronomic advance. Add, for good measure, such dishes as pumpkins, squashes, turkeys, cranberries, maple syrup, blackberries, blueberries, raspberries, strawberries, crab apples, chestnuts and peanuts. If historians dealt more with the simple annals of life and less with great affairs of state, they might well consider this transformation of mankind's bill of fare as marking the transition from medieval to modern times. In the four and a half centuries since Columbus blundered into the Western Hemisphere the American has not developed a single indigenous staple beyond those he derived from the Indians. Today, it is estimated, four sevenths of the country's agricultural output consists of plants (including tobacco and a native species of cotton) which were discovered with the New World.

From the older continent the white man brought wheat and other small grains, many kinds of vegetables and the larger fruits, but by introducing domestic poultry, hogs and cattle he probably made his major contribution, since apart from turkeys the wilderness contained no comparable animals. Moreover, some of the native food plants, notably the white potato and the tomato, were slow in becoming known to the English settlers. The potato, immemorially grown by the Peruvian Indians, reached the British in North America after an odyssey of two hundred years involving four crossings of the Atlantic. Carried to Spain in the early sixteenth century after Pizarro conquered the Incas, it was quickly naturalized there, and, probably in the 1560's, Spanish colonizers bore it with them to Florida. Some marauding Englishmen under Sir John Hawkins, coming upon the tuber in its new habitat, next conveyed it to the British Isles, where in due course it displaced the parsnip as Ireland's basic food crop. Early in the eighteenth century settlers from Erin took it on its fourth transatlantic voyage, this time to the Anglo-American colonies, where, thanks to its latest port of call, it was labeled the Irish potato, a name it has retained in America ever since.

The tomato had almost as singular a history. Though the Indians of Mexico and South America had eaten it for untold ages, the white man in both Europe and America believed it poisonous, and for more than three centuries cultivated it only as an ornamental garden plant. Not till the second quarter of the nineteenth century did the "love apple," as it was called, reach the American table. Then, as if to make up for past neglect, it leaped into tremendous favor, being consumed both raw and in soups, in "catchup" and other culinary forms. Anticipating the twentieth-century vogue, physicians proclaimed its medicinal properties, and patent-medicine vendors cashed in on the popularity with "Compound Tomato Pills" and "Compound Extract of Tomato."

Unlike the potato and tomato, corn or maize was known to the colonials from the start and indeed profoundly influenced the spread of settlement. The whites learned its many uses and methods of tillage from the aborigines, and after the native fashion they ate it in the form of mush, hominy and grits, stewed corn, syrup, bread, pudding, roasting ears, popcorn and dried kernels. Moreover, as befitted apostles of the more advanced civilization, they quickly discovered how to convert it into an intoxicating drink. Thanks to Indian stores of the vegetable, the first arrivals at Jamestown and Plymouth escaped starvation; and many years afterward, when the first frontiersmen pushed across the Alleghenies, they too managed to survive by supplementing occasional wild game with supplies obtained from the savages. No crop could have better suited the settler's need. More quickly

grown than wheat, requiring comparatively little seed or attention and yielding three or four times as large a return, corn also
furnished his table with a greater variety of dishes. "Suppose our
fathers had to depend on wheat for their bread," reflected a Ten-
nessean of later days with pardonable exaggeration. "It would
have taken them a hundred years longer to reach the Rockies."

Indirectly, maize also provided the settler with pork, his principal article of meat, since hogs, fed on corn fodder and needing
slight care, grew to full size in a single season. Preserved in brine,
this flesh became his mainstay three times a day and seven days
a week. Under the circumstances salt acquired an enormous importance even apart from its use in the fisheries. As the difficulty
of obtaining it increased with greater distance from the briny Atlantic, the pioneers faced in reverse the problem confronting their
spice-seeking forebears in Europe: they were discouraged from
venturing afar. At first they sent pack trains back to the coast for
an annual supply, but after a time this became impracticable.
They then sought out the saline springs and deposits which the
savages and wild animals used. Not the least of Daniel Boone's
services in breaking the path for civilization was his skill in finding salt licks. Westward migration did not gather real momentum, however, till the backwoodsman in the 1790's and later developed his own saltworks on a commercial scale — in central
New York, in western Pennsylvania and particularly in the Great
Kanawha basin of present West Virginia. Ohio and Kentucky,
seeking population, early passed legislation to promote local
production. By 1810 the districts along the Ohio River and its
branches provided nearly three quarters of the country's total
output, with Cincinnati, famed as "Porkopolis," the chief distributing center. The West, assured of abundant and cheap salt,
looked confidently to the future.

II

That the new West was an appendage of an American republic
rather than of imperial England reveals another dietary influence
in United States history. The thirteen colonies renounced the
mother country when, as Anthony Trollope put it, they felt "big
enough to go it alone." Though many things had nurtured this

feeling of self-reliance, a major factor was the self-sufficient food supply. Indeed, besides raising enough for themselves, the people had developed a profitable export trade out of the surplus of their grain, pork and beef and the catches of the Newfoundland fisheries. They came to believe, without conscious disloyalty to Britain, that they possessed the economic sinews for a free national existence. As Tom Paine summed up the argument in *Common Sense* in January, 1776, their commerce consisted of "the necessaries of life" and would "always have a market while eating is the custom of Europe."

Because of this dormant sense of independence, England's policy of colonial control, introduced after her long struggle with France for North America, inevitably encountered difficulties, and the difficulties proved all the greater because of restraints placed upon certain imported articles of diet to which the people had become attached. The supplying of these products, moreover, had grown into a considerable business. Though they were mere accessories to the American table, the restrictions created irritations that aroused the colonists to re-examine their constitutional relations with King and Parliament.

The first dispute involved West India molasses, whose importance arose from the fact that it was the poor man's substitute for sugar as well as the stuff from which rum, the most popular tipple, was made. When England in 1764 laid a revenue duty on molasses from the foreign West Indies and proceeded to enforce it, an uproar followed, especially in New England. The people, seeing no alternative but to shut down the distilleries, foretold drastic unemployment, prohibitive prices and the loss of the African slave trade — where rum served as a key commodity of exchange — and, seemingly as an afterthought, they also contended that the tax was illegal. The passage of the Stamp Act the next year heightened the anger, and in 1766 Parliament backed down, reducing the molasses impost and repealing the stamp duties. Long afterward John Adams wrote, "I know not why we should blush to confess that molasses was an essential ingredient in American independence."

No sooner did this crisis pass than tea took the center of the stage. As in England, this beverage was the favorite nonalcoholic drink. Hence when the Townshend Act of 1767 imposed a duty on it and a few less significant commodities, the ministry, discounting American objections to taxation without representation, confidently expected the colonists' palates to overcome their principles. But the patriots retaliated by boycotting all British trade and endeavored to popularize substitute brews made from native plants. Then smugglers discovered ways of bringing in sufficient amounts from Dutch sources, thus enabling people to imbibe the genuine article without the hated tax and, besides, at a lower price. In 1770 Parliament tried a new tack, revoking all the duties but the one on tea, which was retained, the King said, "to keep up the right." Had Britain been content with this move, the final break might have been long postponed, for opposition had now subsided in most of the colonies and even John Adams admitted that at John Hancock's he "drank green tea, from Holland, I hope, but don't know."

In 1773, however, Parliament empowered the East India Company to import the herb through its own agents — to the wrath of both smuggling and legitimate merchants. The people in the leading ports promptly organized to keep the offending leaves from going on sale, and in Boston the famous Tea Party ensued. Parliament in reprisal shut the port of Boston in 1774 till the act of vandalism should be paid for, and altered permanently the Massachusetts form of government. But these measures, instead of isolating the Bay Colony, as had been hoped, rallied the other provinces to her side. In the onrush of events peaceful resistance changed into armed rebellion and then into open revolution. Tea, in John Adams's phrase, was thus another essential ingredient in American independence.

Ironically, a situation involving food also provoked the first forcible defiance of the United States government under the Constitution. The farmers on what was then the frontier, being hampered by the mountains in sending their bulky corn and other cereals to the seaboard, had made it a practice to convert their surplus grain into whisky, a commodity both easy to transport and highly remunerative. Because of this, a federal excise in 1791 on distilled liquors incensed them as much as the molasses and tea duties had the colonists. North Carolina, Virginia and Maryland contented themselves with legislative protests; but in western Pennsylvania the inhabitants mobbed revenue collectors and excise payers, and finally, in 1794, the government, not knowing how far the "Whisky Insurrection" might go, mobilized fifteen thousand militia, a show of strength which brought the turbulence to a bloodless close. Though Congress did not remove the tax for another eight years, the hard-pressed farmer had by that time developed a new market in the burgeoning settlements of the Ohio Valley, where he could sell his corn in the form of hogs instead of hogsheads. Never again did a controversy turning on food challenge the national authority.

III

What the average person ate never failed to fascinate European observers. Coming from countries where the fertility of the people outran the fertility of the soil, they marveled at the profusion of dishes which any American regarded as his birthright. Captain Basil Hall, visiting New York in 1827, reported that breakfast consisted of shad, mutton cutlets, "a great steaming, juicy beefsteak," rolls and "regiments of hot toast, with oceans of tea and coffee." The American's noon and evening repasts merely expanded upon the morning's fare. Corn in various guises could always be counted on along with multitudinous pastries and sweetmeats, while the more substantial viands ordinarily included, according to one traveler, "pork, salt-fish, tough poultry, and little birds of all descriptions." Consistently absent were milk, fresh fruit and leafy vegetables.

Hurry marked both the cooking and consuming of food. The housewife, having many dishes to prepare, fried everything she could in order to save time, while the bread and pastry would have wrecked the constitution of a less hardy people. The supplanting of the oven-flanked open fireplace by the cookstove in the 1820's and 1830's seemed only to 'worsen matters, encouraging still greater haste in cooking, and providing new and irresistible opportunities for robbing victuals of nutriment and flavor. A mid-century English visitor somberly recalled Brillat-Savarin's aphorism: "The destiny of nations depends upon the manner in which they nourish themselves"; and as late as 1880 the author of *The American Code of Manners* lamented, "To cook indigestible lumps of pastry, to feed a nation on pies, on heavy bread —

who can expect greatness, wisdom or honesty from a nation of moody dyspeptics?" Under the circumstances eating was a grim business characterized by resolute application and a ban on conversation. The national motto, according to one European, was "gobble, gulp, and go."

This ill-balanced, ill-cooked, hastily devoured fare impaired physical fitness. Medical men and others, though ignorant as yet of such dietary constituents as minerals, proteins and vitamins, blamed the food for the ravages of scurvy and dyspepsia, the bad teeth, the quick fading of women and the high infant mortality. Perhaps it was more than a mere convention of speech that people generally eschewed the bluff English salutation of "Good morning!" for the solicitous inquiry "How do you do?" It has been suggested that America's early pre-eminence in dentistry stemmed from the dire need and the exceptional opportunities for practice, while thirst-provoking salt meat probably explains the overindulgence in hard liquor which shocked early nineteenth-century humanitarians into organizing the temperance movement.

It is likely, also, that the characteristic American physique resulted largely from what and how people ate — the women "lean as greyhounds," remarked by Thackeray in the 1850's, and the typical male, whom George William Curtis described as thin, "sharp-faced, thought-furrowed," with "anxious eye and sallow complexion." The day was to come when improved cookery, better balanced meals and a leisurely enjoyment of the table would render this wiry, wrinkle-cheeked figure less in evidence, but meanwhile he was enshrined as a national symbol in Uncle Sam.

The reform enthusiasts of the 1830's and 1840's, assailing man's inhumanity to man wherever found, did not overlook America's reckless table habits. One ardent soul went so far as to propose a Society for the Suppression of Eating, though all he really intended was to suppress gluttony. Sylvester Graham, a more persuasive champion, advocated both less and wiser eating, espousing a meatless diet with rough cereals and whole-wheat products along with vegetables, fresh fruits and milk. Grahamism, though exposing the master on one occasion to the violent hands of Boston butchers and bakers, won an instant response in humanitarian circles. Knots of disciples set up societies and boardinghouses

on the new principles; and if most persons remained unconvinced, still the cause did not wholly fail, for it won a modest im-
mortality in the form of Graham bread and Graham crackers.

More important in bringing about an improved diet were the
changing conditions of American life. As more and more people
crowded into cities and worked at sedentary jobs, they felt less
need for meat and heavy victuals, while the rapid extension of
steam locomotion, beginning in the 1830's, greatly enlarged the
range of alternatives, including edibles brought from afar. To
protect perishable foods the railroads about 1840 began to install
iceboxes, and late in the fifties they introduced the refrigerator
car, which attained its fullest use after the Civil War when a
standard gauge of track made possible longer continuous transportation. Every year increased the availability of fresh fruits,
vegetables and milk in the cities. Meanwhile, the advent of the
household refrigerator and of the commercial cold-storage plant
weaned people away from salt-cured meats. Another boon, in
the forties, was the introduction of canned goods, which the Civil
War helped to popularize when the government supplied the
troops with condensed milk and canned fruits and vegetables.
Between 1860 and 1870 the output of these articles rose from five
million to thirty million cans. A few years later, beef, tongue and
soups could be bought in tin containers, and improved refrigerator cars were speeding dressed meat from the Chicago packing
houses to every part of the land.

A Vermont farm wife itemizing her baking for the year 1877
listed 152 cakes, 421 pies, 1038 loaves of bread and 2140 doughnuts. By contrast, her urban cousin could obtain all these over
a counter and avoid, moreover, the time-consuming labor of putting up a family supply of meat, vegetables and fruits. "Housekeeping is getting to be ready made, as well as clothing," crowed
Good Housekeeping magazine in 1887. As a consequence, mid-
dle-class women in the cities were freed for a larger participation in the world beyond their doors. Also, if they preferred, they
could pay greater attention to the art and science of cooking.
That many availed themselves of the latter opportunity is shown
by the space which both magazines and newspapers now devoted
to recipes and the planning of meals. Another sign of the times
was the establishment of cookery schools in the seventies under

such authorities as Juliet Corson in New York, Maria Parloa in Boston and Sarah T. Rorer in Philadelphia, whose names became household words from coast to coast. In the eighties courses on the subject entered the public schools. Meanwhile a host of new and better cookbooks flooded the market. Unlike the older treatises they fortified the novice by specifying exact measurements of ingredients.

Not unexpectedly, observers began to notice alterations in the American physique. During the eighties dealers in ready-to-wear clothing had to adopt a larger scale of sizes. An Easterner, familiar with New York and Boston over a period of fifty years, declared in 1895, "The men are more robust and more erect, the women have greatly improved both in feature and carriage; and in the care and condition of the teeth in both sexes a surprising change has taken place." Lanky Uncle Sam was coming less and less to resemble his devoted compatriots. In bringing this about, undoubtedly the major agency was more wholesome and better cooked meals.

IV

If a dietary need led to the discovery of America by Columbus, a dietary need of a different kind contributed to the repeated rediscovery of America by immigrants. Many things during the nineteenth century drew them across the Atlantic, but none epitomized the land of opportunity so concretely or affected living conditions so directly as the abundance and cheapness of provisions. "America letters," written back to the old country, and handed about among relatives and friends until the pages wore thin, brought the exciting news to a people haunted by the specter of want. "Tell Thomas Arann to come to America," exhorted a British arrival, "and tell him to leave his strap what he wears when he has nothing to eat in England, for some other half-starved slave. Tell Miriam there's no sending children to bed without supper." "There is a great many ill conveniences here," wrote an Irishman, "but no empty bellies." "The poorest family," added another immigrant, plainly risking his reputation for veracity, "adorn the table three times a day like a wedding dinner — tea, coffee, beef, fowls, pies, eggs, pickles, good bread."

The failure of Europe's potato crop in 1845, 1846 and 1848 suddenly converted these disparities into tragedy. This calamity, which spread woe through England and much of the Continent, fell hardest on the Irish, who relied almost solely upon the potato. Goaded by hunger, families roamed the countryside, devouring what they could find — nettle tops, water cress, wild herbs, even the carcasses of dogs and diseased cattle. Nearly a quarter of the Irish people perished. Relief ships from the United States brought not only money and provisions, but also the incentive to make a new start in a new land. Between 1846 and 1849 more than 212,000 fled to America, with 650,000 following in the next decade. Emigration increased also from England, Germany and other afflicted countries. For the time being, starvation overbore all other reasons for settling in the United States.

The European newcomer, although ever the chief gainer in the matter of food, atoned in some degree by enriching the national menu with his own traditional dishes. In this sense the melting pot was also a cooking pot. The Germans, early on the scene, contributed such items as frankfurters, hamburgers, liverwurst, sauerkraut, cottage cheese, rye bread, pumpernickel, zwieback, strudel, pretzels and dill pickles. The Irish introduced corned beef and cabbage and Irish stew; the Scots, oatmeal and barley broth; the Dutch, doughnuts and waffles; the French, consommé and fried frog legs; the Italians, macaroni, spaghetti, ravioli, minestrone and antipasto; the Hungarians, goulash; and the Russians, caviar and borsch. From the other side of the world came chow mein, egg fu-yung, preserved kumquats and other Chinese culinary delicacies, while from south of the United States, largely by way of former Mexican territory, came chile con carne, tamales and tortillas.

Foreign influences affected the national dietary in other ways as well. Even in colonial days traders imported dried prunes, currants and raisins from the Mediterranean, not to mention tea from the Orient. Shortly after 1800 the first bananas appeared — thirty bunches from the West Indies — and in the 1830's the first cargoes of Sicilian oranges and lemons. Over the years the list was expanded to include such products as olives, figs, pineapples, tropical nuts, cane sugar, spinach and soybeans. As soon as these novelties attracted sufficient custom, the wide range of climate and soil led in most instances to their being grown in the United States; and local production, by lowering the price, in turn greatly stimulated their consumption.

With an unexampled array of native and foreign viands to choose from, people nevertheless tended to prefer some to others, and these in the course of time came to give a distinctive stamp to the American bill of fare. According to a Gallup poll in 1947, the favorite dinner features plain rather than fancy dishes: fruit or shrimp cocktail, vegetable soup or chicken broth, steak with peas and French fried or mashed potatoes, rolls, coffee, and apple pie capped with ice cream. Perhaps still more typical is the standard American breakfast. Once hardly distinguishable from the noon and evening meals, it has become a simple repast consisting usually of fresh fruit or fruit juice, cooked or uncooked cereal, toast and coffee, perhaps topped off with bacon and eggs. Great new industries have arisen from this change in breakfast habits.

v

The dietary influence, potent in so many other respects, counted also in political life. No student has yet explored the implications for American history of Voltaire's remark, "The fate of a nation often depends upon the digestion of the minister," but the possibilities are inviting. Politicians long ago discovered the value of a well-cooked meal in softening asperities and composing personal and factional differences. Probably the fathers of the American party system, Thomas Jefferson and Alexander Hamilton, set the example with the famous dinner in 1790 at which the Virginian obtained the promise of a southern site for the national capital in return for his influence in carrying through Congress Hamilton's scheme for assuming state debts. Gastronomy also proved effective with the rank and file. Through most of the nineteenth century the institution known as the barbecue proved a magnet for rural political gatherings. Huge crowds, attracted from miles around by a feast of roasted hogs or oxen, lingered on while stump speakers roasted the opposition candidates.

Not often, however, did a dietary question figure as a cam-

paign issue. In 1840 the Whigs, acclaiming the simple rustic
virtues of William Henry Harrison living allegedly in a log cabin,
contrasted in song his ways with those of his Democratic rival
Van Buren:

> See the Farmer to his meal
>   Joyfully repair;
> Crackers, cheese, and cider too,
>   A hard but homely fare.
> Martin to his breakfast comes
>   At the hour of noon;
> Sipping from a china cup,
>   With a golden spoon.

And in 1900 the Republicans, switching the emphasis to
hearty living, helped sweep William McKinley to victory with
their slogan of the "full dinner pail." Again in 1928 Republican
spellbinders capitalized upon the party's supposed patent on
prosperity by promising "a chicken in every pot and two cars in
every garage." Their candidate, Herbert Hoover, blind to the impending economic collapse, confidently proclaimed the day at
hand when hunger would be unknown and poverty "be banished
from this nation."

Food as a political factor made a much bigger dent on legislation, however, than on elections. Governmental intervention on
behalf of the consumer began early and increased with the years.
It signalized society's waxing concern with the conservation and
quality of the food supply and thereby helped to undermine the
traditional laissez-faire conception of government. The march of
the pioneer had left a bloody trail in the wasteful slaying of
game. The great awk and the heath hen, birds whose toothsome
flesh had tickled Yankee colonial palates, completely vanished,
the awk by the mid-nineteenth century and the heath hen not
long after. Similarly the sky-darkening flocks of passenger pi-
geons, observed in the Mississippi Valley as late as the eighties,
dwindled from millions to nothing within the span of a single
human generation. The rise of industrialism had further baneful
results, for factory wastes polluting streams and shore waters
helped exterminate the salmon along the Atlantic Coast, while
no less harmful in checking Nature's powers of replenishment

was the rapid expansion of commercial canning and packing.

In the interest of protecting food resources Massachusetts is said to have prescribed a closed season for deer as early as 1694, but such legislation did not become common till the nineteenth century revealed the growing need. In 1818 Massachusetts acted to preserve game birds, Virginia followed in 1832, and within another thirty years most of the states adopted like measures. In 1878 California and New Hampshire took the next step by setting up game departments. The federal government helped out by creating the office of Commissioner of Fish and Fisheries in 1871 and by establishing the first national forest reserve in 1891, partly to foster wild life. Other gains, incidental or direct, came from the militant conservation movement which the first Roosevelt launched early in the twentieth century. In 1913, for example, Congress stretched its interstate commerce powers to include the protection of migratory game birds, and in 1916 an Anglo-American treaty (afterward extended to Mexico) accomplished a similar end with reference to Canada. By such gradual stages the public became in time fully alive to the need of conserving the nation's natural resources, animate as well as inanimate.

Concern with the quality of food apparently started with milk. In 1856 Massachusetts headed the procession of legislatures by prohibiting adulteration, and in 1882 Newark, New Jersey, began the practice of inspecting dairies. In 1874 Illinois went further by enacting a general food law. As other parts of the country fell into line, the national government's co-operation became essential in order to prevent the regulations from being defeated by products from less enlightened states. Dr. Harvey W. Wiley, chief chemist of the Department of Agriculture, pointed the way in 1883 by organizing a continuing study of food adulteration; and a generation later Upton Sinclair's best seller *The Jungle*, exposing noisome conditions in the Chicago packing houses, prodded Congress into action. The legislation of 1906 provided for federal inspection of meat in interstate commerce and forbade interstate shipments of any "adulterated, misbranded or poisonous" foods. Later statutes, notably one in 1938, extended and strengthened the restrictions. Today at least twenty federal agencies deal directly or indirectly with questions involving foodstuffs or diet.

Long before the migratory-birds treaties with England and

Mexico the dietary issue had figured in foreign relations. No diplomatic dispute in United States history ever ran so protracted and tortuous a course as that over fishing rights off the Newfoundland Banks and in Canadian-American waters — from the peace negotiations at the close of the Revolution to the agreement eventually worked out with the help of The Hague Court in 1912. Sugar provided a shorter and more dramatic chapter. American citizens had developed extensive cane plantations in Hawaii and Cuba; and when Congress in 1890 and 1894 took away their principal market by legislation discriminating against foreign sugar in the United States, the resulting low prices precipitated uprisings which landed Hawaii in Uncle Sam's lap and helped convert Cuba from a Spanish colony into an independent country. Meat had its innings about the same time. Embargoes by Britain, Germany and other countries against American livestock and meat as being infected engendered a decade or more of controversy which was finally ended in 1891 by the establishment of adequate export inspection in the United States.

VI

In war no less than peace, food has on occasion been a determinant. Some historians hold that England's pro-Southern ministry at the time of the Civil War put off recognizing the Confederacy till too late because crop failures at home created a national need for Northern grain that overbore the manufacturers' need for Southern cotton. Temporarily at least, wheat was King instead of cotton. Be that as it may, the Confederacy itself faced a critical lack of provisions. Addicted to one-crop agriculture, the people had always relied upon the North and Europe for the bulk of their cereals, meats, salt and hay. The tightening federal blockade by land and sea steadily strangled these sources of supply, forcing the South to divert plantation land to the raising of food and forage. Not only did these efforts not go far enough, but the invading foe cut off areas desirable for the purpose, while faulty transportation and an inefficient commissariat often kept existing stocks from reaching the troops. As the struggle continued, Confederate army rations had to be reduced, and the men sometimes marched and fought on empty stomachs. Behind the lines, mobs in Atlanta, Mobile, Richmond and elsewhere on occasion pillaged food shops.

The shortage of salt created particular concern as outside possibilities of supply vanished and Union forces seized or destroyed local saltworks in the Great Kanawha and Holston valleys and other places. This dietary deficiency, affecting the health of both soldiers and civilians, also weakened Robert E. Lee's striking power by ravaging his horses with hoof and tongue diseases. Moreover, the dearth of brine caused untold quantities of bacon and other foodstuffs to spoil. As Basil Gildersleeve, soldier-professor at the University of Virginia, later observed, "Hunger was the dominant note of life in the Confederacy, civil as well as military." It can hardly be doubted that this circumstance contributed to the South's ultimate defeat.

Although salt was no longer important as a preservative of army fare when the Spanish War broke out, the newer methods of processing food — refrigeration and canning — touched off the main scandal of that short conflict. According to the Rough Rider Theodore Roosevelt, not a quarter or even a tenth of the meat sent to Cuba was fit for human consumption. Protests against "embalmed beef" issued from press, public and Congress. Though two commissions of inquiry whitewashed the Secretary of War, the critics remained unconvinced, and President McKinley in the end fired him. The fault was really twofold. Compounding incompetence in Washington, the officers in the field handled the supplies without due regard to the tropical heat.

The two great struggles of the twentieth century gave food a central role. Under conditions of total war, civilians had to save food for the mass armies, while the government on its part had to make certain that the stay-at-homes ate enough to be able to produce prodigious quantities of arms and machines as well as to raise an agricultural surplus for feeding the Allied countries in addition to their own. In the first war the United States Food Administration under Herbert Hoover discharged these duties. To lessen domestic consumption it imposed licensing controls on processors and wholesalers; and spurring the public with the slogan "Food will win the war," it sponsored wheatless and meatless days, which everybody observed. To increase the production of vegetables it encouraged vacant-lot gardening, and to stimulate grain production Congress put a guaranteed price on wheat.

The later and greater war carried the country further along the same path. Even before the United States entered the fight, lend-lease shipments speeded an increasing quantity of food to the Axis-resisting powers, and thenceforth the unprecedented size of America's own armed forces intensified the drain. In meeting the astronomical need, the administration resolved to avoid two crying injustices which the civilian population had endured in the previous conflict: runaway prices and an unfair distribution of the available stock of provisions. The Office of Price Administration, which exercised most of the necessary powers, clamped restrictions upon the wholesale and retail prices of many articles and rationed essential foods. (To occasional grumblers it addressed the following admonition: "Our forefathers did without sugar until the 13th century, without coal until the 14th, without butter until the 15th, and without tea, coffee or soap until the 17th. What was it you were complaining about?") To boost output, the government offset the disadvantage which the farmer suffered from fixed prices on his commodities by paying subsidies to producers of meat, butter and other staples. And, as in the earlier struggle, these efforts achieved the purpose.

VII

Through the ages an adequate food supply has been humanity's greatest need and most tenacious goal. Until the eighteenth century hunger was man's almost constant companion in the Old World. Famines breeding epidemics scourged one European country after another; and even after the eighteenth century the danger did not wholly cease, as the plight of the Irish in the 1840's shows. Happily, the discovery of America opened new possibilities of which mankind took increasing advantage. North America became a granary for the Old World, and the Europeans who settled across the Atlantic left behind them the dread of want. True, local and temporary starvation sometimes occurred as an incident of reckless pioneering or of Indian attacks or of setbacks to business, and, more often perhaps, because of floods or other natural disasters; but these happenings only underscored the normal condition of plenty.

As G. Stanley Hall remarked, "When food is abundant and fit, men tend to be contented; and when it is scanty or ill-adapted to their nutritive needs they become uneasy, restless, and seize upon anything however untoward to objectify and justify their discontent." Nature's guarantee of a full stomach to all people willing to work moderated or cured extreme radical tendencies and helped deflect reform energies into orderly democratic channels. Werner Sombart, the German economist, comparing the progress of socialism in the two countries during the nineteenth century, attributed its backwardness in the United States to the fact that the Yankee worker consumed almost three times as much bread and meat and four times as much sugar as the German. He concluded, "On the shoals of roast beef and apple pie all socialistic Utopias founder."

Not till the Great Depression of 1929 did widespread starvation threaten the American people. In earlier slumps, local private and public charitable agencies and improvised soup kitchens had proved equal to the need; but the new crisis, sowing ruin deep and wide in every direction, soon exhausted community and state funds, rendering thirteen million breadwinners idle and hungry through no fault of their own. These with their dependents numbered a quarter or third of the population. Yet there was no general shortage of food, for while urban families went mealless, the farmers piled up unsalable crops. As the nation looked vainly to the Hoover administration for effective action, a mounting resentment swept over the land. Why, people asked, could not a country with ample to eat and men eager to work guarantee the impoverished at least the right of survival? Portents of social upheaval appeared. Armed bands of Western farmers resisted foreclosure sales. A "Bonus Expeditionary Force" of jobless veterans descended upon Washington, only to be expelled with gas bombs and army tanks.

Franklin D. Roosevelt, raised to the presidency in 1932 by an angry electorate, mastered the emergency. Disregarding constitutional scruples, he proclaimed that humanity and justice forbade the nation to let citizens starve; and Congress responded by pouring billions into relief, supplying the needy with food and jobs through the WPA and like agencies, and restoring the common man's faith in democratic processes. Other New Deal measures undertook to assure better wages for labor and provide unemployment insurance, as well as to reinvigorate business, banking and agriculture. In the face of peacetime disaster the government under bold leadership showed itself the people's protector, provider and friend, setting a precedent which no future administration is likely to ignore.

The relation of food to human welfare, emphasized by the Great Depression and also by the two world wars, high-lighted the investigations scientists were making into dietary ingredients. These researches disclosed that malnutrition might arise from ill-chosen fare as well as from too little — from the "hidden hunger" of the gourmand quite as much as from the enforced abstinence of the destitute. Early in the century nutritional experts concentrated upon calories, tiny heat units due chiefly to fats, proteins and carbohydrates (starch and sugar), which serve the human engine as fuel. They next discovered vitamins, chemical constituents necessary for the body's health, including life itself. By 1920 three had been identified: A, which improves eyesight; B, a deterrent of beriberi; and C, which prevents scurvy. Later years saw other letters added to the vitamin alphabet and some of the older ones subdivided. By a proper respect for these factors men could facilitate bone growth, fortify themselves against many physical and mental disorders and enhance their morale; and since these values exist in common foods, the poor might profit as well as the rich.

The public, always receptive to suggestion and idolizing science, embraced these findings almost too eagerly. Housewives gave anxious thought to a correct balance of food elements; persons who had never had to worry about their next meal began to worry about their last one; and multitudes dosed themselves with vitamin pills, yeast products, mineral capsules, liver extracts and other preparations which alert manufacturers supplied. The consumption of vitamin-rich articles like leafy vegetables, dairy products, fresh fruits and fruit juices reached new highs, while milk, prized for combining the first six vitamins of the alphabet, became the national beverage. Could Sylvester Graham have returned to earth, he would have particularly rejoiced to see millers artificially restoring to flour the vitamins and minerals which refining processes removed.

Equipped with this new knowledge, the victors over the Axis

powers employed it as an instrument for a durable peace. While the guns were still booming, they set up the United Nations Relief and Rehabilitation Administration in 1943 to succor the victims of war and invasion and thereby avert civil convulsions harmful to a return of normal conditions. By mid-1947 UNRRA had shipped nearly nine million tons of provisions, besides supplying machinery, materials and technical advice for agricutural revival. Looking to the longer stretch, an international conference at Hot Springs in 1943 concluded that recent progress in nutritional science and farming methods made it possible for all peoples to maintain a healthful subsistence; and the FAO (Food and Agriculture Organization), established two years later as a branch of the United Nations, conducted surveys of global food resources and proposed better modes of distributing available supplies and of raising consumption standards. In the view of Sir John Boyd Orr, the original director general, "Future peace depends first on what is done about foods. . . . If politics will give first attention to what the common people of the world want most — food and a decent living for themselves and their children — I am certain we can find a basis for nations to work together."

When the victors fell to quarreling with each other over the Kremlin-inspired subversion of neighboring countries, the United States and Western Europe again turned to food as a trump card for international order and security. In his famous address at Harvard in June, 1947, Secretary of State George C. Marshall stated, "Our policy is directed not against any country or doctrine but against hunger, poverty, desperation and chaos . . . so as to permit the emergence of political and social conditions in which free institutions can exist." In response to his suggestion sixteen powers (Russia and her satellites declining) drew up a general plan for restoring their economic health, and Congress in the spring of 1948 voted $5,055,000,000 as a first installment of working capital for a four-year European Recovery Plan, nearly a billion of the initial sum going into foodstuffs. And even before the program was successfully completed the same principle of promoting democracy and peace began to be applied to the underdeveloped areas of the globe, not only through the FAO but also by the United States and, later on, by other free nations. By

1963, indeed, surplus American farm products were going to more than a hundred countries with a total population of one and a third billion.

Thus, as the long record shows, the dietary influence had manifold ramifications in American history from the days of Columbus to the present. Molière's dancing master in *Le Bourgeois Gentilhomme* insisted that "all the mistakes of men, the fatal reverses that fill the world's annals, the shortcomings of statesmen and the blunders of great captains arise from not knowing how to dance." Without going so far, it must nevertheless be clear that food has been a powerful and persistent, if neglected, factor in the making of America.

13

Casting the national horoscope

HISTORY is hindsight; prophecy, foresight. America has never failed to pay honor to her historians, but where is the beadroll of her prophets? Does the ability to chart the unknown deserve less well of society than the ability to retrace the known, or is this supposed gift merely a delusion of the superstitious and ignorant? The answer is not simple. In our personal lives we are not satisfied to let the future take care of itself, for, consciously or unconsciously, we are continually acting upon some assumption as to events yet undisclosed. In this spirit we buy property, conduct business, plant crops, send our children to college, purchase stocks, vote in elections.

True, educational institutions have still to recognize the prophetic function by establishing chairs to foster the art, but nonetheless they maintain departments in which the element of soothsaying bulks large. Thus the student of meteorology is taught how to predict winds, tides, heat and cold; the beginner in astronomy learns to foretell an eclipse or a comet five hundred years away; and courses in public health trace the probable movement of epidemics. Similarly, the social scientist through his study of business cycles seeks to plot the economic road ahead. But even without benefit of scholarship Americans have always indulged in prophecy. It is not that with Shelley they felt,

> The world is weary of the past,
> Oh, might it die or rest at last!

but, rather, that in a country still being finished the future is more exciting than the past. The utterances and writings that resulted illumine a neglected facet of the many-sided national character. This essay suggests the variety and scope of this abundant literature with some reflections on its significance.

I

A lively sense of contemporaneity with the future permeated the American spirit from the beginning. Living in a new and richly endowed land, the people constantly visioned marvels to come. Granted a fair interval of time, nothing man could hope for appeared beyond realization. It was George Berkeley, Irish prelate and philosopher, about to set sail for Rhode Island, who in 1726 gave immortal expression to one of the bravest of these anticipations. Writing his "Verses, on the Prospect of Planting Arts and Learning in America," he predicted an accomplishment,

> Not such as Europe breeds in her decay;
> Such as she bred when fresh and young,
> When heavenly flame did animate her clay . . .
> Westward the course of empire takes its way.

Dean Berkeley's seed fell on well-prepared soil. By common report the Pilgrims, more than a century before, had carved on a rock at Plymouth the lines:

> The eastern nations sink, their glory ends,
> And empire rises where the sun descends.

This couplet, John Adams said, had "been repeated with rapture" as long as he could remember. The colonists, loath to consider themselves exiles on the fringes of civilization, stoutly believed they were destined to be the heirs of the ages. The Englishman Andrew Burnaby, visiting the North American settlements some thirty years after Berkeley's forecast, again and again encountered the view — to him "strange as it is visionary" — that "empire is traveling westward" and that America in due course would "give law to the rest of the world."

This conviction of future ascendancy undoubtedly helped

nerve the colonists for the political struggles leading to the break with England. In Berkeleyan spirit the youthful patriot Philip Freneau chose as his graduation theme at Princeton in 1771 "The Rising Glory of America," and by the same sign newspaper editors continually reprinted Berkeley's prediction as well as others of similar import. The *Essex Gazette* on March 1, 1774, for example, quoted the Duke of Orrery as declaring that "the ball of empire might roll westward and stop in America; a world unknown when Rome was in its meridian splendor." Tom Paine's trumpet call to independence, *Common Sense*, published early in 1776, played skillfully upon the same note. Nor did the actual attainment of freedom dim the memory of Berkeley's prevision. Many years later Daniel Webster paid tribute to his "intuitive glance into futurity," and Charles Sumner, recalling the lines after nearly a century of nationhood, asserted, "There is nothing from any oracle, there is little from any prophecy, which can compare with them." Americans in the middle of the twentieth century can appreciate even more greatly Dean Berkeley's clear-sightedness.

Taken literally, however, the westward course of empire, even if foreordained, did not necessarily imply the creation of an independent nation in the west; but the alternative was almost as odious to Britain's ruling class. From the time of Berkeley's poem onward, if Josiah Tucker, the English economist and divine, is right, the colonists expected that, short of independence, the imperial capital would sooner or later be shifted from Great Britain to "Great America." (Tucker himself jeered that "the *English* would rather submit to a *French* yoke, than to an *American;* as being the lesser Indignity of the two.") By the 1770's the idea was very much in the air, a writer in the *Pennsylvania Gazette*, July 4, 1774, assigning as the reason the older country's obvious senility. John Adams, masquerading as "Novanglus" in the *Boston Gazette* about the same time, dated the consummation as no more than four decades off. Adams, of course, was presently to arrive at a different notion of the relations of Britain and America; but Adam Smith, the Scottish political economist, publishing his famous *Wealth of Nations* in the very year of independence, was of the same opinion still, though allowing "little more than a century" for the accomplishment.

Predictions of the yet bolder step of a separate existence reached back to earliest times. John Adams, reminiscing to Benjamin West in 1807, derided the supposition that in 1776 American independence was "a novel idea" or "a modern discovery." On the contrary, "The idea of it as a possible thing, as a probable event, nay, as a necessary and unavoidable measure, in case Great Britain should assume an unconstitutional authority over us, has been familiar to Americans from the first settlement of the country." Numerous pamphlets, sermons and newspaper articles document Adams's view. Even before the successive crises that precipitated the Revolution, the Swedish botanist Peter Kalm, traveling in the colonies in 1748, reported people as saying that in thirty or fifty years they would set up a free state.

But prognostications on the other side were no less emphatic. In 1721 Jeremiah Dummer, the Massachusetts colonial agent, expressed the opinion, soon to be hackneyed through repetition, that deep-seated antagonisms rendered it inconceivable that the colonies should ever unite against England. Franklin himself in 1760 dismissed the notion of such a combination as "not merely improbable, it is impossible." But the palm goes to Andrew Burnaby, who at about the same time found that "fire and water are not more heterogeneous than the different colonies in North America. . . . In short, such is the difference of character, of manners, of religion, of interest," that, "were they left to themselves, there would soon be a civil war from one end of the continent to the other; while the Indians and negroes would, with better reason, impatiently watch the opportunity of exterminating them all together." When history failed to take heed, he altered his view only to the extent of affirming that the newly established union would "not be permanent or last for any considerable length of time."

II

Graver perils even than Burnaby envisaged hung over the nation, according to another school of thought — no less than the end of the world. For many centuries the pious had been anticipating the Lord's second coming as something foretold by certain allegorical passages in Holy Writ. Long before Columbus made his voyage, people in Europe had expected the year 1000 to inaugurate the millennium — Christ's thousand-year reign on earth. Thenceforth speculation continued undampened, since the obscurities of the Biblical language were deemed to have excused the original calculation.

In the colonial and early national periods Americans of religion and learning added to the discussion. Jonathan Edwards, the great theologian, the Reverend Joseph Bellamy (who in 1758 wrote a book on the subject) and President Eliphalet Nott of Union College fixed on the year 2000 as the approximate time. In fact, according to Timothy Dwight, president of Yale and Edwards's grandson, writing in 1813, "Almost all judicious commentators have agreed, that the Millennium, in the full and perfect sense, will begin at a period, not far from the year 2000." A minority nevertheless dissented. Three New England clergymen — Jedidiah Morse, Edward D. Griffin and Ethan Smith — plumped for 1866; Professor John McKnight of Columbia, for 1900; Professor William Linn of Rutgers, for 1916; while Ezra Stiles, Dwight's predecessor at Yale, put off the fulfillment till around the year 2500. Judge John Bacon of Berkshire County, Massachusetts, reviewing the scriptural evidence in 1799 with an open-mindedness alien to most millenarians, discovered support for 1941 in Daniel, for 1975 in Ezekiel, and a possibility of 1926, 1956 or 2001 in Revelation. And there, without delivering a judicial decision, he left the matter.

Such persons, choosing dates for the Second Advent beyond their probable or possible lifetimes, ran no risk of seeing their predictions explode in their faces; but others proved less cautious. The Reverend David Austin of Elizabethtown, New Jersey, airing his views in *The Millennium; or, the Thousand Years of Prosperity* (1794), imprudently set the event for May 15, 1796, and when he was disappointed, removed to New Haven, the seat of his alma mater, where he prepared houses and a wharf for the Jews whom he expected soon to arrive on their way to greet the Messiah in the Holy Land. With equal assurance Nathaniel Wood of Middletown, Vermont, designated January 14, 1801, a few months off, at which time an earthquake should dispose of the unregenerate. Others of the ilk included Joseph Dylks of Salesville, Ohio, who proclaimed 1832, then just four years away;

George Rapp, founder of a communistic society, who survived his prediction of the Second Advent in 1836 by eleven years; and Harriet Livermore, daughter of a Massachusetts Congressman, who picked 1847 but lived on till 1868. Harriet expounded her views even in the Hall of the House of Representatives and later in Europe. A friend told John Greenleaf Whittier of finding her, "when quite an old woman, wandering in Syria with a tribe of Arabs, who with the Oriental notion that madness is inspiration, accepted her as their prophetess and leader."

Perhaps this latest evangel would have won a wider hearing if a rival seer had not stolen her audience. William Miller, veteran of the War of 1812 and a devout student of the Bible, set out from his farm at Low Hampton, New York, in 1831 to warn his countrymen that the millennium would start "about the year 1843" when a rain of fire would destroy all the wicked. Celestial omens — an hour's display of shooting stars in 1833 and a huge comet at noon just ten years later — lent credence to his message, and the hard times following the Panic of 1837 seemed a further "sign of the last days" foretold in the Second Book of Timothy. Meanwhile, in 1839, the simple old man fell in with a high-pressure organizer, the Reverend Joshua V. Himes of Boston, who played Aaron to the prophet's Moses, staging meetings for Miller in the leading towns under a vast tent, briefing apostles and inspiring the publication of Adventist journals as far west as Cincinnati.

When, however, 1843 passed just as other years, Miller decided he had erred in using the Christian instead of the Jewish calendar in his computations, which meant that the Second Advent might be delayed till Thursday, March 21, 1844. That night his devoted followers, convinced that the moment was at last at hand, gathered in places throughout the North from the Atlantic seaboard to Illinois for the occasion. The fresh disappointment merely redoubled the zeal of the prophet's aides, who persuaded their aged leader, much against his will, to venture still another date — Tuesday, October 22. Excitement now rose to a new pitch; men closed their shops or neglected their crops; many, it was reported, provided themselves with ascension robes. When the appointed night arrived, the Millerites took up the vigil once more, some on hilltops and in trees, only to see the dawn again come without the anticipated event. A further revision of the timetable

seemed ill-advised, so those in authority contented themselves
with insisting that the millennium was still imminent but of indef-
inite date. Most of the converts deserted the fold, and the founder
himself survived the denouement by but five years. In aftertimes
small isolated groups continued to believe they had unlocked the
secret. Even in the enlightened twentieth century a band of Reformed Seventh Day Adventists at East Patchogue, Long Island,
bore watch through the night of February 6, 1925.

The *Boston Transcript* in 1844 remarked of the Millerite frenzy,
"This is a free country and men have a sort of natural right to be
fools." James Brisbane of Batavia, New York, when admonished
by a neighbor that the world was about to end, replied crustily,
"Damned glad of it. This experiment of the human race is a total
failure!" In more sober mood the poet-reformer Whittier de-
plored a doctrine derived from "Oriental imagery and obscure
Hebrew texts," whose only effect was to distract attention from
the urgent needs of the living. Yet, when due allowance is made
for the overwhelming bulk of people who jeered or condemned,
the episode occupies a unique place in American history, for no
other seer ever succeeded in creating a nation-wide movement or
in working on the popular mind with such hypnotic force.

III

Granted the unlikelihood of divine interference, how long
would the United States endure? Until the Civil War revealed
the strength of the Union, no question aroused more frequent
discussion. In the Constitutional Convention of 1787 Nathaniel
Gorham of Massachusetts spoke the thought of many when he remarked, "Can it be supposed that this vast country, including the
western territory, will remain one nation one hundred and fifty
years hence?" And, as its boundaries expanded ever farther westward and huge gaps came to separate the settled regions, an increasing number shared his skepticism. In the opinion of the San
Francisco newspaper *Alta California* in 1851, "California and
Oregon cannot be expected to remain attached to a government
which has its seat at a month's journey from them. The bonds of
empire must become feeble in proportion to the distance over
which they are extended." That such predictions went amiss was

due in considerable part to the rapid introduction of improved means of communication — roads, canals, railways and the telegraph — which helped to offset the very real dangers of wide dispersion.

A more obvious threat to a durable Union was the spreading chasm between North and South occasioned by differences growing out of the institution of Negro slavery. The distances here were economic, social and ideological rather than physical and, as such, defied bridging by mere technological means. In the resulting contest for political dominance both sides resorted to dire prophecies of what would happen if the other continued obdurate. The South as the weaker party became increasingly strident in these exchanges; but apart from a handful of proslavery extremists, predictions of this contingent character were generally gambits in a well-understood political game — a sort of blackmail to force concessions.

Two of the most elaborate Southern prognostications assumed the form of fiction. *The Partisan Leader; a Tale of the Future,* appeared in the summer of 1836 in an effort to head off Martin Van Buren's election to the presidency, though, as befitted the subtitle, the volume bore the publication date 1856. The writer, who adopted the pseudonym "Edward William Sidney," was Nathaniel Beverley Tucker, professor of law at the College of William and Mary and a half-brother of the fiery political jouster John Randolph of Roanoke. The project had actually originated with Duff Green, editor of the *United States Telegraph* in Washington, who, with his patron saint John C. Calhoun, Tucker and other states-rights Democrats, had recently broken with the Jackson administration over the issue of nullification. The book wove love interest and thrilling adventure into what purported to be a preview of the consequences to Virginia and the South should Van Buren get the opportunity to perpetuate Old Hickory's policies. The story tells how the people of the Lower South, casting off the manacles of Yankee abolitionist and manufacturing interests, seceded from the Union and formed a confederacy when Van Buren sought a fourth term in 1848. Enjoying free trade with England, they at once achieved unparalleled prosperity. Van Buren, however, through the use of troops, bribery and federal patronage, kept Virginia from following suit; but as capital and commerce gravitated from the state to the new Southern nation, secessionist sentiment increased. In support of it, the Partisan Leader (otherwise not identified) organized guerrilla resistance in the mountain districts, and in two battles in November, 1849, routed Van Buren's minions. The Leader himself, however, was captured and taken to Washington, where, as the book closes, preparations were being made for his escape. Despite this inconclusive ending the fable makes it clear that in the long run Virginia managed to throw off the Northern yoke.

For obvious reasons the novel was reprinted as propaganda by both sides after the Civil War began, but before that time it was joined by an even more sensational volume, *Anticipations of the Future, to Serve as Lessons for the Present Time.* Published anonymously in Richmond during the stormy preliminaries of the presidential election of 1860, it was cast in the form of letters supposedly written by an American correspondent of the London *Times* from 1864 to 1870. The author, Edmund Ruffin, was a well-known Virginia planter and long-time friend of Nathaniel Tucker's, who would soon fire the first shell against Fort Sumter.

The book pictures in realistic detail the successive steps leading to the disruption of the Union. Abraham Lincoln, though carrying the 1860 election, so disappointed the abolitionists by his timorous policy toward slavery that in 1864 he was replaced by William H. Seward. Under the aggressive New Yorker, Congress raised the tariff to the detriment of the South, created new offices for administration henchmen, excluded slavery from the territories by the device of free homesteads, packed the judiciary with Negrophiles and augmented the North's military defenses. In December, 1867, six Northern legislatures, to ensure the total destruction of slavery, obtained Congress's consent to divide each of these states into two states, thus manufacturing the necessary three-fourths majority for a constitutional amendment for the purpose. Enraged beyond endurance by this last reckless stroke, the Lower South seceded and established a confederacy in January, 1868, which Virginia and the other slave states promptly joined when President Seward began an invasion. The Union forces encountered trouble from the start. The sea blockade proved futile. Seward's appeal for a servile insurrection failed. The invaders, moreover, were hampered not only by distance from their sources of supply, but also by the constant diversion of troops to quell bread riots in Northern cities, where the loss of Southern trade had idled the workers. In July the New York mob, forty thousand strong, repulsed the soldiers, burning the city to the ground. Two months later peace negotiations were begun, but the Northern people would neither accept the South's terms nor continue the fight. As the story concludes, the Pacific Coast seemed about to set up as a separate nation, while the Midwest and the Middle Atlantic states appeared on the point of adhering to the Southern confederacy, which was now flourishing like the proverbial bay tree as a result of direct trade with Europe. It looked as though "fanatical New England" alone would perpetuate the once glorious name of the United States.

By demonstrating that a Northern sectional party in power could inflict "bondage, degradation and ruin" upon the South while still observing constitutional forms, Ruffin brilliantly illumined the weakness of Calhoun's elaborate legalistic defense of Southern rights. As a prophet, moreover, Ruffin ranked with Nathaniel Tucker in foretelling secession, the order in which the Deep South and the border states would act, and the creation of a Southern confederacy. Both blundered, however, in specifying dates, persons and incidents and, even more importantly, in not foreseeing the North's military triumph and the extinction of slavery.

The errors of these extremists seem more excusable than the conjectures of two men who were more sober analysts of the unfolding scene. Professor George Tucker, the able political economist at the University of Virginia, declared in 1843 that, owing to steadily climbing overhead costs, slavery would come to an end probably between 1900 and 1920. With no prevision of Fort Sumter just eighteen years away, he believed, "It will be abolished with the consent of the master no less than the wishes of the slave." His failure to foresee the Civil War as the effective agency classes him with Alexis de Tocqueville, who in the 1830's deemed the South's need for federal protection against the formidable black population a sufficient reason why that section would never secede. If the improbable should happen, however, the Frenchman considered it "unquestionable" that the Northerners "would not be able, nor indeed would they try, to prevent it."

IV

Edmund Ruffin was not alone in viewing Northern society as a smoking volcano. Time and again Calhoun expressed the belief that the growing antagonism between capital and labor portended "hostility and conflict, ending in civil war," with the North headed for "a state of social dissolution." E. N. Elliott, a Southern college president, went so far in 1860 as to charge Northern businessmen with having abetted antislavery agitation in order to divert attention from their own oppressive doings. "When the mob shall have tasted the sweets of plunder and rapine in their raids upon the South," he warned, "will they spare the hoarded millions of the money-princes and nabobs of the North?"

Such premonitions of disaster could be discounted as reflecting a sectional bias; but another prediction of these years, emanating from England, still disturbs the minds of some to the present day. Thomas Babington Macaulay, the famous historian, divulged his view of the future of the United States — a country he had never visited — in a letter of May 23, 1857, to Henry S. Randall, an early biographer of Thomas Jefferson. "As long as you have a boundless extent of fertile and unoccupied land," he said, "your labouring population will be far more at ease than the labouring population of the old world," but the time will arrive when you too will have your Manchesters and Birminghams teeming with men embittered by starvation wages and unemployment. Then will come the demagogue, "ranting about the tyranny of capitalists and usurers, and asking why anybody should be permitted to drink Champagne and to ride in a carriage, while thousands of honest folks are in want of necessaries." His desperate followers will overturn the government, despoil the rich and, by so doing, destroy the springs of national prosperity. Two possibilities will then remain:

Either some Caesar or Napoleon will seize the reins of government with a strong hand; or your republic will be as fearfully plundered and laid waste by barbarians in the twentieth Century as the Roman Empire was in the fifth; — with this difference, that the Huns and Vandals who ravaged the Roman Empire came from without, and that your Huns and

Vandals will have been engendered within your own country
by your own institutions.

Lord Macaulay's death sentence on American democracy first
saw print in March, 1860, in the *Southern Literary Messenger,*
where it neatly dovetailed with the editor's own aristocratic predilections and fears. The *New York Times* copied the piece with
disapproving comment as did one or two other Northern journals, but interest in the matter was quickly smothered by the onset of the sectional war. Yet, as the sequel was to reveal, Macaulay's prophecy was a ghost that could not be laid. Every great
economic upset in the years that followed redirected attention to
it. His ominous words were cited either in a mood of resignation,
or to underline the danger of entrusting power to the unproper-
tied, or to show why remedial action should be undertaken before
it was too late.

In 1877, when the depression following the Panic of 1873 was
at its worst, *Harper's Magazine* republished the letter, and perhaps there it came to the eyes of Henry George, who used it to
reinforce his argument for the single tax in *Progress and Poverty*
(1879). Though normal conditions returned before the next
presidential election, James A. Garfield, the Republican nominee,
nonetheless took occasion to pronounce the prognostication as
the "most formidable indictment of democratic principles ever
penned." Again, in the midst of the business recession of 1884–
1885, Josiah Strong harked back to it. In his influential work *Our
Country: Its Possible Future and Its Present Crisis* (1885) he
agreed that "The time is coming when the pressure of population
on the means of subsistence will be felt here as it is now felt in
Europe and Asia," but he believed that the perils Macaulay foresaw would be averted by America's imperialistic expansion into
Latin America and Africa. And the social distress spawned by
the hard times of 1893 and culminating in Bryan's free-silver crusade prompted *Gunton's Magazine* a few months before election day in 1896 to recall the prophecy with the pointed comment
that political democracy could survive only through instant and
intelligent correction of economic injustices.

For the next quarter of a century the letter gathered dust; then
the sharp postwar business revulsion of 1920–1921 put it in cir-

culation again. This time a conservative, appalled by labor's increasing power at home and abroad, used it as a text for warning *Sewanee Review* readers against "dangers now indicated by things too obvious to be ignored," and Macaulay's words, despite the lapse of years, were rated newsworthy by papers as far apart as New York and Des Moines. The Great Depression of the thirties resuscitated the document once more. In the *Review of Reviews* in 1934 a contributor portrayed "Macaulay as a New Deal Prophet," while the *American Mercury* and a variety of newspapers reprinted the forecast with mixed emotions. Who can say that the future will not see the famous ghost walk again?

The singular longevity of the somber augury arose in part from the fact that the underlying premise harmonized with a long-held American opinion. As far back as 1787 Jefferson had foretold grave difficulties when the vacant lands should be gone and the people "get piled upon one another in large cities, as in Europe." "If some of our cities are not like Birmingham and Manchester," declared the historian George Bancroft in 1834, "it is owing not to our legislation, but to the happy accident of our possessing the West." As more and more of the public domain passed into private hands, fear of the consequences found repeated expression. Even the usually optimistic James Bryce wrote in the 1880's of "mists and shadows" looming on the nation's horizon because of the exhaustion of the free lands, and early in the nineties Professor Frederick Jackson Turner in his celebrated essay "The Significance of the Frontier in American History" announced that "the frontier is gone, and with its going has closed the first period of American history."

But was dictatorship or chaos the necessary outcome, as Macaulay had affirmed? Must the choice be between Caesar and the Huns and Vandals, or was there a third force, a middle way of orderly evolution? Yes, said the widely read *New York Ledger* to the latter proposition when the forecast first appeared: in America, unlike England, "every man expects to be rich" and hence has a personal stake in bringing about changes peaceably and lawfully. Yes, said James A. Garfield when he turned to the subject, because universal education serves as a brake on hasty and reckless action by the masses. Yes, said the forecaster's own countryman Matthew Arnold, because hatred of the wealthy can never attain great virulence in a country lacking Europe's permanent class divisions. Persuasive though such assurances were, the lurking possibility that Macaulay might nevertheless be right re-awakened apprehension whenever the economic skies unexpectedly turned black.

Edward Bellamy's *Looking Backward, 2000–1887,* William Dean Howells's *A Traveller from Altruria* (1894) and most of the other fictional portrayals of a future Utopia published in the last two decades of the nineteenth century dwelt rather upon what the authors wanted to see happen than upon what they confidently expected. Notwithstanding, they too prescribed a solution of class antagonisms by gradual and democratic means and usually allowed a hundred years or more for the accomplishment.

Their successors in the early twentieth century wrote with a greater sense of urgency and, in two of the three conspicuous instances, with less confidence in the capacity of the people. In 1907 the young Socialist writer Upton Sinclair told in *The Industrial Republic, a Study of the America of Ten Years Hence* how William Howard Taft's victory over William Jennings Bryan in the campaign of 1908 turned the country over to a plutocracy whose oppressions so aroused the people that they elected William Randolph Hearst in 1912 on a platform denouncing class rule. Then, as a cyclical depression attended with bloodshed and business prostration fell upon the land, President Hearst — cast in a singular role as his career in real life was to show — took over the railways as a first step toward the socialization of other forms of capitalistic enterprise.

But Jack London, who published *The Iron Heel* in the same year as his fellow Socialist's screed, took a very different view. According to his crystal ball the plutocracy, or "Oligarchy," turning to account the social despair bred by the depression of 1912, gained a strangle hold on the country which secret revolutionary bands sought vainly to break in 1917 and again in 1932. Though the story actually ends at the latter date, the author notes that many later revolts, "all drowned in seas of blood," proved necessary before the socialist republic was finally achieved in the year 2212.

Edward M. House, the third of the trio, set forth his conception anonymously in *Philip Dru: Administrator, a Tale of Tomorrow,*

1920–1935, published shortly after Woodrow Wilson's election in 1912. As sensitive to the economic omens as the Socialist writers, Colonel House, soon to be influential in working out Wilson's own far-reaching reform program, foretold a violent revolution in 1928 as the result of President James R. Rockland's use of troops at the polls to perpetuate his tyrannical regime. Leading the forces of resistance, Philip Dru, a high-minded ex-army officer, overcame the government troops at the battle of Elma in New York, forthwith declared himself "Administrator of the Republic," and in this self-appointed post dispensed with Congress, decreed sweeping changes of an enlightened character, promulgated a new Constitution incorporating the principle of ministerial responsibility and then, in 1935, obligingly handed the government back to the people. Many of Dru's reforms, it should be noted, foreshadowed President Wilson's legislative accomplishments, and some even anticipated the New Deal.

The growing social unrest, which in politics produced the progressive movement of the early twentieth century, tinged these later writings with Macaulayan forebodings. Nevertheless they too rejected both Caesar and the Huns and Vandals except possibly as a painful interlude. Far from taking a defeatist attitude, they revealed their authors' essential Americanism by subscribing to the traditional national belief in a happy ending.

V

In no branch of soothsaying did Americans display greater gusto than in depicting future developments in science and technology. From the start they had been a race of tinkers and gadgeteers, finding in homemade appliances a means of saving time for doing more work. After the successful contriving of the cotton gin and the steamboat around the year 1800, they turned increasingly to inventions that affected society at large. By 1843 the Commissioner of Patents could say, "The advancement of the arts from year to year taxes our credulity," and he rashly concluded that this progress seemed "to presage the arrival of that period when human improvement must end."

But neither of his sentiments represented the popular view. Far from having his credulity taxed, the ordinary American took in his stride scientific miracles which an earlier time would have denounced as witchcraft, and he looked forward to more and more of them. Forecasts of new marvels just around the corner constantly reinforced this expectation. Thus in 1812, seventeen years before the first practical use of the locomotive in England, Oliver Evans of Philadelphia, a pioneer engine builder, foretold the day "when people will travel in stages moved by steam engines from one city to another almost as fast as birds fly — fifteen to twenty miles an hour."

The man who outshone all his contemporaries at such predictions was Andrew Jackson Davis, the ill-educated son of an illiterate shoemaker in Blooming Grove, New York, who discovered that while in a trance he could learn from the spirit world "things past, present, and to come." By 1845, when but nineteen, he felt warranted in asserting, "I have now arrived at the highest degree of knowledge which the human mind is capable of acquiring." So fortified, he penned a whole shelf of mystical treatises reinterpreting God's universe at the instance of the supposed shade of Emanuel Swedenborg. Davis's ingrained practicality, however, caused him to connect man's regeneration with the leisure made possible for spiritual contemplation by the introduction of preordained inventions; and to these he devoted loving attention, notably in *The Penetralia,* published in 1856. In the field of transportation he listed double-decker railway cars with rooms for concerts and balls, spanning the continent in four days; road vehicles powered by a "simple admixture of aqueous and atmospheric gases"; and "aerial cars," similarly run, which would "sail as easily, and safely, and pleasantly, as birds." For agriculture he envisioned a quadrupling of production per acre, thanks not only to improved machinery but to man's control over climate. ("By arrangements of electricity and magnetism, he may prevent extreme heat or cold; also drouths and disastrous storms.") Among his other vaticinations were apartment houses, portable dwellings and synthetic wearing apparel. ("Great trees will be wrought up into beautiful fabrics!") How many oracles have forecast the future as well?

Later seers took up where Davis left off. Dr. Linus P. Brockett, graduate of Brown and Yale, promised in 1870 that the next hundred years would bring forth conveyances "propelled under the

earth in tubes" by a "new motive-power"; ships driven across the
Atlantic in four days by "hot or condensed air, solar heat, or some
application of electricity"; an improved mode of illumination,
"either the electric light, the magnesian light, or some yet undis-
covered illuminator"; and a great variety of other inventions, including devices for "reducing the mechanical labor of writing,"
better methods of food preservation, and the substitution "of
new materials to take the place of wood, leather, stone, or some
of the metals now in use." Edward Bellamy in *Looking Backward* (1887) foretold the radio, while Ignatius Donnelly in *Caesar's Column* (1890) added television.

Air navigation appeared on almost everyone's list, at least
from Davis's time onward. Edmund Clarence Stedman, poet and
Wall Street broker, predicted in 1879 that the airship would wipe
out all trade barriers and usher in the long-dreamed-of Congress
of the Nations. "Troops, aërial squadrons, death-dealing armaments," he said, "will be maintained only for police surveillance
over barbarous races, and for instantly enforcing the judicial decrees of the world's international court of appeal." Similarly, the
writers of Utopian fiction usually took aviation for granted, some
even to the extent of interplanetary travel. John Jacob Astor IV,
for instance, in *A Journey in Other Worlds* (1894) described the
first round trip to Saturn and Jupiter as taking place between
December 21, 2000, and June 10, 2001. A few persons, however,
being better informed as to the technical difficulties, scoffed at
the dream of flying. As late as 1903 the world-famous astronomer
Simon Newcomb admonished the public: "The example of the
bird does not prove that man can fly. . . . May not our mechani-
cians . . . be ultimately forced to admit that aerial flight is one
of that great class of problems with which man can never cope,
and give up all attempts to grapple with it?" Just two months
later Wilbur Wright winged off the ground at Kitty Hawk, North
Carolina.

While most laymen avoided the realm of pure science, a notable exception was Mme. Helena Petrovna Blavatsky, the Rus-
sian-born theosophist, who in 1888 affirmed that between that
date and 1897 there "will be a large rent in the veil of Nature, and
materialistic science will receive a death blow." The phrasing was
cryptic, but events seemed to spell out the meaning. In the years

indicated, momentous advances occurred in science — the discoveries of the Roentgen ray, radioactivity and the electron —
which did actually modify basic conceptions of the nature of matter.

More than a century after the Commissioner of Patents pronounced his obituary over science and invention, the end of human improvement did not yet appear to be in sight. The shoe,
indeed, was now on the other foot. People were anxiously inquir-
ing whether society could adjust itself quickly and wisely enough
to the dynamic changes which the progressive dominion over
Nature necessitated. Was man's servant becoming his master?
Whatever the future held in store, no responsible American found
the solution in a moratorium on human ingenuity.

VI

Almost any American, it seemed, considered himself the seventh son of a seventh son, and few subjects, domestic or international, religious or secular, escaped his scrutiny. It was natural
for a pioneer people to want to anticipate the next page of history, and the lapse of years, bringing supposedly greater sophisti-
cation, did nothing to dampen the curiosity. On the contrary, society's mounting problems — the uneasy relations of capital and
labor, the giant strides of technology, the dislocation of rural
life, the increasing strains on government, the nation's steady drift
into world affairs — only heightened the propensity. If a few
shivered at the future they saw, most warmed their hands before
it. But, whatever the nature of the glimpses, the public at large
listened with undisguised fascination.

The evidence of this interest since the Civil War is impressive,
even if only occasional examples be considered. In 1867 Senator
Charles Sumner of Massachusetts reviewed in the *Atlantic
Monthly* a sheaf of early prognostications about America, including some asserting the New World's existence long before
Columbus discovered it; and these Sumner afterward expanded
into a book, *Prophetic Voices Concerning America,* in anticipa-
tion of the centennial of Independence. In 1870 Linus P. Brockett devoted a bulky chapter to "Marvels Which Our Grandchil-
dren Will See" in *One Hundred Years' Progress of the United*

States, a work by Charles L. Flint and others. After specifying political, economic, intellectual and spiritual developments Brockett closed by itemizing a typical day in the life of an American in 1970. In 1887 William Barrows ventured his *The United States of Yesterday and of To-morrow,* while James Bryce the same year put forth a critical appraisal of *The Predictions of Hamilton and De Tocqueville* as a springboard for offering some of his own in *The American Commonwealth* a year later. In 1888 David G. Croly, after serving a novitiate in the "Prophetic Department" of a New York realtors' journal, published his *Glimpses of the Future, Suggestions as to the Drift of Things (To Be Read Now and Judged in the Year* 2000). Josiah Strong in 1893 added his bit in *The New Era,* and the same year Andrew Carnegie, taking "A Look Ahead" in the *North American Review,* foretold a merger of the English and American peoples in a "Reunited States."

The twentieth century, if anything, displayed even greater inquisitiveness. The *New York Times,* the *New York World* and other papers ran articles from time to time featuring the second sight of men like Thomas A. Edison, Hudson Maxim, Charles P. Steinmetz and Vannevar Bush, and magazines did likewise. Children learned of jet planes and atomic bombs long before their elders, thanks to the daily cartoon strip picturing Buck Rogers's adventures in the twenty-fifth century. In the booming 1920's business forecasting became a highly remunerative profession, though the unpredicted Great Depression presently discredited most of the "prophets of profits."

The next decade brought to the microphone Drew Pearson and Robert S. Allen, who as Washington journalists "in the know" entranced millions of listeners with their weekly "Predictions of Things to Come" in American politics. The New York World's Fair in 1939 shrewdly mined the same vein of curiosity by taking as its theme "The World of Tomorrow." Four years later Philip A. Brown of Baltimore campaigned for municipal office on a platform assuring his fellow townsmen that by 1968 their homes would be warmed and cooled by air radioed respectively from the equator and the poles. Not enough voters, however, were convinced by his contention that "Men of this type with a vision are sorely needed in the City Council during the next 4 years."

In 1947 about sixty leaders of business, education, religion and social welfare deposited in the cornerstone of the New York Advertising Club's new building their expectations of what the world would be like in 2004. Among the books in recent years concentrating upon prophecy have been Joseph N. Leonard, *Tools of Tomorrow* (1935), C. C. Furnas, *The Next Hundred Years, the Unfinished Business of Science* (1936), Roger W. Babson, *Looking Ahead Fifty Years* (1942), Leo Cherne, *The Rest of Your Life* (1944) and A. W. Zelomek, *Here Comes Tomorrow* (1944).

VII

"I like the dreams of the future better than the history of the past," declared the Sage of Monticello; but for neither Jefferson nor his countrymen was this partiality mere escapism, substituting reverie for action. A wise people, like a wise individual, takes counsel of things in the making as well as of those already entered on the books. Indeed, it may always hope to devise or revise the future whereas the past lies beyond recall. Some prophecies have pointed toward Great Expectations, others toward Bleak House; but whatever the degree of optimism or despair, they tended to tinge men's thinking and in some manner to condition the course of events. A rosy forecast like Dean Berkeley's set up a goal of achievement; a somber one like Lord Macaulay's conveyed timely warning against possible disaster. The effect of millennial anticipations is more difficult to assess (though Whittier has earlier been quoted on the matter), for in the most notable instance the prediction was confuted too quickly for it to have much influence good or bad.

Despite the continuing interest in prophecy the United States has never produced an oracle of the stature of Nostradamus in sixteenth-century France or even of that of the perhaps legendary Mother Shipton in England of about the same time. Moreover, some of the most significant prognostications emanated from foreign observers or visitors. America's own seers, like her philosophers, have dealt rather with fragments than with wholes, commenting on those aspects of affairs which particularly engaged their attention. Collectively, however, they covered every important phase of life.

Within the limits thus set, their record for accuracy proved extremely good. Although a man looking into the mirror of the future unavoidably sees truth in his own image, that image has generally been one of hope and self-confidence, as in the case of his fellow Americans. In a land distinguished by unparalleled social and material progress the improbable has always seemed possible and has tended to become actual. "With regard to this country," observed Daniel Webster with understandable exaggeration, "there is no poetry like the poetry of events, and all the prophecies lag behind the fulfilment." It has been the prophet of doom who most often came a cropper.

Those who set out to read the future usually mapped the road ahead from knowledge of the road behind. Consciously or unconsciously, they sought to extrapolate a trend. But trends in human affairs sometimes turn in unexpected directions, for the unanticipated may always intervene and discredit the forecast. Hence, as Poor Richard remarked, "He that knows nothing of it may by chance be a prophet, while the wisest that is may happen to miss." This is the moral that Anatole France slyly imparts in his fable of ancient Athens. One evening Gallio and some friends were learnedly pondering the future of the gods when a street riot called away Gallio to discharge his duties as Roman proconsul. Returning after a brief absence, he shrugged off the affair as a silly brawl between two groups of Hebrews about an uncouth fellow, a certain Paul or Saul of Tarsus, who was declaiming the doctrines of an alleged Messiah, whose name Gallio had forgotten. Let's not waste our breath over the mouthings of this "Jew weaver" of Tarsus, he said, for not from such a source can we ever learn what deity will supplant Jupiter.

FOR FURTHER
READING

INDEX

For further
reading

READERS accustomed to scholarly writings in which, to quote Samuel McChord Crothers, "at the foot of every page the notes run along, like little angry dogs barking at the text," will feel a sense of incompleteness in essays that ignore the convention. This final section is a gesture in extenuation. The commentary which follows seeks to accomplish four things. It gives the principal sources for each chapter; it tells which ones have appeared elsewhere fully annotated; it contains suggestions for additional reading; and it includes some material which in the author's judgment would have clogged the main narrative. Any obligation to continue with the volume ceases at this point. Ocean travelers will recall the familiar warning just before the ship leaves port: "All ashore who are going ashore!" That warning is now given the reader.

I am indebted to various people for a critical reading of parts of the first edition of this book and for other help, notably my Harvard colleagues Donald C. McKay, David Owen and Arthur M. Schlesinger, Jr.; Francis W. Coker of Yale University; Richard W. Leopold of Northwestern University; Stewart Mitchell of the Massachusetts Historical Society; Charles I. Foster of the Worcester Historical Society; and, last but not least, my wife, Elizabeth Bancroft Schlesinger. My secretary, Elizabeth F. Hoxie, rendered invaluable assistance at every stage of the research and writing and, in addition, prepared the index and guided the volume through the press.

1. "WHAT THEN IS THE AMERICAN, THIS NEW MAN?"

This essay appeared originally in the *American Historical Review*, XLVIII (1942–1943), 225–244, was reprinted as a booklet by the Macmillan Company, and under the title "Der amerikanische Charakter" appeared in condensed form in the *Amerikanische Rundschau*, no. 2

(1947). It is reproduced here unchanged except for occasional verbal revisions and the omission of footnotes. The quotation that supplies the title is from *Letters from an American Farmer* (London, 1782) by "J. Hector St. John," the pen name of Michel-Guillaume Jean de Crève-cœur, a Frenchman who lived and traveled in various parts of the Atlantic seaboard from 1759 to 1780 and again from 1783 to 1790, becoming a naturalized citizen and marrying an American.

Notable among the foreign-born commentators who in the next century settled in the United States, and hence wrote out of familiarity with American life, were Francis Lieber, Francis J. Grund and Philip Schaff. Dissatisfied with the catch-as-catch-can reports of hasty travelers, they decided to do a more faithful job. Lieber, finding Germany too hot for him as a liberal, removed to America in 1827 at the age of twenty-seven and was carrying on literary work in Philadelphia in 1834 when he wrote *The Stranger in America; or, Letters to a Gentleman in Germany: Comprising Sketches of the Manners, Society, and National Peculiarities of the United States* (Philadelphia, 1835). Grund, born in Bohemia in 1805 and educated in Vienna, lived in Philadelphia from the early 1820's, where he engaged in journalism. He recorded his findings in *The Americans in Their Moral, Social, and Political Relations* (London, 1837). Schaff, a Swiss who migrated in 1844 when he was twenty-five, joined the faculty of the seminary of the German Reformed Church at Mercersberg, Pennsylvania. On a visit to Berlin in 1854 he delivered two lectures on his experiences and observations, and these, after being published in German, were revised and translated into English under the title *America, a Sketch of the Political, Social, and Religious Character of the United States* (New York, 1855). All three became men of note in their adopted country.

Besides these general accounts by Americans of foreign birth, there is a host of autobiographical narratives written mostly in the twentieth century, which, though delineating intimate personal experiences, offer indirect testimony on American characteristics and behavior. Especially noteworthy are Mary Antin, *The Promised Land* (Boston, 1912); Edward Bok, *The Americanization of Edward Bok* (New York, 1922); Stoyan Christowe, *My American Pilgrimage* (Boston, 1947); Pascal D'Angelo, *Son of Italy* (New York, 1924); Samuel Gompers, *Seventy Years of Life and Labor* (New York, 1925); C. C. Jensen, *An American Saga* (Boston, 1927); Theodore Laer, *Forty Years of the Most Phenomenal Progress in the Annals of the United States and of the World* (New York, 1936); Hans Mattson, *Reminiscences* (St. Paul, 1891); C. M. Panunzio, *The Soul of an Immigrant* (New York, 1921); M. E. Ravage, *An American in the Making* (New York, 1917); Jacob Riis,

The Making of an American (New York, 1901); E. A. Steiner, *From Alien to Citizen* (New York, 1914); Goldie Stone, *My Caravan of Years* (New York, 1945); Andreas Ueland, *Recollections of an Immigrant* (New York, 1929); and Anzia Yezeirska, *Children of Loneliness* (New York, 1923). For a fuller list, see M. R. Davie, *World Immigration* (New York, 1936), 563–567.

Still other points of view are afforded by the multitudinous works by foreign sojourners who, as Francis Lieber put it, have been "thrown on our shore, almost periodically like the eruptions of the Geysers on Iceland." Beginning in early colonial times, these books have continued in unbroken succession down to the present, with all continents and nearly all countries contributing. The "new man" working out his destiny in far-off North America never ceased to excite the curiosity, admiration, hostility or fear of the outside world. H. S. Commager, ed., *America in Perspective* (New York, 1947), presents estimates of American national traits by thirty-five European visitors from the later eighteenth century to the twentieth. A complete Baedeker of such writings has never been compiled, but the following lists indicate the richness of the field: Lane Cooper, comp., "Travellers and Observers, 1763–1846," in W. P. Trent and others, eds., *The Cambridge History of American Literature*, I (New York, 1917–1921), 468–490, including local as well as foreign travelers; the annotated bibliography in Allan Nevins, ed., *America Through British Eyes* (New York, 1948); and Frank Monaghan, ed., *French Travellers in the United States, 1765–1932* (New York, 1933). Four works summarizing the observations of such tourists are H. T. Tuckerman, *America and Her Commentators* (New York, 1864); J. G. Brooks, *As Others See Us* (New York, 1908); Jane L. Mesick, *The English Traveller in America, 1785–1835* (New York, 1922); and Max Berger, *The British Traveller in America, 1836–1860* (New York, 1943).

These works fall into two general classes. Most are of the nature of travelogues, sometimes interlarded with general impressions and interpretations. The smaller number consist of systematic over-all discussions after the manner of Lieber, Grund and Schaff. As the writings of these three show, success in evaluating an unfamiliar way of life requires intimate acquaintance, a musing mind, unusual humility and a willingness to take pains. Not many travelers possessed these qualifications, though only Count Hermann Keyserling attempted the task while parading his unfitness for it. In his widely read volume *America Set Free* (New York, 1929) this German declares, "During my travels about the country, I guarded myself with almost old-maidish precaution against information. . . . I went out little; I read hardly any papers." In his four months' stay (which he considered needlessly long) he "used exclusively the faculty of intuition." Perhaps this is why he commends Dr. Carl G. Jung's conception of the American as "a European with the manners of a negro and the soul of an Indian."

Fortunately, other visitors went about the matter differently. Two are outstanding in the nineteenth century. Alexis de Tocqueville, while investigating prison practices in the United States for his government in 1831–1832, took advantage of his nine months' sojourn to study conditions in general. His treatise *De la Démocratie en Amérique* (the first installment of which appeared in Paris, 1835; then in Henry Reeve's translation for London publication the same year under the title *Democracy in America;* and next in a New York edition, 1838, with an introduction by J. C. Spencer) is a thoughtful and comprehensive critique. Phillips Bradley has prepared the most recent and best edition of the complete work (2 v., New York, 1945). In *Tocqueville and Beaumont in America* (New York, 1938) G. W. Pierson describes Tocqueville's methods of collecting information. The Frenchman's abstract and theoretical approach — what Lord Acton has called his "chill sententiousness" — caused him sometimes to ignore the humbler indications of the facts and rendered him singularly blind to the strength of economic forces in American life. Yet, when all deductions are made, his analysis unveils far more truth than it cloaks, and his treatise surpassed any similar one until James Bryce brought forth *The American Commonwealth* (London and New York, 1888).

The Briton enjoyed definite advantages over his predecessor: a better scholarly preparation; greater maturity (Bryce was fifty as compared with Tocqueville's twenty-nine); a more realistic temper; a perfect acquaintance with the language; and longer familiarity with the country. "When I first visited America eighteen years ago," Bryce says in his first chapter, "I brought home a swarm of bold generalizations. Half of them were thrown overboard after a second visit in 1881. Of the half that remained, some were dropped into the Atlantic when I returned across it after a third visit in 1883–84: and although the two later journeys gave birth to some new views, these views are fewer and more discreetly cautious than their departed sisters of 1870." F. W. Coker tells in detail "How Bryce Gathered His Materials and What Contemporary Reviewers Thought of the Work" in *Bryce's American Commonwealth, Fiftieth Anniversary* (R. C. Brooks, ed., New York, 1939), 155–168. In 1893–1895 Bryce published a revised and much enlarged edition and, after making minor corrections and additions in later printings, he issued what he called a "further complete revision" in 1910. Meanwhile he wrote two articles for the *Outlook,* March 25 and April 1, 1905, on "America Revisited — Changes of a Quarter Century." These various endeavors to retouch the original picture, while not without interest, lack the authority of the original work.

Of twentieth-century surveys of the American scene, two by English scholars are of particular note: Denis Brogan, *The American Character* (New York, 1944), and H. J. Laski, *The American Democracy* (New York, 1948).

In addition to appraisals by outsiders, the American people have frequently sat for self-portraits. Journalists, sociologists, anthropologists, biologists, literary scholars, clergymen, philosophers — all these and others have looked into the mirror. The list of works includes J. T. Adams, *The American* (New York, 1943); Hamilton Basso, *Mainstream* (New York, 1943); Jerome Dowd, *Democracy in America* (Oklahoma City, 1921); John Erskine, *American Character and Other Essays* (Chautauqua, 1927); A. B. Hart, *National Ideals Historically Traced* (New York, 1907); F. E. Hill, *What Is American?* (New York, 1933); Max Lerner, *America as a Civilization* (New York, 1957); Margaret Mead, *And Keep Your Powder Dry* (New York, 1942); Alexander Meikeljohn, *What Does America Mean?* (New York, 1935); Bliss Perry, *The American Mind* (Boston, 1912); A. H. Quinn, *The Soul of America, Yesterday and Today* (Philadelphia, 1932); Monroe Royce, *The Passing of the American* (New York, 1911); Leon Samson, *The American Mind, a Study in Socio-analysis* (New York, 1932); P. B. Sears, *Who Are These Americans?* (New York, 1939); Simeon Strunsky, *The Living Tradition* (New York, 1939); and Henry van Dyke, *The Spirit of America* (New York, 1910).

Because of the stress which the present essay puts on the agricultural underpinnings of the American people, three other books may prove of interest: J. M. Williams, *Our Rural Heritage, the Social Psychology of Rural Development* (New York, 1925); F. J. Turner's collection of essays in *The Frontier in American History* (New York, 1920); and D. M. Potter, *People of Plenty* (Chicago, 1954). Those who would like greater emphasis on the Southern variant of the national character should not fail to read W. J. Cash, *The Mind of the South* (New York, 1941).

Interesting comments on the present essay have come from naturalized citizens, who, from their special backgrounds, called attention to traits and attitudes which they felt had been overlooked or understressed. An Italo-American waxed eloquent over the beauty of the young girls, while adding reluctantly that their bloom fades sooner than that of European women. An Anglo-American emphasized the difference between the motor impulses of the two peoples by recalling that in his native country candidates "stand" for office, whereas in the United States they "run" for office. A friend who grew up in pre-Communist Russia considered the lack of privacy a distinguishing mark of American life, while another Russian-American held that boastfulness has been equally characteristic of the two peoples. In support of this contention he cited the following passage from Roger Dow's article, "Prostor, a Geopolitical Study of Russia and the United States," in the *Russian Review*, I, 17 (November, 1941):

> Americans and Russians have had a certain love of vastness for its own sake. When the Russians built their railroads they insisted that the tracks must have a wider gauge than elsewhere — "Russia is so much bigger," they explained to the harassed engineers. It is exemplified in the reports of Russian resources, for great as they are, they never quite equal the optimism of the official statistics. . . . When Twain was travelling in Russia he got into a discussion with Baron Ungern-Sternberg, the Minister of Railways, who all but overwhelmed him with statistics. At one point, the minister said there were ten thousand convicts working on railway gradings and right-of-ways, at which point the American sized him up for a minute and then blandly replied that in the United States there were *eighty thousand* convicts working on the railways, and that every one was under sentence of death for first-degree murder! "That closed *him* out," he said happily.

2. BIOGRAPHY OF A NATION OF JOINERS

Except for the absence of footnotes and some verbal changes, this essay appears substantially as published in the *American Historical Review*, L (1944–1945), 1–25. Under the title "Der Amerikaner als Vereinmensch" it was also published in the *Amerikanische Rundschau*, no. 10 (1947). Charles I. Foster, commenting on the article in the *American Historical Review*, L, 434–436, properly points out that the subject, if exhaustively explored, would include the family, the plantation, the indenture system and spontaneous, informal groups, and that government itself is a manifestation of the associative spirit, though in a different sense from that here used. The list of inclusions might further be extended to embrace international associations, as J. C. Faries evidences in *The Rise of Internationalism* (New York, 1915).

General historical works refer repeatedly to voluntary organizations, and some of these bodies have been studied intensively. For those in the religious field see W. W. Sweet, *The Story of Religion in America* (rev. ed., New York, 1939); Albert Post, *Popular Freethought in*

America, 1825–1850 (New York, 1943); C. I. Foster, *An Errand of Mercy, the Evangelical United Front, 1790–1837* (Chapel Hill, 1960); and Fergus MacDonald, *The Catholic Church and the Secret Societies in the United States* (New York, 1946). In politics E. E. Robinson, *The Evolution of American Political Parties* (New York, 1924), affords a functional analysis, while special studies include E. D. Collins, "Committees of Correspondence of the American Revolution," American Historical Association, *Report for 1901*, I, 243–271; E. P. Link, *Democratic-Republican Societies, 1790–1800* (New York, 1942); S. A. Rice, *Farmers and Workers in American Politics* (New York, 1930); and Nathan Fine, *Farmer and Labor Parties in the United States, 1828–1928* (New York, 1928).

Particularly useful for reform movements are the following: Janet Wilson (James), "The Early Anti-Slavery Propaganda," *More Books*, XIX (1944), 343–359, 393–405, XX (1945), 51–67; Benjamin Quarles, "Sources of Abolitionist Income," *Mississippi Valley Historical Review*, XXXII (1945–1946), 63–76; G. H. Barnes, *The Anti-Slavery Impulse, 1830–1844* (New York, 1934), which also discusses religiously inspired benevolent societies; D. L. Colvin, *Prohibition in the United States* (New York, 1926); J. A. Krout, *The Origins of Prohibition* (New York, 1925); P. H. Odegard, *Pressure Politics: the Story of the Anti-Saloon League* (New York, 1928); Merle Curti, *Peace or War, the American Struggle* (New York, 1936); Eleanor Flexner, *Century of Struggle: the Woman's Rights Movement* (Cambridge, 1959); Blake McKelvey, *American Prisons* (Chicago, 1936); and F. D. Watson, *The Charity Organization Movement in the United States* (New York, 1922).

The advent of capitalistic associations is traced in J. S. Davis, *Essays in the Earlier History of American Corporations* (2 v., Cambridge, 1917); C. C. Abbott, *The Rise of the Business Corporation* (Ann Arbor, 1936); Shaw Livermore, *Early American Land Companies* (New York, 1939); and Oscar and Mary F. Handlin, "Origins of the American Business Corporation," *Journal of Economic History*, V (1945–1946), 1–23. Later developments are delineated in Kenneth Sturges, *American Chambers of Commerce* (New York, 1915), C. E. Bonnett, *Employers' Associations in the United States* (New York, 1922), and the many works on trusts and combinations.

The encyclopedestrian *History of Labour in the United States* (4 v., New York, 1918–1935) by J. R. Commons and others and *The American Federation of Labor* (Washington, 1933) by L. L. Lorwin contain valuable data on trade unions, while H. L. Childs contrasts the pressure activities of the AFL and the United States Chamber of Com-

merce in *Labor and Capital in National Politics* (Columbus, 1930).
Agrarian associations figure prominently in S. J. Buck, *The Granger
Movement* (Cambridge, 1913); J. D. Hicks, *The Populist Revolt*
(Minneapolis, 1931); and Edward Wiest, *Agricultural Organization in
the United States* (Lexington, 1923). Among the relatively few works
on scientific, learned and professional societies are R. S. Bates, *The
Rise of Scientific Societies in the United States* (Cambridge, 1943);
Morris Fishbein, *A History of the American Medical Association, 1847
to 1947* (Philadelphia, 1947); and L. W. Dunlap, *American Historical
Societies, 1790–1860* (Madison, 1944). For a comparison of the roles
and methods of professional and business organizations, with some
attention to labor associations and farm co-operatives, see C. F.
Taeusch, *Professional and Business Ethics* (New York, 1926).

Fraternal orders are treated from various points of view in N. P. Gist,
Secret Societies, a Cultural Study of Fraternalism (Columbia, Mo.,
1940); C. W. Ferguson, *Fifty Million Brothers* (New York, 1937);
Walter Basye, *History and Operation of Fraternal Insurance* (Rochester, 1919); and H. B. Meyer, "Fraternal Beneficiary Societies in
the United States," *American Journal of Sociology*, VI (1901), 646–
661. These should be supplemented by more particular accounts, such
as M. M. Johnson, *The Beginnings of Freemasonry in America* (New
York, 1924); A. G. Stevens, comp., *The Cyclopædia of Fraternities*
(rev. ed., New York, 1907); and Arthur Preuss, comp., *A Dictionary
of Secret and Other Societies* (St. Louis, 1924). Charles McCarthy,
"The Antimasonic Party," American Historical Association, *Report for
1902*, I, 365–574, and J. C. Palmer, *The Morgan Affair and Anti-
Masonry* (Washington, 1924), describe the uprising against that order.
Other leisure-time organizations are portrayed in Jane C. Croly, *The
History of the Woman's Club Movement in America* (New York,
1898); C. F. Marden, *Rotary and Its Brothers* (Princeton, 1935); and
W. E. Davies, *Patriotism on Parade, the Story of Veterans' and Heredi-
tary Organizations* (Cambridge, 1959); while frequent references to
sports and other recreational associations appear in F. R. Dulles,
America Learns to Play (New York, 1940). For a description of
mutual-aid societies, cultural organizations and fraternal orders among
ethnic groups, see W. C. Smith, *Americans in the Making* (New York,
1939), 96–113. Conspiratorial bodies form the subject matter of Wood
Gray, *The Hidden Civil War* (New York, 1942); S. K. Horn, *Invisible
Empire, the Story of the Ku Klux Klan, 1866–1871* (Boston, 1939);
J. M. Mecklin, *The Ku Klux Klan* (New York, 1924), dealing with the
twentieth-century reincarnation; and Michael Sayers and A. E. Kahn,
Sabotage! (New York, 1942), and Arthur Derounian ("John Roy Carl-

son"), *Under Cover* (New York, 1943) and *The Plotters* (New York, 1946), treating the period of the Axis war and its aftermath.

The role of associations as "self-government by the people outside of government" — Herbert Hoover's phrase — is considered historically and sociologically in Oscar and Mary Handlin, *Dimensions of Liberty* (Cambridge, 1961), chaps. v–vi. The increasing importance of pressure activities in recent years is depicted in E. P. Herring, *Group Representation before Congress* (Baltimore, 1929); K. C. Crawford, *The Pressure Boys* (New York, 1939); and Stuart Chase, *Democracy under Pressure* (New York, 1945). Joseph Paul-Boncour, J. N. Figgis, H. J. Laski, A. D. Lindsay, G. D. H. Cole, S. G. Hobson and other European political thinkers have gone so far as to advocate changing the structure of government in order to give voluntary associations direct and official representation; but this doctrine of pluralism, curiously enough, has mustered little support in the country where the organizational process has gone furthest. These theoretical proposals are concisely reviewed and appraised by F. W. Coker in the *Encyclopaedia of the Social Sciences* (New York, 1930–1934), XII, 170–174.

3. AMERICAN CONTRIBUTIONS TO CIVILIZATION

This chapter is essentially the article which appeared in the *Atlantic Monthly*, CCIII (1959), 65–69, under the title "America's Influence: Our Ten Contributions to Civilization." It has been reprinted in anthologies and circulated by the United States Information Agency in translation in Germany, Japan, South Vietnam and elsewhere. The subject has received little consideration from historians or others. President Charles W. Eliot of Harvard included an address on "American Contributions to Civilization" in a book of that title (New York, 1898). These were, he said, the substitution of negotiation and arbitration for war, religious toleration, the step-by-step attainment of manhood suffrage, the peaceable assimilation of immigrants and the wide diffusion of material well-being.

Four years afterward, in 1902, William T. Stead, editor of the London *Review of Reviews*, devoted a whole volume to the theme and in prophetic mood called it *The Americanization of the World, or, The Trend of the Twentieth Century*. The Englishman included all of Eliot's items with many others in a diversity of fields and of varying degrees of importance. Nearly fifty years later another European made somewhat comparable claims for the United States, though with more scholarly caution. This was the Norwegian historian Halvdan Koht in his book *The American Spirit in Europe* (Philadelphia, 1949). In

Professor Koht's opinion, "it is scarcely possible to point to a single aspect of modern civilization in which America has not exerted a certain degree of influence; in many matters it has been the determining influence." But again he did not distinguish the one kind from the other. Apart from these rare attempts at a general discussion, there is, however, an abundance of books, too numerous to list here, on each of the basic contributions noticed in the present essay.

4. THE ROLE OF THE IMMIGRANT

This is the third form of a piece originally appearing in *New Viewpoints in American History* (New York, 1922) under the title "The Influence of Immigration in American History." The second was prepared for *Common Ground,* I (1940–1941), 19–28, where it was called "Immigrants in America." This latest version, though presenting essentially the same point of view, covers additional matter and bears only a rough family resemblance to its predecessors. A bibliography of the subject is *Immigration in the United States: a Selected List of Recent References* (Washington, 1943), compiled for the Library of Congress by Anne L. Baden. A useful shorter list is in D. F. Bowers, ed., *Foreign Influences in American Life* (Princeton, 1944), part ii. For a critical discussion of historical writings on immigration, see E. N. Saveth, *American Historians and European Immigrants, 1875–1925* (New York, 1948). The following highly selective list omits all references antedating the bibliographical note appended to the essay of 1922.

Comprehensive surveys include G. M. Stephenson, *A History of American Immigration, 1820–1924* (Boston, 1926); R. L. Garis, *Immigration Restriction* (New York, 1927); Carl Wittke, *We Who Built America* (New York, 1939); and E. L. Jordan, *Americans* (New York, 1939). More limited as to period but still general in scope are M. L. Hansen, *The Atlantic Migration, 1607–1860* (Cambridge, 1940); Ella Lonn, *Foreigners in the Confederacy* (Chapel Hill, 1940); and M. R. Davie, *Refugees in America* (New York, 1947), dealing with fugitives from the totalitarian upheavals in the twentieth century. M. L. Hansen, *The Immigrant in American History* (Cambridge, 1940), and Oscar Handlin, *Race and Nationality in American Life* (Boston, 1957), are collections of essays touching many aspects of the subject.

Particular groups are more intensively studied in D. C. Graham, *Colonists from Scotland . . . 1707–1783* (Ithaca, 1956); W. A. Knittle, *The Early Eighteenth Century Palatine Emigration* (Philadelphia, 1936); Ralph Wood, ed., *The Pennsylvania Germans* (Princeton, 1942); J. A. Hawgood, *The Tragedy of German America: the Germans in the United States of America during the Nineteenth Century and After* (New York, 1940); C. J. Child, *The German-Americans in Politics, 1914–1917* (Madison, 1939); Carl Wittke, *German-Americans and the World War* (Columbus, 1936); W. F. Adams, *Ireland and Irish Emigration to the New World from 1815 to the Famine* (New Haven, 1932); E. F. Roberts, *Ireland in America* (New York, 1931); T. C. Blegen, *Norwegian Migration to America, 1825–1860* (2 v., Northfield, 1931–1940); C. C. Qualey, *Norwegian Settlement in the United States* (Northfield, 1938); A. B. Benson and Naboth Hedin, eds., *Swedes in America, 1638–1938* (New Haven, 1938); Arnold Mulder, *Americans from Holland* (Philadelphia, 1947); B. H. Wabeke, *Dutch Emigration to North America, 1624–1860* (New York, 1944); Giovanni Schiavo, *The Italians in America before the Civil War* (New York, 1934); P. K. Hitti, *The Syrians in America* (New York, 1924); Wasyl Halich, *Ukrainians in the United States* (Chicago, 1937); Oscar Handlin, *Adventure in Freedom: Three Hundred Years of Jewish Life in America* (New York, 1954); Manuel Gamio, *Mexican Immigration to the United States* (Chicago, 1930); M. L. Hansen, *The Mingling of the Canadian and American Peoples* (New Haven, 1940); Bruno Lasker, *Filipino Immigration to Continental United States and to Hawaii* (Chicago, 1931); Yamato Ichihashi, *Japanese in the United States* (Stanford University, 1932); and J. H. Franklin, *From Slavery to Freedom* (New York, 1947), the best history of the American Negro.

The process of acculturation, though discussed in other works, is the main concern of Donald Young, *American Minority Peoples* (New York, 1932); T. J. Woofter, *Races and Ethnic Groups in American Life* (New York, 1933); M. R. Davie, *World Immigration* (New York, 1936); Bertram Schrieke, *Alien Americans* (New York, 1936); W. C. Smith, *Americans in the Making* (New York, 1939); Oscar Handlin, *Boston's Immigrants, 1790–1865* (Cambridge, 1941) and *The Uprooted* (Boston, 1951); Carey McWilliams, *Brothers under the Skin* (Boston, 1943); Gunnar Myrdal, *An American Dilemma: the Negro Problem and Modern Democracy* (2 v., New York, 1944); and F. J. Brown and J. S. Roucek, eds., *One America* (rev. ed., New York, 1945). Nativist attitudes and movements are studied in Gustavus Myers, *History of Bigotry in the United States* (New York, 1943), and, with reference to particular instances, in R. A. Billington, *The Protestant Crusade, 1800–1860* (New York, 1938); John Higham, *Strangers in the Land. Patterns of American Nativism, 1860–1925* (New Brunswick, 1955); L. J. Levinger, *The Causes of Anti-Semitism in the United States* (Philadelphia, 1925), and Carey McWilliams, *Prejudice, Japanese-Americans: Symbol of Racial Intolerance* (Boston, 1944).

For immigrant autobiographies, see the bibliography for chapter I of the present volume. T. C. Blegen, *Grass Roots History* (Minneapolis, 1947), pays special attention to immigrant experiences in America.

Immigrant contributions to American civilization form the subject matter of R. E. Stauffer, ed., *The American Spirit in the Writings of Americans of Foreign Birth* (Boston, 1922); O. G. Villard and others, *The Influence of Immigration on American Culture* (New York, 1929); A. H. Eaton, *Immigrant Gifts to American Life* (New York, 1932); William Seabrook, *These Foreigners* (New York, 1938); and Louis Adamic, *A Nation of Nations* (New York, 1947). B. J. Hovde, "Notes on the Effects of Emigration upon Scandinavia," *Journal of Modern History*, VI (1934), 253–279, is one of the few studies exploring the reflex action of emigration upon the countries of origin.

5. THE TIDES OF NATIONAL POLITICS

This chapter, appearing in its first form in the *Yale Review*, XXIX, 217–230 (December, 1939), under the title "Tides of American Politics" excited a good deal of editorial comment at the time. Most of the commentators accepted the underlying thesis, "T. R. B." in the *New Republic*, CII (March 11, 1940), 344, going so far as to say of the article, "It is worth a freight-train-load of Washington dispatches." But the *St. Louis Post-Dispatch*, December 25, 1939, wondered whether so "mechanistic" a view does not violate "all our concepts of democracy. Are we ruled by the calendar or by our thinking? Do we admit Emerson's dictum that 'things are in the saddle and ride mankind'? Or is all this just an interesting accident?" *Time* in its issue of April 15, 1940, brooding over the prediction that "the political mood known loosely as New Dealism" would "last until 1947 or 1948, with a possible error of a year or so one way or the other," hopefully cited as evidence to the contrary the indications of a Gallup poll. The essay as now revised amplifies certain points in the original piece and continues the analysis through the restoration of conservative Republican leadership to Congress in 1947. Readers familiar with the author's discussion of "Radicalism and Conservatism in American History" in *New Viewpoints in American History* (New York, 1922) will discover that in both the *Yale Review* article and the present essay he offers a different and, he thinks, sounder explanation of the alternation of these trends.

The search for recurrent patterns and rhythms in human history has occupied many minds, though only a few writers have examined such phenomena with specific reference to the American past. William Allen White, *Some Cycles of Cathay* (Chapel Hill, 1925), divides

United States history into three broad periods — the Revolutionary, the Anti-Slavery and the Populist — which he regards as "a part of a larger cycle of democratic growth in the peoples and governments controlled by the English speaking races." Also concerned with American history are two able statistical analyses of party turnover in elections: S. A. Rice, *Quantitative Methods in Politics* (New York, 1928), chaps. xx–xxii, and L. H. Bean, *How to Predict Elections* (New York, 1948). Though these studies deal with the fortunes of parties rather than with political trends in the sense of the present essay, Bean questioned the inevitability of a fifteen-year conservative tide after 1947, holding that "the opposite is possible, that the 1950's might again see the dominance of liberalism."

Cyclical theories from ancient Babylon to modern times are summarized by A. J. Toynbee in *A Study of History*, IV (London, 1939), 23–39, who then presents his own views. Of other recent writings in this general field, R. H. Wheeler argues the case for "The Effect of Climate on Human Behavior and History" in Kansas Academy of Science, *Transactions*, XLVI (1943), 33–51. But the lion's share of attention has been given to economic cycles. W. C. Mitchell digests the earlier literature on the subject in the *Encyclopaedia of the Social Sciences* (New York, 1930–1934), III, 92–107. Later studies include Mitchell, *Business Cycles* (New York, 1927); W. I. King, *The Causes of Economic Fluctuations* (New York, 1938); E. L. Smith, *Tides in the Affairs of Men* (New York, 1939); J. A. Schumpeter, *Business Cycles* (2 v., New York, 1939); Ellsworth Huntington, *Mainsprings of Civilization* (New York, 1945), chaps. xxiv–xxviii; and E. R. Dewey and E. F. Dakin, *Cycles, the Science of Prediction* (New York, 1947).

Unfortunately, comparable phenomena in intellectual and artistic fields have had little study. Friedrich Meinecke, *Die Entstehung des Historismus*, II (2 v., Munich, 1936), 480–631, discusses Goethe's conception of alternating currents in religion, in literature and in art. A short but suggestive article on the creative work of selected individuals is J. H. D. Webster, "Periodic Inspiration in Poetry and Music," *Poetry Review*, XXXIV (1943), 137–140. Jane Richardson and A. L. Kroeber, going further afield, offer a "quantitative analysis" of *Three Centuries of Women's Dress Fashions* (Berkeley, 1940).

6. RATING THE PRESIDENTS

This essay replaces the chapter on "A Yardstick for Presidents" in the original edition of this book, being based upon the later and more comprehensive survey of 1962. It somewhat amplifies the article "Our

Presidents: a Rating by 75 Historians" in the *New York Times Magazine*, July 29, 1962, which also appeared in the *Courier-Journal Magazine* (Louisville, Ky.), August 19. The participants in the poll were Lewis E. Atherton, University of Missouri; James P. Baxter, 3d, former president of Williams College; Ray A. Billington, Northwestern University; Wilfred E. Binkley, Ohio Northern University; Theodore C. Blegen, University of Minnesota; John M. Blum, Yale University; Denis W. Brogan, Peterhouse, Cambridge University, England; Paul H. Buck, Harvard University; Solon J. Buck, former National Archivist, Washington, D.C.; James M. Burns, Williams College; Francis W. Coker, Yale University; Henry S. Commager, Amherst College; James B. Conant, former President of Harvard University; Marcus Cunliffe, University of Manchester, Manchester, England; Richard N. Current, University of Wisconsin; Merle Curti, University of Wisconsin; Virginius Dabney, ed., *Richmond Times-Dispatch;* Chester M. Destler, Connecticut College, New London; David Donald, Princeton University; Dwight L. Dumond, University of Michigan; Clement Eaton, University of Kentucky; Harold U. Faulkner, Smith College; Gilbert C. Fite, University of Oklahoma; Felix Frankfurter, United States Supreme Court; John Hope Franklin, Brooklyn College; Frank Freidel, Harvard University; Ralph H. Gabriel, American University, Washington, D.C.; Paul W. Gates, Cornell University; Norman A. Graebner, University of Illinois; Fletcher M. Green, University of North Carolina; Oscar Handlin, Harvard University; James B. Hedges, Brown University; Pendleton Herring, President, Social Science Research Council; John D. Hicks, University of California at Berkeley; John Higham, University of Michigan; Richard Hofstadter, Columbia University; Arthur N. Holcombe, Harvard University; Sidney Hyman, political analyst, Washington, D.C.; Gerald W. Johnson, journalist and historian, Baltimore; Walter Johnson, University of Chicago; Arthur S. Link, Princeton University; Dumas Malone, University of Virginia; Asa E. Martin, Pennsylvania State University; Reginald C. McGrane, University of Cincinnati; Frederick Merk, Harvard University; Elting E. Morison, Massachusetts Institute of Technology; Samuel E. Morison, Harvard University; George E. Mowry, University of California at Los Angeles; Curtis Nettels, Cornell University; Roy F. Nichols, University of Pennsylvania; Russell B. Nye, Michigan State College; John W. Oliver, University of Pittsburgh; Bradford Perkins, University of Michigan; Dexter Perkins, Cornell University; Stow Persons, University of Iowa; Earl Pomeroy, University of Oregon; David M. Potter, Stanford University; Edgar E. Robinson, Stanford University; Lindsay Rogers, Columbia University; Eugene H. Roseboom, Ohio State University;

Clinton Rossiter, Cornell University; Arthur M. Schlesinger, Jr., Harvard University; Charles G. Sellers, Jr., University of California at Berkeley; Fred A. Shannon, University of Illinois; James W. Silver, University of Mississippi; Henry Nash Smith, University of California at Berkeley; Kenneth M. Stampp, University of California at Berkeley; Irving Stone, biographer and historian; Glyndon G. Van Deusen, University of Rochester; Richard C. Wade, University of Chicago; Walter P. Webb, University of Texas; Thomas J. Wertenbaker, Princeton University; T. Harry Williams, Louisiana State University; Harvey Wish, Western Reserve University; and C. Vann Woodward, Yale University.

Two foreign scholars have earlier sat in judgment on our chief executives. James Bryce, who gloomily entitled a chapter in *The American Commonwealth* "Why Great Men Are Not Chosen Presidents," attributed this to many circumstances: the tendency of natural leaders to avoid public life for business and the law, where the material rewards are greater; the timidity which usually causes parties to prefer "safe" candidates to strong-minded ones; the political advantage of confining nominations to the more populous states; the voters' meager appraisal of the qualities needed for the position; and the habit of party regularity at the polls. Many persons, moreover, who might have made good Presidents, lost the chance because they would have made poor candidates. Comparing the twenty elected to the office down to 1900 with the twenty English prime ministers of the same period, he considered that "only Washington, Jefferson, Lincoln, and Grant can claim to belong to a front rank represented in the English list by 7 or possibly 8 names." A later English student, however, entered a sharp dissent. Better grounded in American history than Bryce, and writing also from a longer perspective, Harold J. Laski in *The American Presidency* (1940) maintained that eleven of the thirty-one Presidents down to that time had been "extraordinary men," a proportion rivaling that of his own country. On the whole, he thought the advantage lay actually with the United States, since the best American executives averaged longer in power than their British counterparts and hence were able to do more to effectuate their policies.

Other evidences and estimates of presidential greatness may prove of interest. Twenty-nine states have named counties after Washington, twenty-six after Jefferson, twenty-four after Lincoln, twenty-two after Jackson and twelve after Adams; but this is a type of recognition for which later executives could hardly qualify as the country filled up and no counties remained to be christened. Franklin D. Roosevelt a week after his first election offered his own list of great predecessors, which, as reported in the *New York Times*, November 13, 1932, consisted of Washington, Jefferson, Jackson, Lincoln, Cleveland, Theodore Roosevelt and Wilson, who, he said, "were leaders of thought at times when certain historic ideas in the life of the nation had to be clarified."

In most instances, however, the interest in greatness has gone beyond presidential performance to include lifelong services. On this broader basis, thirteen historians, asked "Who Are the Three Greatest Americans?" could agree on only two, Washington and Lincoln, as reported in the *New York Times*, March 24, 1907; and Arthur H. Vandenberg, afterward United States Senator from Michigan, found that a hundred leading citizens in 1921 rated Lincoln as foremost, with Washington next and all other choices trailing far in the rear. He announced the results in a book whose title voiced his own dissent: *The Greatest American: Alexander Hamilton* (New York, 1921). In 1903 J. M. Cattel spread a wider net in his "Statistical Study of Eminent Men" in *Popular Science Monthly*, LXII, 359–377. Determining the one thousand outstanding figures in world history by the proportion of space they occupied in six biographical cyclopedias in four different countries, he found eight American Presidents to be in the list: Washington, Lincoln and Jefferson, who qualified in the first group of one hundred, Grant and John Adams in the second hundred, Jackson in the third, and Madison and John Quincy Adams in the fifth. Here again, the estimates were not confined to presidential performance.

Morton Borden has edited *America's Ten Greatest Presidents* (Chicago, 1961), a series of sketches of the ones rated above the average by the poll of 1948 (and again by that of 1962). D. C. Coyle relates the verbal abuse suffered by the Presidents in *Ordeal of the Presidency* (Washington, 1960); and F. L. Mott reviews statistically the line-up of the press in "Newspapers in Presidential Campaigns," *Public Opinion Quarterly*, VIII (1944–1945), 348–367.

7. PERSISTING PROBLEMS OF THE PRESIDENCY

Outstanding among recent historical and analytical studies of the presidency are, in order of publication, W. E. Binkley, *The Powers of the President* (Garden City, 1937, revised in 1947 as *President and Congress*); E. S. Corwin, *The President: Office and Powers* (New York, 1940); E. P. Herring, *Presidential Leadership* (New York, 1940); H. J. Laski, *The American Presidency, an Interpretation* (New York, 1940); Irving Stone, *They Also Ran. The Story of the Men Who Were Defeated for the Presidency* (Garden City, 1943); G. F. Milton, *The Use of Presidential Power, 1789–1943* (Boston, 1944); Dorothy G.

and Julius Goebel, *Generals in the White House* (New York, 1945); E. T. Booth, *Country Life in America as Lived by Ten Presidents of the United States* (New York, 1947); C. P. Patterson, *Presidential Government in the United States* (Chapel Hill, 1947); J. E. Pollard, *The Presidents and the Press* (Washington, 1947); P. R. Levin, *Seven by Chance: the Accidental Presidents* (New York, 1948); K. H. Young and Lamar Middleton, *Heirs Apparent* (New York, 1948); Sidney Hyman, *The American President* (New York, 1954); E. H. Roseboom, *A History of Presidential Elections* (New York, 1957); Jack Bell, *The Splendid Misery* (New York, 1960); L. W. Koenig, *The Invisible Presidency* (New York, 1960); Clinton Rossiter, *The American Presidency* (rev. ed., New York, 1960); and Vincent Wilson, Jr., *The Book of the Presidents* (Silver Spring, Md., 1962). For presidential health and longevity, see L. I. Dublin and A. J. Lotka, *Length of Life* (New York, 1936); anon., "Does the Presidency Shorten Life?" Metropolitan Life Insurance Company, *Statistical Bulletin*, XXVII, no. 10 (October, 1956), 1–3; and Rudolph Marx, *The Health of the Presidents* (New York, 1960).

Some of the older works have continuing value, notably James Bryce, *The American Commonwealth* (3 v., London, 1888, and revisions); Edward Stanwood, *A History of the Presidency* (rev. ed., 2 v., Boston, 1928); C. C. Thach, *The Creation of the Presidency* (Baltimore, 1922); and H. H. Horwill, *Usages of the American Constitution* (Oxford, 1925).

8. AMERICA'S STAKE IN ONE WORLD

This chapter elaborates certain ideas set forth in "War and Peace in American History," an article in the *New Republic*, CVII (September 21, 1942), 337–340, which appeared while the Axis war was still in progress. For discussions of the pragmatic isolationism of the fledgling Republic, see J. F. Rippy and Angie Debo, *The Historical Background of the American Policy of Isolation* (Northampton, 1924); S. F. Bemis, "Washington's Farewell Address: a Foreign Policy of Independence," *American Historical Review*, XXXIX (1933–1934), 250–268; and A. B. Darling, *Our Rising Empire, 1763–1803* (New Haven, 1940).

In *A Study of War* (2 v., Chicago, 1942) Quincy Wright traces the natural history of war in world history as well as the tendency toward coalition conflicts, while the American habit of unpreparedness is made clear in Emory Upton, *The Military Policy of the United States* (rev. ed., Washington, 1917), covering the period to 1865; F. L. Huidekoper, *The Military Unpreparedness of the United States* (New York,

1915); and Harold and Margaret Sprout, *The Rise of American Naval Power, 1776–1918* (Princeton, 1939). D. L. Fleming, *The United States and the League of Nations, 1918–1920* (New York, 1932), and T. A. Bailey, *Woodrow Wilson and the Great Betrayal* (New York, 1945), are accounts of America's failure to enter the League. For the UN, see E. P. Chase, *The United Nations in Action* (New York, 1950), and L. M. Goodrich, *The United Nations* (New York, 1959).

9. WORLD CURRENTS IN AMERICAN HISTORY

This essay is based upon material presented, with full documentation, in "World Currents in American Civilization," a chapter in the collaborative work *Studies in Civilization* (Philadelphia, 1941), published by the University of Pennsylvania Bicentennial Conference. C. J. H. Hayes argues essentially the same thesis in "The American Frontier — Frontier of What?" in the *American Historical Review,* LI (1945–1946), 199–216. Particular aspects of the general theme are dealt with in numerous places. R. R. Palmer, *The Age of the Democratic Revolution* (Princeton, 1959), interrelates the democratic movements in America and Europe during the period 1760–1800. R. B. Mowatt and Preston Slosson, *History of the English-Speaking Peoples* (New York, 1943), is more interesting for the goal set up by the authors than for their success in interweaving the histories of the United States and the British Empire. Other works treating Anglo-American contacts include Edward Eggleston, *The Transit of Civilization from Europe to America in the Seventeenth Century* (New York, 1901); William Cunningham, *English Influence on the United States* (Cambridge, England, 1916); and A. F. Pollard, *Factors in American History* (New York, 1928), which does more adequately what Cunningham's title promises. Bernard Faÿ, *The Revolutionary Spirit in France and America* (New York, 1927), spanning the period 1776–1800, and H. M. Jones, *America and French Culture, 1750–1848* (Chapel Hill, 1927), are useful volumes, and in *Ideas in America* (Cambridge, 1944), chap. vii, Jones discusses, more broadly, "The Influence of European Ideas in Nineteenth-Century America."

E. B. Greene's pamphlet, *American Interest in Popular Government Abroad* (Washington, 1917), should be supplemented by Elizabeth B. White, *American Opinion of France from Lafayette to Poincaré* (New York, 1927); C. D. Hazen, *Contemporary American Opinion of the French Revolution* (Baltimore, 1897); Myrtle A. Cline, *The American Attitude toward the Greek War of Independence, 1821–1828* (Atlanta, 1930); A. J. May, *Contemporary American Opinion of the Mid-Century*

Revolutions in Central Europe (Philadelphia, 1927); J. G. Gazley, *American Opinion of German Unification, 1848–1871* (New York, 1926); and H. R. Marraro, *American Opinion on the Unification of Italy, 1846–1861* (New York, 1932). For the antislavery movement as an international phenomenon, see particularly Annie H. Abel and F. J. Klingberg's introduction to *A Side-Light on Anglo-American Relations, 1839–1858* (Washington, 1927), and Klingberg's article, "Harriet Beecher Stowe and Social Reform in England," *American Historical Review*, XLIII (1937–1938), 542–552.

Transatlantic intellectual and cultural relations have received considerable attention. D. F. Bowers, ed., *Foreign Influences in American Life* (Princeton, 1944), includes chapters on economic theory, the fine arts and the role of Hegel and Darwin. Among other studies are B. A. Hinsdale, "Notes on the History of Foreign Influences upon Education in the United States," United States Commissioner of Education, *Report for 1897–1898*, I, 591–629; C. F. Thwing, *The American and the German University* (New York, 1928); J. A. Walz, *German Influence in American Education and Culture* (New York, 1936); Merle Curti, "The Great Mr. Locke, America's Philosopher, 1783–1861," in *Probing the Past* (New York, 1955), 69–118; Michael Kraus, *The Atlantic Civilization: Eighteenth-Century Origins* (Ithaca, 1949); R. L. Hawkins, *Auguste Comte and the United States, 1816–1853* (Cambridge, 1936); B. J. Loewenberg, "Darwinism Comes to America, 1859–1900," *Mississippi Valley Historical Review*, XXVIII (1940–1941), 339–368; S. T. Williams, "Tradition and Rebellion: European Patterns in the Literature of America," University of Pennsylvania Bicentennial Conference, *Studies in Civilization* (Philadelphia, 1941), 177–200; G. H. Orians, *The Influence of Walter Scott on America and American Literature before 1860* (Urbana, 1929); and S. H. Goodnight, *German Literature in American Magazines Prior to 1846* (Madison, 1907).

10. THE MARTIAL SPIRIT

Merle Curti, *The Roots of American Loyalty* (New York, 1946), examines the American brand of patriotism historically and analytically; and J. H. Franklin, *The Militant South, 1800–1861* (Cambridge, 1956), accounts for the bellicose spirit in that section. Though most general histories of the United States touch incidentally upon wartime opinion, the subject has had, in addition, much monographic study. For internal divisions during the War of Independence, C. H. Van Tyne, *The Loyalists in the American Revolution* (New York, 1902),

Carl Van Doren, *Secret History of the American Revolution* (New York, 1941), and W. H. Nelson, *The American Tory* (Oxford, 1961), are valuable. S. E. Morison, *The Life and Letters of Harrison Gray Otis* (2 v., Boston, 1913), portrays the Federalist opposition to the War of 1812. C. S. Ellsworth, "American Churches and the Mexican War," *American Historical Review*, XLII (1939–1940), 301–326, explores one angle of the popular response to that event.

For Northern dissidence in connection with the Civil War, see Mary Scrugham, *The Peaceable Americans, 1860–1861* (New York, 1921); Mayo Fesler, "Secret Political Societies in the North during the Civil War," *Indiana Magazine of History*, XIV (1918), 183–286; Wood Gray, *The Hidden Civil War* (New York, 1942); and G. F. Milton, *Abraham Lincoln and the Fifth Column* (New York, 1942). Southern conditions — not noticed in the present essay — are described in A. B. Moore, *Conscription and Conflict in the Confederacy* (New York, 1924); F. L. Owsley, *States Rights in the Confederacy* (Chicago, 1925); and Georgia L. Tatum, *Disloyalty in the Confederacy* (Chapel Hill, 1934). Ella Lonn, *Desertion during the Civil War* (New York, 1928), deals with both sides.

Various aspects of American opinion in the neutral period before the first German war are treated in C. J. Childs, *The German-Americans in Politics, 1914–1917* (Madison, 1939); Henry Landau, *The Enemy Within, the Inside Story of German Sabotage in America* (New York, 1937); H. C. Peterson, *Propaganda for War* (Norman, 1939); J. D. Squires, *British Propaganda at Home and in the United States from 1914 to 1917* (Cambridge, 1935); Carl Wittke, *German-Americans and the World War* (Columbus, 1936); and William Preston, Jr., *Aliens and Dissenters: Federal Suppression of Radicals, 1903–1933* (Cambridge, 1963). *Under Cover* (New York, 1943) by Arthur Derounian ("John Roy Carlson") is a firsthand report by an investigator of subversive groups in America before and after Pearl Harbor. W. S. Cole, *America First* (Madison, 1953), describes the work of the principal isolationist organization of this later period. The Gallup and *Fortune* public-opinion polls are summarized in current issues of *Public Opinion Quarterly*.

11. THE CITY IN AMERICAN CIVILIZATION

This essay amplifies an article, "The City in American History," which originally appeared in the *Mississippi Valley Historical Review*, XXVII (1940), 43–66, thickly barnacled with footnotes, and which has been reprinted in a number of anthologies. W. A. Diamond, contributing a chapter "On the Dangers of an Urban Interpretation of History" to *Historiography and Urbanization* (E. F. Goldman, ed., Baltimore, 1941), 67–108, criticized the piece on three grounds: that the terms "city" and "urban" are used loosely; that a city is too diversified a form of society to exert a causal influence on history; and that a more meaningful concept is that of economic or class interests. The reader will judge for himself as to the validity of the first two objections. As for the third, the urban and class interpretations do not seem to the present writer mutually exclusive.

Historical treatments of the American city are so numerous that only a few can be listed. For the world setting, Lewis Mumford, *The City in History* (New York, 1961), A. F. Weber, *The Growth of Cities in the Nineteenth Century* (New York, 1899), and J. A. Fairlie, *Municipal Administration* (New York, 1901), are important. Urban aspects of the colonial era to 1776 are depicted in Carl Bridenbaugh, *Cities in the Wilderness* (New York, 1938), and *Cities in Revolt* (New York, 1955); E. S. Griffith, *History of American City Government: the Colonial Period* (New York, 1938); Michael Kraus, *Intercolonial Aspects of American Culture on the Eve of the Revolution* (New York, 1928); Carl and Jessica Bridenbaugh, *Rebels and Gentlemen* (New York, 1942), an account of Philadelphia life from 1740 to 1775; R. A. East, *Business Enterprise in the American Revolutionary Era* (New York, 1938); Leila Sellers, *Charleston Business on the Eve of the Revolution* (Chapel Hill, 1934); and Virginia D. Harrington, *The New York Merchant on the Eve of the Revolution* (New York, 1935).

For the pre-Civil War years, see S. I. Pomerantz, *New York, an American City, 1783–1803* (New York, 1938); R. G. Albion, *The Rise of New York Port, 1815–1860* (New York, 1939); J. W. Livingood, *The Philadelphia-Baltimore Trade Rivalry, 1780–1860* (Harrisburg, 1947); G. R. Taylor, *The Transportation Revolution, 1815–1860* (New York, 1951); R. C. Wade, *The Urban Frontier: the Rise of Western Cities, 1790–1830* (Cambridge, 1959); W. W. Belcher, *The Economic Rivalry between St. Louis and Chicago, 1850–1880* (New York, 1947); E. C. Kirkland, *Men, Cities, and Transportation, a Study in New England History, 1820–1900* (2 v., Cambridge, 1948), and R. R. Russel, *Economic Aspects of Southern Sectionalism, 1840–1861* (2 v., Urbana, 1924). For the later nineteenth century, see particularly Blake McKelvey, *The Urbanization of America, 1860–1915* (New Brunswick, 1963); Allan Nevins, *The Emergence of Modern America, 1865–1878* (New York, 1927); A. M. Schlesinger, *The Rise of the City, 1878–1898* (New York, 1933); A. I. Abell, *The Urban Impact on American Protestantism, 1865–1900* (Cambridge, 1943); C. W. Patton, *The Bat-*

tle for Municipal Reform, Mobilization and Attack, 1875–1900 (Washington, 1940); and S. B. Warner, Jr., *Streetcar Suburbs: Process of Growth in Boston, 1870–1900* (Cambridge, 1962). The twentieth-century city is discussed from various angles in J. G. Thompson, *Urbanization: Its Effects on Government and Society* (New York, 1927); G. R. Taylor, *Satellite Cities, a Study of Industrial Suburbs* (New York, 1915); H. P. Douglass, *The Suburban Trend* (New York, 1925); N. P. Gist and L. A. Halbert, *Urban Society* (New York, 1933); W. G. Ogburn, *Social Characteristics of Cities* (Chicago, 1937); Urbanism Committee of National Resources Committee, *Our Cities, Their Role in the National Economy* (Washington, 1937); R. D. McKenzie, *The Metropolitan Community* (New York, 1933); Victor Jones, *Metropolitan Government* (Chicago, 1942); M. H. Leiffler, *City and Church in Transition* (Chicago, 1938); E. W. Montgomery, *The Urbanization of Rural Education* (Chicago, 1936); and Alvin Boshoff, *The Sociology of Urban Regions* (New York, 1962).

Three of the best histories of single cities are Bessie L. Pierce, *A History of Chicago* (3 v., New York, 1937–1957, in progress); Blake McKelvey's 4-volume history of Rochester, N.Y. (Cambridge and Rochester, 1945–1961); and Bayrd Still, *Milwaukee* (Madison, 1948). A. N. Holcombe, *The Political Parties of Today* (rev. ed., New York, 1925), considers urban and rural factors in American political history, while literary reactions concern G. A. Dunlap, *The City in the American Novel, 1789–1900* (Philadelphia, 1934), and Morton and Lucia White, *The Intellectual versus the City from Thomas Jefferson to Frank Lloyd Wright* (Cambridge, 1962). For the leadership of the city-born in intellectual and cultural fields, see F. A. Woods, "City Boys versus Country Boys," *Science*, n. s., XXIX (1909), 577–579; E. L. Clarke, *American Men of Letters* (New York, 1916); R. H. Holmes, "A Study of the Origins of Distinguished Living Americans," *American Journal of Sociology*, XXXIV (1928–1929), 670–685; and S. S. Visher, *Geography of American Notables* (Bloomington, 1928), which lists other important studies in the footnotes to pages 7–8.

12. FOOD IN THE MAKING OF AMERICA

This chapter is an abridgment of an exhaustively documented article, "A Dietary Interpretation of American History," published in the Massachusetts Historical Society *Proceedings*, LXVIII (1952), 199–227. The role of food in the history of mankind is delineated in Ellsworth Huntington, *Mainsprings of Civilization* (New York, 1945), chaps. xxii–xxiii; H. E. Jacob, *Six Thousand Years of Bread* (Richard and Clara Winston, translators, Garden City, 1944); E. P. Prentice, *Hunger and History* (New York, 1939); and A. H. Verrill, *Perfumes and Spices* (Boston, 1940). No comparable accounts exist for American history, the closest approximation being R. O. Cummings, *The American and His Food* (Chicago, 1940), which ably summarizes the shifts in popular dietary habits since colonial times but slights the larger social and political consequences.

Many aspects of the subject have had separate treatment, usually from an economic point of view. These works, abounding in grist for the social historian, include A. H. Verrill and O. W. Barrett, *Foods America Gave the World* (Boston, 1937); Gertrude I. Thomas, *Food of Our Forefathers* (Philadelphia, 1941); E. H. S. and H. S. Bailey, *Food Products from Afar* (New York, 1922); Forrest Crissey, *The Story of Foods* (Chicago, 1917); E. C. Brooks, *The Story of Corn and the Westward Migration* (Chicago, 1916); Dorothy Giles, *Singing Valleys, the Story of Corn* (New York, 1940); R. A. Clemen, *The American Livestock and Meat Industry* (New York, 1923); C. B. Kuhlman, *Development of the Flour Milling Industry in the United States* (Boston, 1929); John Storck and W. D. Teague, *Flour for Man's Bread* (Minneapolis, 1952), mostly about the United States; James Collins, *The Story of Canned Goods* (New York, 1924); A. W. Bitting, *Appertizing; or the Art of Canning; Its History and Development* (San Francisco, 1937); and O. E. Anderson, *Refrigeration in America* (Princeton, 1953). The best historical survey of agriculture is E. E. Edwards, "American Agriculture — the First 300 Years," in the *Yearbook of Agriculture for 1940*, 171–276.

Governmental concern for consumer interests receives attention in Charles Elliott, ed., *Fading Trails* (New York, 1942), which treats of the protection of wild life, and Stephen Wilson, *Food & Drug Regulation* (Washington, 1942), while the new nutritional science is made intelligible to lay readers by C. C. and Sparkle M. Furnas, *Men, Bread and Destiny* (New York, 1937), and Mark Graubard, *Man's Food* (New York, 1944). The logistic role of food is depicted in Ella Lonn, *Salt as a Factor in the Confederacy* (New York, 1933), and J. F. Rhodes, *History of the United States* (New York, 1892–1919), V, 359–384, during the Civil War; in M. R. Dickson, *The Food Front in World War I* (Washington, 1944), and W. C. Mullendore, *History of the United States Food Administration* (Stanford University, 1941), during the first German war; and in Roy Hendrickson, *Food "Crisis"* (Garden City, 1944), and E. P. Prentice, *Food, War and the Future* (New York, 1944), during the Axis war. For cookery, which is hardly touched upon in the present essay, there is a plethora of sources as the following references indicate: Katherine G. Bitting, comp., *Gastronomic Bibliography* (San Francisco, 1939), listing cookbooks of many countries; Waldo Lincoln, comp., "Bibliography of American Cookery Books, 1742–1862," American Antiquarian Society, *Proceedings*, n. s., XXXIX (1929), 85–225; and J. E. Gourley, comp., *Regional American Cookery, 1884–1936* (New York, 1936).

13. CASTING THE NATIONAL HOROSCOPE

This essay contains most of the material presented in an article of the same title in American Antiquarian Society, *Proceedings*, LV (1947), 53–94. The chief omissions are the footnotes, references to astrology and an account of population predictions. For soothsaying in general, see H. J. Forman, *The Story of Prophecy* (New York, 1936); Rolfe Boswell, *Nostradamus Speaks* (New York, 1941) and *Prophets and Portents* (New York, 1942); and John Cournos, ed., *A Book of Prophecy from the Egyptians to Hitler* (New York, 1942).

Though no similar surveys exist for the United States, various phases of the subject have been canvassed. Jane L. Mesick, *The English Traveller in America, 1785–1835* (New York, 1922), and Max Berger, *The British Traveller in America, 1836–1860* (New York, 1943), digest the predictions of British visitors; while H. M. Lydenberg, "What Did Macaulay Say about America?" New York Public Library, *Bulletin*, XXIX (1925), 459–481, and H. H. Clark, "The Vogue of Macaulay in America," Wisconsin Academy of Sciences, Arts and Letters, *Transactions*, XXXIV (1942–1943), 237–292, shed light on the most provocative of all foreign prophecies. Elizabeth F. Hoxie discusses a leading millenarian in "Harriet Livermore: 'Vixen and Devotee,'" *New England Quarterly*, XVIII (1945), 39–50; and Clara E. Sears, *Days of Delusion* (Boston, 1924), and F. D. Nichols, *The Midnight Cry* (Washington, 1944), describe the Millerite frenzy. Readers who wish to learn about the Utopian novelists at secondhand should consult A. B. Forbes, "The Literary Quest for Utopia, 1880–1900," *Social Forces*, VI (1927–1928), 179–189; J. F. Normano, "Social Utopias in American Literature," *International Review for Social History*, III (1938), 287–299; W. F. Taylor, *The Economic Novel in America* (Chapel Hill, 1942), especially 189–213, 237–272; and V. L. Parrington, Jr., *American Dreams* (Providence, 1947), chaps. viii–xxi.

Few historians have themselves donned the robe of prophet. With regard to world history, E. P. Cheyney, *Law in History* (New York, 1927), predicted that certain tendencies, such as moral progress and the spread of democracy, will dominate the future. In 1909 Henry Adams, applying to human history what he believed to be the second law of thermodynamics, was more specific, announcing a timetable which fixed 1921 as the year when man's power of thought would reach the "limits of its possibilities," though he prudently reserved 2025 as a possible alternative date. See his *The Tendency of History* (New York, 1928), 172. However, R. F. Nichols, in "The Dynamic Interpretation of History," *New England Quarterly*, VIII (1935), 163–178, maintained among other things that Adams misunderstood the second law of thermodynamics.

Index

Women, status of, 4, 14, 56; demand suffrage, 42, 56, 161

Work, as national trait, 4, 9–11, 22–23

World War I, unpreparedness for, 147; and public opinion, 183–86; food as factor in, 235–36

World War II, manual for soldiers, 20; immigrants in, 81–82; preparedness for, 147–48; steps leading to U.S. entry, 143–44, 152, 190; and national unity, 187–91, 193; food as factor in, 236

SENTRY EDITIONS